D0845322

Broadcasting to the Soviet Union

Maury Lisann

The Praeger Special Studies program—utilizing the most modern and efficient book production techniques and a selective worldwide distribution network—makes available to the academic, government, and business communities significant, timely research in U.S. and international economic, social, and political development.

Broadcasting to the Soviet Union

International Politics and Radio

PRAEGER SPECIAL STUDIES IN INTERNATIONAL POLITICS AND GOVERNMENT

Praeger Publishers New York Washington London

Library of Congress Cataloging in Publication Data

Lisann, Maury.
Broadcasting to the Soviet Union.

(Praeger special studies in international politics and government)
Bibliography: p.
Includes index.
1. Radio in propaganda. 2. International broadcasting.
3. Propaganda, International. I. Title.
JF1525.P8L57 327'.14'0973 74-14046
ISBN 0-275-05590-6

PRAEGER PUBLISHERS
111 Fourth Avenue, New York, N.Y. 10003, U.S.A.

Published in the United States of America in 1975
by Praeger Publishers, Inc.

Printed in the United States of America

PREFACE

Radio broadcasting may account for more communication between the Communist and non-Communist parts of the world than all forms of private and laboriously negotiated intergovernmental exchanges combined. It is also probably the form of contact about which least is known.

In the West it is the most impersonal and probably least glamorous of the various forms of East-West contact. The average Westerner is at least potentially a participant in other forms of exchange, but only the relative handful working in broadcasting can get personally involved or interested. The lack of personal involvement is compounded by the difficulty of knowing what is happening at the receiving end.

Virtually nothing has been published on the subject, except for generalized or anecdotal material. Soviet citizens, however, seem to know relatively little about the behavior and views on politically sensitive matters of their compatriots, except for a small circle of close friends, and tend to attribute to others views different from their own. The Soviet authorities, of course, try to make the subject as impenetrable as possible. Their reaction to foreign broadcasting is a form of censorship, and the first rule of any censorship is to censor information about itself.

Most of the information that is published comes from the broadcasters. Thus, it is often discounted as self-serving, an idealized product of organizations whose survival is in question. International broadcasters depend on public funds, and today they are sometimes thought of as disreputable, a relic of an era when an attempt to speak to someone without his government's permission was not looked upon as aggression, illegal intervention, or an infringement of sovereignty.

It is perhaps a bit ironic that public interest in the West in funding international broadcasting waned at just about the time that broadcasting was becoming a major influence. In the case of the Soviet Union, at least, the evidence is that foreign broadcasting became important only in the 1960s. With the fading of the 1950s' style of Cold War confrontation in broadcasting, however, enthusiasm for a long-term, unglamorous task of providing information for an informed public opinion also faded.

The public perception of the role of international broadcasting in closed societies, which comprise an increasingly large percentage of the world, is vague and uncertain. A reading of the annual Congressional hearing transcripts on the funding of U. S. broadcasting suggests that misconceptions about broadcasting are growing.

The material in this book does not represent the views of any broadcaster. My own peripheral associations with broadcasters began only after work on the book was essentially completed. Most of the material that I did receive from broadcasters has had to be omitted for reasons of space. That material, which relates mainly to patterns of jamming, is useful more for analyzing Soviet foreign policy than for analyzing the rule of broadcasting per se, and it can be found in my dissertation, "The Politics of Broadcasting to the USSR" (Johns Hopkins University, 1973).

I wish to thank James King for his encouragement in beginning this work. Henry Loomis, former director of the Voice of America, was very helpful in guiding me to public, but otherwise obscure, material. Herbert Dinerstein of Johns Hopkins University was always available for valuable counsel during the final organization and writing.

CONTENTS

LIST OF TABLES

Broadcasting to the Soviet Union

CHAPTER

1

INFORMATION AND POLITICS

Information is a key element in the direction and character of modern political life. Every government to a greater or lesser extent seeks to control or manage the flow of information within its country. During revolutions the channels of communication and dissemination of news are among the first targets. Even where a society is accustomed to operate with a relatively free flow of information, the fate of government can still depend on the ability to manipulate or manage the activities of the press, as the course of the Watergate affair has shown.

The general importance of information in political affairs needs no explanation. It should be evident that the more tightly information is controlled in a country, the more central to the leadership of the country is the management of the mechanisms and policies of the means of control. When control of information becomes central to the maintenance of the political system, the processes of that control reflect much more than the diffuse relationship between information and politics. They can show an intimate view of the ongoing conduct of affairs, which leaders strive to conceal.

It would be difficult to specify what countries have the most intense interest in controlling all information within their borders. Among the developed countries with relatively sophisticated and educated populations the Soviet Union has come closest, perhaps, to achieving total control of information. This control attempts to seal off at the border any but "licensed" information about the outside world; internally, it tries to compartmentalize the flow of information, both functionally and geographically. Ideally, no individual will know more than he needs to facilitate his general support of the system and to fulfill his own specialized tasks, or more than he would unavoidably learn because of his particular situation. Thus, general-circulation newspapers cannot report much of what appears in more specialized, low-circulation publications, and in some Communist countries attempts are made to forbid the circulation of the local newspaper beyond its immediate area.

Much has been written about the means of control of information in the Soviet Union. As a reminder of the centrality of information control in the Soviet political system it suffices here to note that Glavlit, the bureaucratic manager of censorship, was virtually the only organ of Czarism whose name and function were both carried over apparently intact into the Soviet bureaucracy.

The Soviets could not totally seal off the country. In the early days of Soviet rule the major "leakages" were probably from foreigners entering the Soviet Union, contacts with relatives abroad, and the limited number of Soviet citizens permitted foreign travel. Eventually, as mass illiteracy was reduced, printed materials replaced the traditional Party reliance on oral agitation as the most important means of disseminating information. Control and censorship of printed materials could be exercised effectively by Glavlit, while there was virtually no means of reproduction or recording within reach of the general population.

The most important exception to the continuity of strict control of information probably occurred during World War II, with mass incursions of friendly and unfriendly foreigners, massive international population movements, and the sequel of the stationing abroad of Soviet troops, but that was followed immediately by a drastic repression and retightening of controls that lasted until Stalin's death. Since World War II the only significant gap in the control of information inside the Soviet Union has been short-wave radio broadcasts from abroad. Most of the time the Soviets have attempted to jam those broadcasts, but the jamming has been only partially effective for both technical and economic reasons, although the Soviet Union may have invested more resources in jamming foreign broadcasts than were spent by the broadcasters themselves. The only areas where jamming has been substantially effective are the central parts of large cities, where local ground wave jammers are installed.

Radio broadcasting has been a significant part of international politics since the 1930s, when Nazi Germany made dramatic use of it. By then the right to broadcast across frontiers had already been firmly, if tacitly, established. Today, if radio were to be reinvented, the majority of the world's countries would probably seek to ban broadcasting across frontiers, just as they are attempting to have direct-broadcast television from space, which is technically, if not economically, feasible, declared illegal.

Elite and governmental opinion in most of the world is hostile to international broadcasting because radio is a much more important means of mass communication and opinion forming in most countries than it is in the United States. This hostility, as it has been expressed in U. N. debates on direct-broadcast television and in the less official arguments about radio broadcasting seems to arise from three different sources. First, the Communist countries and a few other authoritarian states see the dissemination of specific types of information as a direct threat to their political stability. Second, the bulk of the world's less-developed countries, whose means of internal social communications are weak, fear that they will be overwhelmed by generalized foreign influences with which they cannot compete. Third, there are a few developed countries—France is the most prominent—whose hostility to foreign broadcasting seems to be motivated by commercial considerations and the protection of internal monopolies.

The hostility does not extend to the mass public, where the popularity of foreign broadcasts tends to be inversely proportional to the intensity of official hostility in a given country. That relationship is recognized by most governments, and even some of the poorest have been vigorously expanding their international broadcasting since the mid-1960s. The expansion of international broadcasting has far exceeded the availability of frequencies and has led to a race to overcome the mutual interference with ever more powerful transmitters. The tendency simultaneously to proclaim international broadcasting harmful while increasing it is perhaps the best testimony to the importance of broadcasting.

Internationally, there have been few formal efforts to regulate the contents of programs. The League of Nations did vote a convention to regulate broadcasts in 1936, acceded to by 26 countries, which the United Nations unsuccessfully voted to revive in 1954. Neither the United States nor the Soviet Union was ever a party to that convention. Morally, the most important international action underpinning international broadcasting is Article 19 of the Declaration of Human Rights, voted unanimously by the U. N. General Assembly in 1948, which proclaims the right to receive information freely, regardless of frontiers.

Lacking a formal framework of program standards, international broadcasting has been conducted in the rough and tumble marketplace of public opinion and diplomacy. The International Telecommunications Union (ITU) has regulated the technical aspects of international broadcasting, but it has no concern with the contents of programming. However, as will be seen, it has been the unofficial forum for some of the political developments in the conduct of broadcasting.

Inside the Soviet Union foreign broadcasting did not become significant until well after World War II. The signal of concern to the Soviet leaders was the beginning of Russian-language broadcasts by the Voice of America in February 1947. That led to what must have been an urgent program of installing jamming transmitters that began operation against the Voice of America in 1948 and shortly afterwards extended their jamming to other foreign broadcasts in Russian and other Soviet languages.

Prior to this time the Soviet Union had not bothered to jam foreign broadcasts, except for a brief period of mutual jamming with Spain in 1946. Ironically, the Soviet Union had been on the receiving end of the first attempts made to stop foreign broadcasting. The first recorded occasion on which an official diplomatic protest had been made against radio broadcasts had been against the Soviet Union in 1930 (by Germany), [1] and the earliest attempt to jam radio broadcasts intentionally had also been directed at Soviet radio (by Rumania in 1932).[2]

In a practical sense, broadcasting to the Soviet Union could not have been very significant in the late 1940s and early 1950s because there were then fewer than two million short-wave receivers in the country. A survey of Soviet residents of that period by MIT's COMCOM project indicates that very few of those who did have receivers dared to listen to foreign broadcasts during the Stalin era.[3] The paranoiac reaction, perhaps typical of Stalin, must have been triggered by the symbolic portent that it was the United States that for the first time was trying to reach directly into the Soviet Union. Not only were scarce resources poured into a jamming system, but until 1953 it was even forbidden to keep transcripts of foreign broadcasts for official analysis and monitoring.[4]

Unlike certain other countries the Soviet Union has not tried to forbid listening to foreign broadcasts per se or to limit access to short-wave receivers. The practical reason is that the Soviet Union's domestic radio system is dependent on the widespread use of short-wave frequencies; a ban on listening would be virtually unenforceable under post-Stalin conditions in the face of the intense search for reliable information that the Soviet press cannot provide. After 1958 the authorities did forbid the sale of receivers with the higher-frequency short-wave bands (19, 16, and 13 meters), the best for long-distance reception under certain conditions, but the public, with a relatively high level of technical sophistication, has converted its receivers to pick up those bands and has otherwise acquired such receivers.

Broadcasting began to acquire the characteristics of mass media in the Soviet Union in the late 1950s. The number of radio receivers, still only about six million in 1955, exceeded 20 million by 1960 and overtook the number of wired speakers at a level of about 35 million in 1964. Television sets, about five million in 1960, surpassed 30 million by 1970.

Estimates of the number of short-wave receivers in the Soviet Union now range from about 35 million to possibly more than 50 million, the differences depending mainly on the unknown rate at which old sets go out of use. Probably not even the Soviet government knows. Figures in the Soviet press are inconsistent and contradictory. Soviet authorities probably lost track after 1962 when the annual registration and subscription tax on receivers was abolished and replaced by a one-time 15- to 20-percent surcharge on the purchase price.[5]

Annual production has exceeded four million sets for many years. Demand for good-quality short-wave receivers is strong, with foreign receivers worth about $200 in the West selling privately and in Soviet pawn shops for more than $600.

The growth in the number of receivers has been accompanied by an increase in the number of foreign broadcasters with programs in Soviet languages. The Soviets claim that there are at least 35 "hostile" broadcasters,[6] but only about half that number have been specifically named in the Soviet press. The continuity of Soviet press attacks and recently acquired statistics on audience interest show that only four foreign stations account for most of the domestic impact of foreign broadcasting. Those four are the Voice of America (VOA); the British Broadcasting Corporation (BBC); Deutsche Welle (DW, the official station of the Federal Republic of Germany); and Radio Liberty (RL). The last, financed by the United States, is the only broadcaster that has attempted continuous and in-depth coverage of Soviet politics and domestic issues; it also broadcasts in more languages of the Soviet Union (up to 18) than any other foreign station.

Other official broadcasters that have been occasionally attacked in the Soviet press include Canada, Israel, Japan, Peking, Spain, Tirana, and the Vatican. About a half dozen clandestine broadcasters have also been named, mostly some years ago. The most important of those from the Soviet point of view, quoted extensively in the Soviet press, appears to have been Radio Baikal, described as located on Okinawa and pretending to be an underground station inside the Soviet Union.[7]

Except for the first four named, the Soviet press has paid more attention to Radio Free Europe (RFE), which does not broadcast to the Soviet Union, than to the other stations. RFE seems to have been used as a surrogate for RL, which for a number of years the Soviets preferred not to mention directly, apparently not wanting to call the public's attention to it.

Even in the late 1960s, when the Soviet government belatedly realized the popularity of foreign broadcasting, it was unwilling to include radio listening in its list of ideological crimes when it stiffened control over the dissent that became overt after 1966. Popularized accounts of the legal aspects of ideological crimes, while citing foreign radio broadcasts as a cause, carefully avoided mentioning listening as a punishable act, although Articles 70 and 190 of the criminal code, applying to the distribution of critical information and propaganda, are sometimes interpreted to include the repeating of information from foreign broadcasts.[8] Instead, the Soviet Union has attempted to deal with the popularity of foreign broadcasting through a sophisticated combination of jamming, diplomacy, and internal information management. Most of what follows is an account and analysis of that effort, with particular attention to the period 1963-68, when, in the absence of most jamming, foreign broadcasts first made a visible imprint on Soviet society. An epilogue sketches in some later developments and expands the analysis with significant information that became available after 1970.

Because control of information is so basic to the maintenance of the Soviet political system, many of the decisions related to it have to be made at the Politburo level. As a consequence, it turns out that there is a close connection between some of these decisions and major developments in foreign policy and even domestic power relationships. Space does not permit a detailed unraveling of those ramifications, but some are dealt with in summary form, in particular Khrushchev's struggle to maintain his primacy before his downfall, and the evolution of the Soviet decision to sign the nuclear test ban treaty, together with the related turning point in its relations with the PRC.

The partial revision of the conventional Western chronology of that event that results is an illustration of the level at which information policy is handled in the Soviet Union and its place near the core of the Soviet political system. This, in turn, shows that the seemingly technical issues with which much of this book is concerned are tightly interwoven with some basic aspects of Soviet society and may be indicative of its evolution and of underlying trends. It should, at the least, help to clarify the role of broadcasting in the spectrum of international politics.

NOTES

1. B. S. Murty, Propaganda and World Public Order: The Legal Regulation of the Ideological Instrument of Coercion (New Haven, Conn.: Yale University Press, 1968), p. 139.

2. John B. Whitton and Arthur Larson, Propaganda: Towards Disarmament in the War of Words (Dobbs Ferry, N. Y.: Oceana, for the World Rule of Law Center, Duke University, 1964), p. 210.

3. Rosemarie S. Rodgers, "The Soviet Audience: How It Uses the Mass Media" (Ph. D. diss., MIT, 1967), pp. 167-68.

4. Artem Flegontovich Panfilov, Radio SShA v psikhologicheskoi voine (Radio of the U. S. A. in Psychological Warfare) (Moscow, 1967), pp. 89-90.

5. Resolution of the Council of Ministers, August 18, 1961, Spravochnik partiinovo rabotnika (Handbook of the Party Worker), 4th ed. (Moscow, 1963), pp. 370-71.

6. "The Soviet Way of Life," editorial, Sovetskaya Rossiya, May 15, 1970.

7. B. Vasilyev, "Provocateurs at the Microphone," Sovetskoye Radio i Televideniye, No. 5 (1958):28-29.

8. M. P. Mikhailov and V. V. Nazarov, Ideologicheskaya diversiya—vooruzheniye imperializma (Ideological Diversion Is the Armament of Imperialism) (Moscow, 1969), pp. 16, 24, 44-46.

CHAPTER 2
JAMMING AND DIPLOMACY

EARLY DISCUSSIONS

Short of direct repression against radio listeners, which, in view of the growth of listening, had become a practical impossibility by the late 1950s, Soviet authorities had three means of coping with the problem: They could physically obstruct listening by jamming; they could attempt to modify the content of foreign broadcasts at the source through diplomacy; they could attempt to remove the incentive for listening by competing at home for the audience with better information services and by discrediting foreign broadcasts through propaganda. Soviet radio and television were not yet equipped to provide rapid news, however, nor were the Soviet leaders yet ready to agree that news in itself had importance for the public. The traditional Party view was that news should be used only to provide illustrative material for predetermined didactic and propagandistic themes and otherwise ignored. While the merits of increasing the flow of news to the public were being argued, steps were taken, particularly after 1960, to improve the news capability of Soviet broadcasting.

Meanwhile, a combination of jamming and diplomacy was tried to induce foreign broadcasters to restrict the contents of their programming. The Soviets also tried a technique of partial or "selective" jamming in a clever effort to use foreign broadcasts to reinforce the themes of Soviet domestic propaganda.

Up to the late 1950s, with a populace possessing few radios and relatively intimidated from using them, the Soviet Union simply jammed all foreign broadcasts in Soviet languages.* Following

---

*An exception were the broadcasts of the Voice of America in the Baltic languages (Lithuanian, Latvian, and Estonian). For geographic

Khrushchev's visit to Britain in the spring of 1956, jamming of the BBC was suspended, only to be resumed again at the time of the suppression of the Hungarian revolution in November. Influence of foreign radio on public opinion was evident to the Party establishment at that time and may have spurred the leadership to seek more sophisticated means of dealing with foreign broadcasts.[1]

Khrushchev, sensing (probably correctly, although the Soviets had no measurements at the time) that VOA had the largest audience, proposed in a public interview, for broadcast by CBS on June 2, 1957, that if VOA would change its programming it would not be jammed. VOA, now freed of the incubus of Sen. Joseph McCarthy, who had made it one of his prime targets, had already moderated the strident approach forced by the political pressures of the Cold War era. The Soviets acknowledged their motives in the years of conversations that followed by making it clear that they were more interested in linking the end of jamming of VOA to changes in RL and RFE than to changes in VOA's own programming.

Over the next six years there were many informal U. S.-Soviet discussions of the jamming-programming relationship.[2] These took place at the periodic negotiations of the U. S.-Soviet cultural exchange agreements, on the occasion of the opening of the large U. S. exhibition in Moscow in 1959, at various meetings of ITU groups, and on a sporadic but almost continuous basis at the International Frequency Registration Board (IFRB) of the ITU secretariat.

Krushchev introduced an additional tactic by reducing jamming of VOA to almost (but not quite) nothing on the day of his arrival in the United States in September 1959. That set the stage for a discussion at the Camp David meeting of a Soviet proposal for a mutual limitation of broadcasting, with an end to jamming. Accounts of what was proposed differ somewhat, but they agree that the United States rejected the deal, feeling that it would be the beginning of a process of demands for further restrictions on program content.[3] The BBC had a similar experience concerning jamming, on a slightly different schedule.

The very light jamming of VOA and BBC lasted until the U-2 incident in May 1960. Jamming was then intensified and remained

---

reasons the Baltic states were more accessible to larger numbers of foreign broadcasts, making jamming even less effective than elsewhere. Estonia, for example, could receive, and generally understand, Finland's domestic radio and television. Also, the Soviets may have regarded the nonjamming of VOA as a tacit quid pro quo for the nonusage of the Baltic languages by RL. The Soviets wished to link suspension of RL to relaxation of jamming of VOA.

on a highly variable and very selective basis until June 1963. The intensification of jamming on the morning of May 5 occurred before the announcement of the downing of the U-2. It in fact coincided with a Politburo and Central Committee meeting that changed the membership of the Politburo and Secretariat in ways detrimental to Khrushchev's power. Khrushchev later told an American visitor that that was the beginning of his fall.[4] That was one of a number of occasions when decisions concerning jamming or radio broadcasting have been integral parts of major developments in Soviet foreign policy or domestic politics.

SELECTIVE JAMMING

The jamming of VOA and BBC that existed from 1960 to 1963 is called "selective" because it was carefully controlled and varied in accordance with the minute-by-minute news content of the broadcasts. Each individual item in the hourly newscasts as well as all or part of longer analytical features was jammed or not jammed depending on how it furthered or conflicted with Soviet political calculations of the moment. Most of the selections of the jammers are easily predictable from a general knowledge of Soviet policies, but there are a number of cases that show facets of Soviet policy that are otherwise concealed or that signal in advance changes of Soviet policy.

Because foreign broadcasts deal with many topics that the Soviet press cannot touch, the day-by-day logs of the selective jamming patterns are an unusually sensitive, sometimes unique, indicator of the daily concerns of the Politburo or the Secretariat. The main purpose of selective jamming seems to have been to make use of foreign broadcasts to prepare public opinion for policy changes without tipping off the world in advance and to exploit for domestic purposes information that the Soviet press could not handle for ideological or diplomatic reasons. Changes in the jamming pattern might also have been used as a form of diplomatic signaling, but there is no evidence that the Soviet leaders intended that. In any case, this use would have had no practical consequences, because the West was not watching the nuances of the jamming pattern, although gross changes, such as the total suspension or resumption of jamming, were noted and analyzed in the context of their diplomatic significance.

Some of the information conveyed by changes in the pattern of selective jamming cannot be found in the more conventional sources of information about Soviet policy. That fact can be illustrated by brief descriptions of some cases.

The Soviet press does not report Soviet tests of nuclear weapons. However, the selective jamming was arranged so that many of VOA's reports of Soviet nuclear tests were not jammed. (Nonjamming, however, never extended to any of the details, such as references to radioactivity in the atmosphere.) Presumably, the United States was shown to be aware of Soviet tests in order to reinforce the Soviet argument that inspection was not needed to verify a nuclear test ban treaty.

Predictably, news of problems in other Communist countries was jammed. There was one exception: East Germany. Occasionally, unfavorable news about East Germany was not jammed. That policy could have been intended to assuage popular resentment in the Soviet Union about official ties and obligations to the former, and still greatly disliked, enemy, where even the standard of living was higher than in the Soviet Union. This is an example of a type of information that the Soviet leaders wanted to disseminate but that for ideological and diplomatic reasons could not be published openly.

After the construction of the Berlin wall the Soviet threat to sign a separate peace treaty with East Germany by the end of 1961 and turn over control of access to West Berlin was seen as leading to a dangerous, even military, confrontation. Publicly, Khrushchev withdrew the threat on October 17. The selective-jamming pattern was changed, however, around September 15, from depicting the West as preparing only for a military confrontation to depicting a situation that was going to be settled peacefully and safely. The West does not appear to have received even unofficial Soviet reassurances on the intended withdrawal until sometime later, although before October 17. This is an example of preparing the public for a change in policy, in this case almost literally from war to peace, without tipping one's hand prematurely. It may also have been connected with Khrushchev's move, precisely at that time, to establish a secret channel of correspondence with President Kennedy, one that would not be known to Khrushchev's colleagues.[5] The exchange of secret letters that began on September 29, 1961, after a false start, remained clandestine on the Soviet side until the following May 1, when the newly appointed Soviet ambassador, Anatoliy Dobrynin, informed the White House that the exchange was being taken out of Khrushchev's personal control and put into regular diplomatic channels.[6]

THE SUSPENSION OF JAMMING

While the experiment in partial jamming was under way, the Party began an overhaul of the Soviet internal broadcasting system, designed to give it the capacity for news and up-to-date political commentary that it had lacked. While that was certainly needed in itself, in order to exploit the psychological advantages that are unique to broadcasting, as compared to other media, it was made clear that a major motive was to make Soviet radio—and later television—competitive with foreign broadcasts in quantity and speed of news. In the process of the reform Khrushchev gained personal control over the Soviet broadcasting system. He used that control to make the issue of jamming a weapon in fending off the opposing forces closing in on him.

The Party concept of news as nothing more than grist for the ideological mill was first challenged in 1957 with the idea that the attitude of listeners depended in large part on who reported first. That was considered so novel an idea that it had to be presented as an alien (East German) concept.[7] The Soviet establishment eventually accepted it as an important principle of successful use of the press—but always more in theory than in practice.

It was not until four months after the 1959 reduction of jamming that the first major change in Soviet broadcasting was ordered. Amidst injunctions to unmask the falsity of imperialist propaganda, to provide more choice of programs, and to make news and commentary more timely, Soviet radio was to be allowed to provide news before it appeared in the newspapers.[8] In order to do this TASS was directed to provide its services directly to local stations (the broadcast organizations had no significant news capability of their own). One result of this initial emphasis on news was that the State Committee reported that on its main radio channel, the First Program, it had put a news broadcast into the peak evening listening hours for the first time.[9]

The 1960 directive to Soviet radio to speed up news reporting was followed by a series of complaints from local radio administrations that it was still impossible to get news from TASS fast enough or in sufficient quantity. Some of those administrations carefully alluded to the problems that presented in competing with foreign radio broadcasts.[10] The distance that Soviet radio had to go can be seen in the fact that more than two years later one of the Union-republics reported that its contribution to solving the problem of slow news consisted of ending the practice of writing the Sunday and Monday newscasts on the preceding Saturday.[11]

The 1960 Central Committee resolution had been aimed primarily at improving the technical and organizational capacity of Soviet broadcasting. In 1962 measures were undertaken to put Soviet broadcasting in a position to compete with foreign radio for the audience in terms of programming. In retrospect it can be seen that that was part of Khrushchev's struggle with his internal opponents, who made the issue of intellectual freedom a main avenue of attack on him, giving Khrushchev in return an opportunity to depict them as the "heirs of Stalin." As a part of this struggle Khrushchev apparently intended to suspend most jamming around the end of 1962, but his plans were set back by the fiasco of the Cuban missile crisis, and he was on the defensive into the spring of 1963, with the public part of the struggle centering precisely on the issue of ideological controls on intellectual life and the dissemination of information.

Khrushchev gained control of Soviet broadcasting in February 1962 with the appointment of Mikhail Kharlamov as chairman of the State Committee for Radio and Television Broadcasting. Kharlamov was so closely associated with Khrushchev's personal diplomacy that he was one of the handful of officials immediately removed when Khrushchev was ousted in 1964. Kharlamov quickly replaced most of the key personnel of radio and television.[12]

At about the same time that Khrushchev pushed through the decision to put offensive missiles in Cuba a directive was issued to Soviet radio to put itself in a position to compete with "hostile radio propaganda."[13] The position was to include the establishment of a true centralized nationwide network so that the central Moscow programs could reach the whole country at once, a general rearrangement of the radio program schedule, and a large increase in the frequency of news and commentary broadcasts. It was specified that the actions had to be implemented by the end of 1962.

The new schedule, which went into effect October 15, 1962, increased weekly news and commentaries on the First Program alone from 114 to 163.[14] As the head of Lithuania's radio pointed out, the new schedule had to interest listeners in order to attract them away from foreign stations, "tens" of which could be heard clearly there.[15] Even more indicative of the aims of the new schedule was the institution on December 20, 1962, of a program on the main central channel at 9:00 p.m. summarizing items from foreign broadcasts.

The missile crisis set Khrushchev's schedule back, and for the next six months the selective jamming was so heavy that it was hardly selective at all, averaging 70 to 80 percent of all news items. The low point for Khrushchev during the period was the mass meeting of intellectuals and Party officials on March 7 and 8, 1963, called to denounce the ideological laxness of the period of destalinization. Khrushchev had to publicly and tearfully defend his own conduct as one of Stalin's top aides. But while that was taking place, the radio organizations were preparing for a move in the opposite direction, toward more open competition with foreign radio.

Under cover of attending the March 7-8 meeting all local radio-TV administrators down to the oblast level were called to Moscow and immediately afterward convened in a meeting of their own.[16] While engaging in the obligatory calls for ideological vigilance, they in fact discussed practical means of improving their own news so that it would be interesting to the public. Most noteworthy was a report from Estonia, where the local radio administration said that it had discovered by survey that the most popular radio program was the "Latest News," and if it was put on the air at the same time as VOA's Estonian program it would be listened to instead of VOA.[17] That report, or more precisely, its sharply edited publication after a month's delay, was a strong indication that some people, including the leadership of the State Committee, felt that Soviet radio was now capable of standing on its own and competing for the domestic audience without the protection of jamming of foreign stations.

On April 9 it was announced that a Central Committee plenary session devoted to ideology, the first ever on that subject, would be held beginning May 28. Since ideology was the issue on which Khrushchev was being attacked, and since he himself had made it known that he wanted the subject of the plenum to be chemistry, things were looking bleak for him.[18] What would have happened if the nominal leader of the anti-Khrushchev group, Frol Kozlov, had not then been incapacitated by a stroke cannot be known. But Khrushchev was already planning a maneuver, the suspension of jamming of VOA and BBC, that would undermine the basis of the chief issue being used against him (lack of ideological vigilance.)

On April 5 agreement in principle had been reached to establish a Washington-Moscow "hot line," the need for which had been demonstrated by delays in transmission of critical messages during the Cuban crisis. Between then and June 20 technical delegations of the two sides met at the ITU in Geneva to work out a protocol implementing the agreement. Into the Soviet delegation, composed primarily of military men, Khrushchev, it may be presumed, inserted Deputy Minister of Communications Ivan Vassilevich Klokov.

To the visible mystification of the Soviet military men, Klokov took aside the Americans there who were familiar with the past discussions about jamming and reopened the subject. There was now, however, a major difference in the Soviet position. Klokov dropped the previous Soviet insistence that curtailment of Radio Liberty must be included in any arrangement that ended jamming of VOA. Now, he said, jamming of VOA could be ended in return only for restraints on VOA's own programming, and the shutting down of VOA's megawatt long-wave transmitter near Munich.[19] The transmitter, a long-time subject of dispute, operated on a frequency of 173 khz, a frequency that the Soviets wanted exclusively for themselves.

This was a substantial softening of the previous Soviet stance. If it gained any compromise from the United States, Khrushchev could use it to claim that his methods for dealing with the internal ideological situation were more effective than any of the repressive measures being urged by his critics. By May Khrushchev was already regaining the upper hand, however temporarily, and he then began to manipulate jamming in the context of more far-reaching aims.

Beginning with the week of May 14, jamming of VOA was reduced by almost half, from an average of about 70 percent of news subjects to less than 40 percent. On May 28 jamming of VOA was reduced by half again, to about 20 percent. That reduction coincided with a change in the jamming pattern that signified a Soviet interest in signing a limited nuclear test ban treaty. Up to that time the Soviets had insisted that a test ban treaty must be comprehensive and without extensive on-site inspection. Proposals for a limited treaty excluding a ban on underground testing had been adamantly rejected. In accordance with that policy all references to proposals for a limited test ban treaty had been jammed.

On May 28 the jamming pattern was suddenly reversed, and from that time on great care was taken to insure that reports of U. S. proposals for a partial test ban treaty were not jammed. The U. S. government received no indication of a change of Soviet policy on the test ban treaty until weeks after the new pattern had been effected.[20] Until Khrushchev's acceptance of an invitation to negotiate was received on June 8, the administration did not expect the Soviets even to agree to discuss it.[21] President Kennedy, who was preparing his June 10 American University speech as a bid for reconciliation, did not know it would turn out to be something of an anticlimax. Years later Dobrynin told Llewellyn Thompson that a private lunch they had had on May 17 just before Dobrynin's return to the Soviet Union had been instrumental in providing the reassurances of U. S. sincerity on which Moscow's decision was based. The 11-day interval from May 17 to 28, then, is the period of the major Soviet decisions that resulted in the test ban treaty and the subsequent open rupture with China.

Jamming of VOA and BBC after May 28 was more a token operation than a substantive interference with the broadcasts. In Geneva Klokov by that time had announced that he personally had the authority to end jamming if he could get any kind of concession from the United States. About June 8 he became so impatient that he said jamming probably would end anyway, and on June 10 all jamming of BBC ceased. Jamming of VOA continued until June 18, Klokov having informed the Americans on June 14 that it was about to end.

The choice of June 18 was characteristic of Khrushchev. That was the day that the Central Committee plenum on ideology, postponed from May 28, opened. The session was intended to promulgate new restrictions on intellectual activity, more centralized control of the creative unions, and so on. By ending jamming the morning the session began, Khrushchev in effect thumbed his nose at the proposals and their proponents. The proposals were not adopted and were allowed quietly to fade away after the plenum.

The Geneva discussions on jamming apparently did not result in any formal agreement. The United States did immediately reduce the power of the Munich long-wave transmitter from 1,000 kilowatts to 50 kilowatts. The following January an agreement was reached with Hungary to shut down the transmitter in return for cessation of jamming of VOA by Hungary.[22] The transmitter was deactivated on January 31, 1964, and Hungary ceased jamming VOA on February 1, 1964. Czechoslovakia stopped jamming both VOA and BBC on April 1, 1964. Rumania had not waited for any agreements; it stopped jamming not only VOA and BBC but also RFE on July 29, 1963. In Eastern Europe only Bulgaria continued jamming without interruption; it did not suspend jamming of VOA until September 1974. Since 1964 the United States has reactivated and deactivated use of the long-wave frequency in step with subsequent Soviet resumption and suspension of jamming of VOA.

On the technical level the 1963 suspension of jamming also resulted temporarily in close cooperation between the United States and the Soviet Union at the IFRB. From September 1963 until 1965 the United States and the Soviet Union cooperated closely, together with Poland and Pakistan, generally opposed to Britain, France, Argentina, South Africa, and Cuba—a line-up that was rather puzzling to observers.[23]

The Soviets subsequently claimed that jamming was ended as a result of an agreement by the United States to restrain the content of VOA's programs.

> The tone of the programs of "Voice of America" in recent years has undergone significant changes. The leaders themselves of "Voice of America" and the organizers of the foreign policy of the USA explain this only and exclusively because the Soviet Union and the majority of the East European countries ended jamming of the broadcasts and that this "along with the increase in transmitter power gave the possibility of reconsidering the programs and making them more varied in content." In reality, after official assurance was received from the US government of the barring by them of slanderous anti-Soviet broadcasts in the programs of the "Voice of America," the jamming of these programs was ended. But all the reasons for the change in tone of the American radio propaganda to the Soviet Union lie much deeper, and not in the fact itself of the presence or absence of jamming.[24]
>
> In the middle of 1963 the American government officially assured the government of the Soviet Union of its decision not to allow in the future in the programs of the "Voice of America" malicious anti-Soviet attacks. In Washington, apparently, they understood that frantic anti-communism, propagated by the radio station, evokes nothing from the Soviet people except disgust and protest. Since that time the broadcasts to the socialist countries

> also have become more restrained. Appeals for "the overthrow of the communist regime," dirty insinuations and curses, almost disappeared. The basic accent was put on glorifying "the American way of life," the advantages of the so-called "free world."[25]

It appears unlikely, however, that there was any formal agreement about program content. Had there been such an agreement, it is probable that when the Soviet Union resumed jamming VOA in 1968 it would have accused the United States of having violated it. The lack of such accusations shows, too, that the relationship between the Soviet audience and foreign radio is not what it was assumed to be in the passages quoted above. By 1968, as will be shown, the Soviets were well aware of that.

What probably happened in 1963 was that the Soviet Union chose to ascribe tacit formality to the assurances that the United States had been giving verbally for several years, that VOA's programs had already changed. This made it easier, on the rare occasions that jamming was allowed to be publicly acknowledged, to justify Soviet policy. The Soviets recognized that the true guarantee that the United States would not drastically alter its existing radio-broadcasting policies—with which they thought they could live—did not rest on any "official" assurances. It was more firmly based in the political detente that accompanied the nuclear test ban treaty, the greater education and experience of the Soviet audiences, and the changing listening needs that would presumably arise from the mass use of television—which in the Soviet Union did not begin until the mid-1960s. The Soviet judgment was correct in the immediate circumstances, but the long-run consequences turned out to be different than envisioned.

NOTES

1. I. Melenkov, Partiinaya Zhizn (June 1957):48-50.

2. A detailed account, together with methodology and analysis of the related selective jamming is contained in Maury Lisann, "The Politics of Broadcasting to the USSR," Ph. D. dissertation (Johns Hopkins University, 1973), Chs. 3, 4.

3. U. S., Congress, House, Committee on Foreign Affairs, Subcommittee on International Organizations and Movements, Modern Communications and Foreign Policy, Part X, Winning the Cold War: The U. S. Ideological Offensive: Hearings, 90th Cong., 1st sess., 1967, pp. 37-38; Thomas C. Sorensen, The Word War (New York: Harper & Row, 1968), pp. 110-11.

4. A. McGehee Harvey, "A 1969 Conversation with Khrushchev: The Beginning of His Fall from Power," Life (December 18, 1970):48B.

5. C. L. Sulzberger, "Foreign Affairs: The Two Ks and Germany," New York *Times*, November 6, 1966; Pierre Salinger, *With Kennedy* (New York: Doubleday, 1966), pp. 191-92.

6. Salinger, *With Kennedy*, pp. 198, 220-21.

7. G. Uskova, "How to Improve the Broadcasts of 'Latest News,'" *Sovetskoye Radio i Televideniye* No. 3 (1957):6-8.

8. Resolution of the Central Committee, CPSU, January 29, 1960, "On the Improvement of Soviet Radio Broadcasting," in *Spravochnik partiinovo rabotnika* (Handbook of the Party Worker), 3d. ed. (Moscow, 1961), pp. 516-23.

9. *OIRT Information* (October 1960):19.

10. V. Kitayev, "Without Information There Are No Newspapers," *Sovetskaya Pechat'* (January 1961):36; Ye. Domoratskiy, "The Search Ought to Continue," *Sovetskoye Radio i Televideniye* No. 4 (July 1961): 25-27; V. Vlasov, "News Is First of All," *Sovetskoye Radio i Televideniye* (August 1961):11-13; N. Skachko, "Times, Times," *Sovetskaya Pechat'* (January 1962):21.

11. T. Kenzhebayev, "Timeliness Is the Sister of Success," *Sovetskoye Radio i Televideniye* (March 1963):8.

12. *Sovetskoye Radio i Televideniye* (July 1962):1.

13. Resolution of the Central Committee, CPSU, June 6, 1962, "On Measures for the Further Improvement of the Work of Radio Broadcasting and Television," *Spravochnik*, 4th ed. (Moscow, 1963), pp. 423-29.

14. Leonid Kubik, "An Eight-Day Analysis of New Programmes on the Soviet Radio," *Radio Liberty Research Note*, October 25, 1962.

15. I. Yanuitis, "We Work for the Radio Listeners," *Sovetskoye Radio i Televideniye* (October 1962):4-5.

16. *Sovetskaya Pechat'* (March 1963):37.

17. "For the People's-Worker, the People's-Creator," *Sovetskaya Pechat'* (April 1963):33-36.

18. Among the many detailed accounts of this period in Soviet politics are Michel Tatu, *Power in the Kremlin* (New York: Viking Press, 1969), and Carl Linden, "Khrushchev and the Party Battle," *Problems of Communism* 12, 5 (1963):27-35.

19. Based on an account by John H. Gayer, former member and chairman of the IFRB.

20. Max Frankel, "Rusk Says Soviet Avoids Test Ban," New York *Times*, May 30, 1963; letter, Dean Rusk to Maury Lisann, June 1, 1971; interview with Llewellyn Thompson, April 30, 1971.

21. Theodore C. Sorensen, *Kennedy* (New York: Harper & Row, 1965), p. 729; Arthur M. Schlesinger Jr., *A Thousand Days* (Boston: Houghton Mifflin, 1965), p. 900.

22. U. S., Congress, House, Committee on Appropriations, *Departments of State, Justice, and Commerce, the Judiciary, and Related Agencies Appropriations for 1965: Hearings*, 88th Cong., 2nd sess., 1964, pp. 536, 539-40, 545-46.

23. David M. Leive, International Telecommunications and International Law: The Regulation of the Radio Spectrum (Leyden: Sijthoff, 1970; Dobbs Ferry, N. Y.: Oceana, 1970), p. 79.

24. Artem Flegontovich Panfilov, Radio SShA v psikhologicheskoi voine (Radio of the USA in Psychological Warfare) (Moscow, 1967), p. 127.

25. Sergei Golyakov, Voina bes vystrelov (War Without Shots) (Moscow, 1968), pp. 57-58.

CHAPTER 3 BROADCASTING WITHOUT JAMMING: 1963–65

MEDIA PRIORITIES AND POWER

In June 1963 the cessation of jamming of almost all foreign broadcasts except for Radio Liberty created a situation unique in Soviet history. The precise timing of changes in jamming was tied to diplomatic, propaganda, internal political, and other "image" considerations. But underlying the decision there had to be a basic calculation that the Soviet political system had so stabilized itself that relatively large quantities of uncontrolled information could be safely absorbed and that the programs of the leadership could be explained and implemented without great resistance. In 1963, as was later made clear, there had been no detailed research on audience interests and public opinion. The decision was based on impressionistic observations; there were only a few local amateurish polls, mainly in Estonia. Methodical and controlled polling on politically sensitive subjects did not begin until about 1965. By 1966 and later, when results began coming in, the development of overt dissident activities and the proliferation of politically-oriented samizdat made it apparent that the assumptions of 1963 were overly complacent.

Jamming was ended just after the beginning of a rapid upsurge in the number of receivers in the hands of the population—and therefore in the number of potential new listeners, unformed in their habits. In the early 1960s there were about 30 million radio receivers in the Soviet Union, and the number was increasing at the rate of several million per year.

One consideration in discounting the potential new mass radio audience may have come from the arrival of television, which in 1963 was just becoming a mass phenomenon in the Soviet Union. There were eight million television sets in use, and the production rate had just reached four million per year. It would have been plausible to conclude that television would attract away the radio audience in the evenings, especially the audience for foreign radio, which had to contend with difficult and time-consuming conditions of reception and tuning. However, there is no direct evidence that such calculations were systematically analyzed.

On the other hand, there is evidence that had these considerations influenced Soviet thinking, they were far off base.

The differences between Soviet television and radio were greater than those between television and radio elsewhere. This was especially so in the most critical area: news broadcasting. Television news broadcasting in 1963 was primitive, relatively infrequent, and in no position to compete with radio, either Soviet or foreign. It was not until the beginning of 1968 that Soviet television first produced a news program that differed significantly from radio news and took advantage of the special visual capabilities of television.[1] A pre-1968 study of the preferences of former Soviet citizens found that they preferred Soviet radio over television by an overwhelming margin, rating its news coverage more complete by a margin of 19 to 3, quicker by 53 to 1, and more important to them personally by 29 to 6 (the differing totals are accounted for by those who preferred newspapers).[2] However, Soviet polling in the area was just beginning in 1963, and it is unlikely that figures of the type given were available at that time.

The first experiment in nonjamming lasted only five years. It was followed by five more years of resumed jamming, during which time the visible activities of dissident elements were largely suppressed by police actions and controlled emigration of the most active figures, climaxed by the deportation of Aleksandr Solzhenitsyn. Well before the resumption of jamming the tightening of controls in the sphere of information was visible in the form of general purges of editorial boards. The politicalization of samizdat reached a peak in April 1968, when the Chronicle of Current Events, virtually a bimonthly newspaper, began to appear. Much of the samizdat, of course, was produced in the hope that it would be broadcast back to the Soviet Union by foreign radio. The qualitative and quantitative change in the nature of dissident activities occurred rather abruptly in early 1966 on the occasion of the Sinyavsky-Daniel trials. The fact that the resumption of radio jamming was delayed for more than two years after the event indicates the reluctance and seriousness with which this step was regarded, although it was the simplest countermeasure available, probably because it was the most open admission of weakness.

The purpose of the following account is twofold. It is first to investigate the specific factors that led to the resumption of jamming. This can be done by examining the countermeasures, short of jamming, taken by the Soviet media in their attempt to compete with foreign radio. Those steps were accompanied by increasingly open discussion of the problem in professional journals. A chronological reconstruction of those measures produces an incomplete, but coherent, record of the rising level of concern in the official perception of the effects of uncontrolled foreign broadcasting. From this it is possible to infer, with reasonable assurance, the history and motives of the decision to resume jamming.

The second purpose is to look for the reality behind the official Soviet perception of the effects of foreign broadcasting. This is exceedingly difficult to do because of the secrecy drawn over the subject inside the Soviet Union. But it is important because there may be a close connection between the subject and certain broader characteristics of the Soviet state and society. In brief, attitudes toward the media and information services are probably related to attitudes toward the government and the political system. Therefore, any new information that can be derived in this area may throw some light on trends in the development of the Soviet political system.

Much journalistic and academic attention has been given to examining visible dissent inside the Soviet Union. Examination has been possible because of the availability of samizdat literature and the visibility of protest demonstrations and other forms of illegal or semilegal activities, often intended for publicity abroad. Analyses of that material have been extremely cautious in drawing general conclusions about the state of Soviet society. They emphasize the extremely small size of the known protest movements. It is often assumed that protesters and dissenters must be very unrepresentative of larger samples of the population. However, it is possible that any activity that risks consequences ranging from loss of livelihood to prison to incarceration in mental institutions would receive active cooperation from only a very small number of its potential sympathizers. At least some of those who engage in overt activity must be motivated by a sense of spiritual or psychological support from a much larger pool of latent agreement. It is the "silent" part of Soviet society that is thrown into relief by the subjects touched here.

Certainly, the relationship between control of information and the maintenance of Soviet rule, which in 1963 some Soviet leaders evidently felt had become less critical, was thrown into sharp relief after the cessation of jamming, when the underlying processes became the subject of intensive study in the Soviet Union. Only a small portion of that effort is accessible, but it is enough to permit an independent examination of the relationship and some tentative conclusions about the development of the Soviet system from a hitherto unapproachable viewpoint. Particularly interesting is the fact that for the first time the Soviet authorities used polling techniques to measure opinion closely related to basic political attitudes. Those poll results, although only partially published, contain questions that can be interpreted as indicating the respondents' belief in the veracity and credibility of the official media.

If there were any measurable amount of disaffection or skepticism about the quality of the Soviet system among the general population, the respondents' answers would be one manifestation of it. We cannot assume that there is a one-for-one relationship between the credibility of the authorities and attitudes toward the official media and a more generalized unhappiness about the Soviet system, nor can an exact enumeration of the factors defining a generalized dissatisfaction be undertaken. But almost certainly there is a relationship, and the fact that almost total censorship was clamped down on the results of this type of polling shortly after it was adjudged a reliable and acceptable form of investigation suggests that the authorities saw a connection.

Another connection may be suggested by the continued Soviet repression of even mild signs of dissent, despite the resulting propaganda beating in world opinion, and the adamant refusal at the Conference on European Security and Cooperation and other forums to consider any relaxation in the flow of information in return for Western concessions on security and trade issues. If dissenters are a small and isolated group, as they do indeed appear to be by conventional observation, the question arises as to why Soviet authorities show continued fear of even slight relaxations of internal controls. The figures from the information and media polls are one possible answer.

The method of deriving the figures from the polling data and related information cannot be as rigorous or exact as is possible with polling material from more open societies, but the effort seems worthwhile because of the rarity and importance of such figures. In fact, there may not be any other comparable information. In the absence of competitive elections and the concealment of other indicators analysis of this data may come as close as is possible in assessing the level of contentment with Soviet life among the population at large.

Material on the Soviet polls has been collected in Chapter 5, which includes a consideration of the validity of broader or narrower interpretations of their results. That chapter, based primarily on Soviet materials available up to 1971, has been left substantially as it was originally written. Since that time new material on radio listening based on non-Soviet surveys has become available. That material has been analyzed separately in an epilogue, which also includes a brief account of some post-1971 developments. An independent comparison and cross-check of the interpretation of the Soviet polls is thus possible, while the non-Soviet data can be extended to provide a more detailed breakdown of the size of the Soviet audience of the separate foreign broadcasters.

EARLY COMPLACENCY

It could be expected in 1963 that the simultaneous combination of the end of most jamming and the rapid increase in number of radio receivers would lead to increased listening, not only because it became physically easier to obtain intelligible reception, especially in the cities, but because the psychological stigma had been removed when the government suspended jamming, thus implicitly signalling that while it might not approve, it no longer considered the broadcasts so harmful as before. That state of affairs was evident in numerous comments made by Soviet citizens at the time. It was strikingly confirmed by an incident later related by a former Soviet scientist who had held sensitive positions throughout the period. At Moscow University there was a section restricted to students with security clearances for classified information, a group heavily sprinkled with sons of high KGB officials and other elite groups. One of those students brought to English-language class, for use in oral translation, a copy of U. S. News and World Report, left in his home by his father, who used it in his work. The instructor listened to the reading with increasing puzzlement until the student came to an item about a Soviet soldier who had defected in Berlin. Halting the reading, she inquired about the source of the magazine, and began a lecture about the harmfulness and impermissibility of becoming involved with such reactionary material. Her lecture provoked a discussion and argument, with the instructor conceding that perhaps she had been wrong to object, because, "after all, since jamming had been ended, it was now all right to listen to the Voice of America."

Reactions of that type must have been known or foreseen by the Soviet authorities at the time of the decision to cease jamming. Yet there were few visible expressions of concern and no apparent counteractions. The popular press, as it had for several years immediately preceding the 1963 decision, generally remained silent about foreign radio stations. That policy was no doubt motivated by the sound reasoning that any publicity, no matter how negative, would only call attention to the broadcasts and, by adding an exotic aura to them, possibly increase listener interest.

Some reinforcement for this supposition can be found in the effects of one theme that never entirely disappeared from the press, although it, as all matters related to foreign radio, was treated in relatively low key during the early 1960s. The reference is to the continuing reminders in the Soviet press that RL and RFE were creatures of the CIA and that VOA and other governments' official radio stations could be assumed to be connected to intelligence organs. Those assertions may have increased interest in and the credibility of the radio stations. They seem to have been generally accepted by the audience, and in a society where permeation of the culture by security and intelligence services was an expected state of affairs, the attacks had the effect of associating the broadcasts with authoritative institutions considered to be closer than any others to sources of power and information. In the case of Eastern Europe this association certainly enhanced the credibility of the radio stations. Surveys of Eastern European refugees, especially after the controversy over RFE's role in Hungary, showed that RFE was respected all the more, and its credibility raised, by allegations of its CIA connections. This was most notable among Hungarians, and to a lesser extent in the rest of Eastern Europe.[3] Conditions in the Soviet Union are not precisely comparable, but comments heard there indicate that on balance the net effect of the awareness of the intelligence connections on listener attitudes was probably more favorable than unfavorable.

In any case, Soviet concern about foreign broadcasting was certainly not manifested during the first year after the suspension of jamming. This was evident not only in the absence of comment in the mass press and the sanguine tone of the professional press but also in the complacent stance taken in the one discovered reference to the size of the audience for foreign radio published during this period:

> The Soviet people long ago saw through the methods of bourgeois propaganda and with disgust turned away from it. In our country there are millions of radio receivers able to pick up all the radio stations of the world. But if you ask their owners whether they listen to the broadcasts from the so called "free world," then the answer will not be comforting for the inspirers and organizers of "psychological warfare." The absolute majority of Soviet radio listeners are completely uninterested in such broadcasts, which they now and then come across in the ether on the wavelengths of the hostile stations and which they immediately tune out. These broadcasts are listened to more or less regularly only by an insignificant number of jaundiced Philistines and callow grovelers, seeking sensations and cacophonous jazz music. Consequently, tens of millions of dollars, expended on anticommunist radio propaganda, are in effect being poured down the drain, not bringing the imperialists the desired results.[4]

Rather modestly, that passage merely claims that at least 51 percent ("the absolute majority") of respondents to a presumed, but unspecified, poll stated that they had no interest in foreign broadcasts. Thus, theoretically, the statement admits the possibility of 49-percent interest in foreign broadcasts. Percentages are not to the point, however, since the intention of the passage is clearly to express confidence that foreign radio broadcasts are an almost negligible problem. It was written in 1963 or early 1964 (sent to printer September 28, 1964).

Standing by itself, the passage could be dismissed as idiosyncratic, but when it is placed in chronological context there can be no doubt that it reflects a genuine belief. It is particularly notable because, as a product of the military-security sector of Soviet society, published by the Ministry of Defense, it presumably reflects the views of a sector that consistently has been most unhappy about suspensions of jamming. The military and the KGB were soon to be among the earliest and most extreme criers of alarm and the advocates of strong counterefforts against the effects of foreign broadcasts. Within two years the deputy chief of the political department of the armed forces was calling for action not only against the broadcasts and their influence but also against listeners personally.[5] This was farther than the civilian leaders were willing to go.

The 1964 statement, so strikingly in opposition to the later views from the same sources combined with the silence of the popular press and the optimistic analyses of the journalism and broadcasting professions, confirms that the Soviet leaders neither foresaw the consequences of suspending jamming (leaving aside the possibility that jamming would have made little difference) nor had prepared any significant compensatory actions.

The lack of serious concern or countermeasures could also be seen in the low level of activity and comment in the Soviet broadcasting organization. E. N. Mamedov, the deputy chairman responsible for internal programming, did inform his planning board in July or August 1963 that it was "especially important to strengthen timely commentaries" and to follow the example of the foreign department of Soviet radio in being more prompt, presumably because internal radio now had free competition, as the foreign department always had.[6]

At about the same time the Ukrainians, who had previously been at the forefront of those who had warned of the slowness of TASS in supplying the news, returned to the attack. The head of the Ukraine's broadcast system noted that they had improved their news operation by adding two more evening newscasts but that TASS was still disregarding its obligation to supply prompt news to the republic-level broadcasting organizations. The indictment was fairly severe and openly connected the entire issue with the competition from foreign radio by noting that the delays in news reporting facilitated the spread of lies and slander by foreign radio. Disingenuously, perhaps, TASS was described as almost the only source of foreign and all-Union news, but one that was operating according to the schedule of local newspapers, leaving its special radio materials for last. The Ukraine, he said, had lost all hope that TASS would reform itself and was suggesting that the central radio establish its own news department with independent collection and distribution of news.[7] This was just about the only serious discussion during the latter part of 1963 that raised a problem related to the end of jamming, although in December a Kirghiz radio official slipped in a comment that bad programs might drive listeners to "transoceanic jazz."[8] The year-end editorial of the State Committee was a rather routine affair, giving no hint of any dissatisfaction or awareness of problems connected with competition from foreign broadcasting.[9]

Probably the most confidence-inspiring experience the Soviets had in dealing with foreign broadcasting was in Estonia. The Estonians were frequently put forth as examples worthy of emulation, in respect to both their practice and the quality of their research and analysis. Just before the suspension of jamming they had delivered a highly encouraging report on their ability to attract listeners from VOA (see p. 13), which was probably an element in the decision to compete with foreign broadcasts. In 1968 a much more detailed report was released.

The Estonians were especially sensitive to the implications of foreign broadcasting because their geographic location enabled European long- and medium-wave broadcasts, as well as short-wave, to reach them. Furthermore, Finland's domestic radio was easily heard in Estonia and, because of the similarity of the Finnish and Estonian languages, widely understood. Finnish television could also be picked up in the coastal areas of Estonia. The fact that Estonian polls showed that Finnish radio provided the most popular foreign programs was of no concern, the Estonians said, because they knew that the Finns would censor their internal services to conform with Soviet desires. It was not made clear whether there was an explicit agreement with Finland to this effect or whether voluntary cooperation could be safely assumed. In any case, the only problem with Finland was that occasionally dispatches from Western news agencies were broadcast without sufficient care and "evoked quickly spreading rumors." But evidently, Finland radio's general deference was sufficiently appreciated for its lapses to be forgiven, for the Estonians carefully stated that they did not criticize it.

In second place among foreign broadcasters in popularity was VOA's Estonian-language program. It was claimed that foreign broadcasts, in the amount of listening, were not serious competition to Estonian radio. But the account then goes on to describe the measures used to combat VOA, and it would not be unreasonable to conclude from the painstaking efforts revealed that VOA was uppermost in the minds of Estonia's radio authorities. Estonian radio created a new evening news program, "Echo of the Day," in 1959. Later polls showed that that newscast had become the most popular radio program in Estonia, with 70 percent of the potential audience in a republic that had one radio receiver for every three inhabitants. The newscast was deliberately timed to begin at the same moment as VOA's Estonian program. Twice its schedule was transferred to VOA's hour, and each time VOA, in a move that was described as "hardly coincidental," transferred its broadcast to an earlier hour. It was probably experiences of this type that provided the greatest encouragement to those sectors of Soviet leading circles that supported the idea of easing up on jamming.

The importance of VOA in the Estonian authorities' thinking was revealed in the description of the production process of "Echo of the Day," which, it turned out, virtually revolved around foreign radio broadcasts. Every morning its planning session surveyed the transcripts of the foreign programs of the preceding 24 hours. Throughout the day the survey was continually updated and the staff formulated decisions on the material that should be answered on that night's newscast. The matter of promptness was constantly emphasized, for the Estonians well understood the maxim that the first source of news dominates, that it is harder to "relearn" than to learn, and that it is difficult to catch up with false news that continues to spread from mouth to mouth, "friend to friend." Nevertheless, the polls eventually revealed that a sizable number was dissatisfied with the promptness of Radio Estonia's news. Finally, probably in 1966 or 1967, the Estonians gave up on TASS as being hopelessly slow on foreign news and resorted to the expedient of cribbing from the central Moscow newscasts. If they could not get a direct relay, they set up in the studio a television set tuned to Moscow television and had the announcer repeat live in Estonian what he saw on television.

The sophisticated Estonians also had a special ploy of their own. Normally, the Soviet press never mentions accidents, natural disasters, or untoward events of an unplanned nature, except for a select few chosen for the purpose of illustrating moral lessons or when their scale is so large that many people would learn of them anyway. The Estonians, however, citing the fact that such a policy leads to exaggerated rumors, reported that they made a point of trying to include some such event on every newscast. The ostensible purpose of doing so was to point out the need for observing safety rules, but they also mentioned the building up of trust in the listener that the Estonian radio always tells the whole truth.[10] It may be suspected that the latter point was closer to the primary motive for this notable departure from Soviet practice, and that the Estonians, although they could not state it directly, were mainly concerned with ways of building up the credibility of their broadcast operations.

The outward appearance of the Soviet broadcasting world remained calm through the early months of 1964. In April the first deputy director of the Ideological Department of the Central Committee published a long survey of the state of the Soviet press and radio and, in effect, issued the department's general instructions for the current period. That disquisition was most notable for what it did not contain: It had nothing to say about foreign radio and made only a passing reference to the possible penetration of foreign ideology.[11] Since this was soon to become one of the main themes of Soviet ideological discourse, the omission must be considered significant.

The director of TASS published a long article the next month that was probably a condensation of the speech he had delivered on Press Day, May 5. Its content and tone also lacked any sense of alarm about Western broadcasts. It did contain a section on bourgeois press and radio attacks against the USSR and went into some detail on how they had exploited an incident in which an African student in the Soviet Union had frozen to death after an incident on a train. But he did not mention Western radio broadcasts to the Soviet Union at all. In vivid contrast to the low-key treatment of Western propaganda, he denounced the Chinese press and radio at length. He was especially indignant about Chinese radio broadcasts to the Soviet Union, singling out an article of February 4, which had been broadcast in Russian 125 times. This, he said, can only evoke "disgust."[12] Sino-Soviet relations had reached a new low, aggravated by fruitless territorial negotiations. About this time the Soviets began selectively jamming Chinese broadcasts to the Soviet Union, concentrating on derogatory attacks on Khrushchev's person. The weight of concern in the speech was clearly tilted toward the Chinese, rather than the Western, propaganda efforts.

THE FIRST POSTJAMMING COUNTERMEASURES

Within weeks of the TASS director's assessment the situation abruptly reversed. The change was total and came without visible warning. The occasion was the gathering in Moscow in early June 1964 of most of the country's ideological and media officials, leading editors and commentators, in what was styled the "All-Union Creative Conference of Publicists." The published version of the proceedings of this conference was replete with warnings of the influence of foreign radio and complaints of the ineffectiveness of the Soviet response. The published proceedings were probably a much laundered version of the full proceedings, and it may be imagined that the private conversations of the participants were more worrisome than either version. The seriousness and importance of the event was underscored when almost immediately afterward, the Soviet radio broadcast system was rearranged and the most radical change yet instituted was introduced.

Mikhail Kharlamov, chairman of the State Committee for Radio Broadcasting and Television, spoke at this conference, but only a general, uninformative, version of his remarks was released. However, others were permitted to speak on the record more to the point. V. D. Tregubov, the chief of news broadcasting of the central radio, was apparently the first to bring up the subject:

> Journalists of the capitalist West are at the microphone day and night, they use radio to the utmost, particularly in broadcasts to the Soviet Union.
>
> Radio exerts a great influence on enormous sectors of the population, and all our journalists should keep this firmly in mind.
>
> We must make broad use of informational material for publicistic statements in the press and on radio and must answer foreign broadcasts more effectively and sharply.[13]

This theme then was taken up at slightly greater length and with markedly greater emphasis by others. G. Zimanas, chief editor of the newspaper of the Communist Party of Lithuania and one who appeared as a regular spokesman on East-West ideological conflict, spoke not only of the problem, but of some of the barriers to responding to it:

> One must respond quickly to various, perhaps unpleasant, manifestations and events which occur in our life. Or else it turns out that we are silent and people learn about it from foreign radio broadcasts, and they learn an incorrect, distorted version. We still consider ourselves monopolists in the field of information. But this is not so. And we, lagging behind in information, are involuntarily orienting people toward foreign radio, and if we let any version get around, later it is difficult to stamp it out. That is why it is important for us to inform readers quickly, correctly, in order that our truthful version goes out first, and not the made up, false one.[14]

Zimanas then went on to describe an incident illustrative of the inability to "overcome barriers." They had wanted to print news of the West German embassy's activities in Lithuania, but had been unable to get full information or a release on it. Only after a letter of complaint had been printed by Pravda was the problem resolved. The barriers involved may have been as much bureaucratic as political—a subject about which Zimanas could not speak openly. The fact that the Soviet news system was inhibited by its inherent bureaucratic structure, as well as voluntary political factors, was soon to be vividly demonstrated.

The strongest expression of concern was delivered by Pravda commentator Yuri Zhukov:

> Our press is now operating in conditions where Soviet citizens are subjected to intensive pressures from the propaganda of our political opponents that reaches over the air and by other methods. Our responsibility is especially great in these conditions.
>
> Our most important task now is to give the reader effective help in finding answers to those questions that occur to him when the bourgeois propaganda reaches him, in not waiting to obtain agreements or "visas" of approval on articles etc., but in always keeping a finger on the pulse of life and delivering prompt and effective counterblows to the enemy. Unfortunately, the inertia of our newspaper life is such that this instantaneous reaction is by no means always in evidence.[15]

No one at the conference openly mentioned the absence of jamming, but it is clear that that was the key fact that prompted those observations. Another characteristic of the comments was that the farther the speaker was from direct responsibility in the broadcasting area, the more insistent he was about the criticalness of the situation. Whereas the radio executive described the combating of foreign broadcasts as one task of the Soviet press and radio, the newspaper editor described it as an important task, and the political commentator described it as the most important task of the Soviet journalism establishment. Regardless of the degree of alarm expressed by different individuals, at the decision-making level action was already being taken.

The reasons for the sudden transition from confidence to alarm are not clear. It may be that the conference itself, perhaps routinely scheduled, was the cause. The interaction and exchange of experience among the participants could conceivably have clarified a picture heretofore only dimly perceived, or known only as isolated parts, at the higher levels of authority. On the other hand some unknown incident or revelation in the preceding weeks might have sparked the convening of the conference for purposes of fuller analysis. Perhaps an unreported incident suddenly revealed much, or, more likely, internal analyses and studies based on a gradual accumulation of information culminated in May and were reinforced by the personal experiences related by the practitioners who gathered together in June. With the available information there is no way of knowing. But it is clear that a decision was almost immediately reached to take new measures to counteract the influence of foreign radio, and the decision was implemented with record speed.

Since the resolution of the Central Committee was dated June 24, 1964, it was probably under active consideration several weeks earlier, at least since the time of the publicists' conference. This resolution established a new schedule of broadcasting for the central radio system. Its key provision was to set up a new round-the-clock channel called Mayak (Beacon) that had to "contain prompt [operativnaya] information (not less than twice per hour)" on both internal and external affairs. The creation of additional facilities was ordered to ensure that Mayak could be heard everywhere in the Soviet Union. An extremely short lead time of five weeks was allowed, with the new program to begin on August 1. (Previous changes of this magnitude usually required more than five months of preparation.) Mayak was to take over the second channel, formerly used for programs designed for the European part of the Russian Republic. The new schedule was then to be as follows: First Program (general central radio channel), 20 hours per day; Second Program (Mayak), round the clock; Third Program (literary-cultural), 12 hours per day; Fourth Program (repetition of portions of the First and Third Programs timed for the Far East, Siberia, and Central Asia), round the clock; Fifth Program (Mayak and specialized material, intended for seamen, Russians abroad, and foreigners studying Russian), round the clock. Emphasizing the increased attention being given to the importance of nationwide ideological cohesion, the quantity of local broadcasting was ordered decreased, although its quality was ordered to be raised.[16]

Mayak went on the air exactly on the ordered deadline: August 1, 1964. So rapid was the rush to begin, there apparently was no advance publicity at all. Even the professional organ of the journalists' union was unable to take advance notice of it, first announcing the new program only in its August issue, which went to press on August 10. The Central Committee's resolution did not explain the reasons for establishing the new program, although such resolutions frequently include a rationale. It was published with the notation that there were "insignificant abbreviations," a procedure that is very unusual, if not unique in this case: Central Committee resolutions, if published at all, are either published in full or in summary form. So it appears that there was at least one sensitive point, possibly relating to the situation that gave rise to the resolution, on which silence was considered preferable. Subsequent Central Committee resolutions on radio programming were not published.

Although official texts were reticent, there is not the slightest doubt about the reasons for the changes. Mayak was established primarily, if not solely, to be a counterattraction to foreign radio broadcasts. The format and contents of the program showed that. Its early format was described as being patterned after foreign news broadcasts, but this was said to have later changed.[17] In fact, insofar as VOA was concerned, Mayak preceded it in adopting the informal arrangement of frequent newscasts interspersed with short, irregularly-placed items of music, interviews, commentary, and so on. VOA did not adopt that format until November 1966, and then, for the time being, mainly on its English-language programs.[18]

It was only several years later that the real purposes of Mayak could be discussed openly. The deputy chief editor of the program said that it was created to meet the demand for news caused by the competition of foreign radio.[19] M. Barmankulov, a prominent journalism dean and a regular commentator on the subject of foreign radio, described Mayak's role in countering the so called Western radio specialty of "agitation by naked facts." He referred to accusations that Mayak, other radio programs, and some newspapers had even harmed their own propaganda functions by giving too much time and space to news, presumably in rebutting news heard on foreign broadcasts.[20]

A deputy chairman of the State Committee fully disclosed the prime role of Mayak in the struggle against foreign broadcasting. In the process he also provided an encapsulated summary of the basic Soviet strategy for dealing with foreign broadcasts without the protection of jamming. Noting that there were 32 foreign radio stations broadcasting to the Soviet Union (he named only VOA, BBC, and DW, in that order), he enumerated the counterefforts that were demanded, the most important of which was Mayak, followed by the regular newscasts on the other programs. Third place in the four-pronged counteroffensive against foreign radio belonged to specially designed anti-American programs. Bringing up the rear were prompt commentaries and analyses.[21]

Besides confirming the motivation behind the decision in 1964 to create Mayak, the rank order of importance of the various countermoves against foreign broadcasts is of enormous interest in that it points toward the central concern of the Soviet perception of what foreign broadcasting was all about. Simple presentation of the spot news occupies the first two places on the list. Denunciations of the biases of the stations and of the United States were used, and also analyses and interpretations of the news, but in Soviet eyes those were secondary. It was the Soviet concept of "agitation by facts" that most agitated—in the Western sense—the guardians of the Soviet regime. This subject will be considered in greater detail later; the operational implications of it mean that the simple availability of the news had greater immediate importance than the ideas or interpretations that it might carry. Foreign radio made known the existence of facts that the Soviet media reported late or not at all. It was not so much a matter of whether the facts could convey a possibly anti-Soviet interpretation, although, of course, they might, but that, as the polls were to hint, their simple existence undermined trust in the Soviet media, which inevitably meant undermined trust in the government and in the system itself.

The Soviets understood in 1968 as they had not in 1963 that the situation was not one that could be resolved by inducing, explicitly or tacitly, any feasible restraint on the part of the foreign stations. The coolness and ostensible objectivity of the major Western stations, particularly VOA and BBC, came to be seen by the Soviets as a deceptive and dangerous trick, rather than a sign of moderation. The only internal solution would be a complete overhaul of the Soviet news distribution system, in both its basic principles and operational procedures. This overhaul was attempted, but it was strictly limited, for both political and bureaucratic reasons.

Mayak, at least in its early days, had an additional function that was never mentioned. It was broadcast, often in distorted form, on frequencies above the 25-meter band, where, normally, Soviet internal broadcasting never operated. All those frequencies were exactly those being used by RL. In other words, it was being used as an auxiliary jammer. It may have been that that was done because at the time there were surplus jamming transmitters that the Soviets wished to keep on a stand-by status, and their use for Mayak could be considered a form of readiness practice.

Although the Central Committee had specified that Mayak should broadcast news not less than twice per hour, its news schedule was actually on an hourly basis for at least its first year. That may have been for technical reasons; in any case, at a later date it did go over to a schedule of 48 newscasts per day.[22] But even on the original schedule there was no shortage of news. A compilation of June through July 1965 showed the following daily quantities of news and related materials: Mayak had 25 newscasts per day, totalling 305 minutes, eight press reviews of 80 minutes, and six commentaries of 45 minutes; simultaneously, the First Program had eight newscasts of 120 minutes, two press reviews of 25 minutes, and one commentary of 20 minutes.[23] Thus, Mayak alone was broadcasting more than seven hours of news and commentary per day, and the First Program's total of news-related material had reached almost three hours per day. And those totals were in a country that only four years earlier had broadcast no news at all during prime-time hours. The strategy of increasing the distribution of news as the first line of defense against foreign radio was being thoroughly implemented.

The early reviews of Mayak were generally favorable, with some reservations. Mayak's success, it was said, consisted in getting out an unending flow of news, and TASS had made special arrangements for Mayak's supply. Although there were initial difficulties with the literary and music portions of the program, it was reported: "The new program is solving the main problem—to report promptly on all events taking place in our country and abroad."[24]

Letters specifically praising the availability of news on Mayak were published. But they were accompanied by a review that tempered the praise with the observation that the number of letters received in response to Mayak in the first four months—1,020—was considered to be low; and half of those were requests for musical works. Mayak, the review said, was often lagging behind foreign radio stations with the news. In addition, a more varied format was needed.[25]

Summing up the first full year of Mayak, when Mayak was said to have found its own voice, the main criticism had become less that Mayak's news was too late than that it was too narrow. The early-morning newscasts, in particular, were repetitions of previous newscasts. Mayak needed more contact with the local press. Its August 9, 1965 programs were based solely on TASS and Novosti material. Mayak had nothing of its own. Mayak's listeners were said to want news from it, not the interpretations of capitalist radio stations "which put out inauthentic facts with far-reaching goals." The ether is an arena of struggle, and the capitalist radio "must always be unmasked with timely broadcast information."[26]

In the midst of this period of assessment and experimentation with Mayak, Khrushchev was ousted from power in October 1964. That event appears to have had no immediate effect on broadcasting policies. It is true that Mikhail Kharlamov was one of the handful of officials who were removed simultaneously with Khrushchev's downfall, but that seems to have had more to do with Kharlamov's well-known close connections with Khrushchev and his role as Khrushchev's errand boy in backstage maneuvers than with his administration of the Soviet broadcasting system. In any case, Kharlamov's removal does not seem to have caused upheavals in the broadcasting organization, and it has not been possible to detect significant changes in programming policies at that time. One change that did occur was the end of selective jamming of Radio Peking (for a little more than two years, as it turned out), but inasmuch as that jamming had been directed mainly at personal denigrations of Khrushchev, his ouster made the whole operation moot for both the Chinese and the jammers.

The new chairman of the State Committee for Radiobroadcasting and Television was Nikolai N. Mesyatsev. He is not known to have become involved in political maneuvering the way Kharlamov did. He held the post until the spring of 1970, when he was fired, probably in connection with the propaganda fiasco of the overdone hundredth anniversary of the birth of Lenin, as well as with the general malaise that brought about a widespread sweepout of ideological officials.

The experience with Mayak was probably followed at high levels. The suspension of jamming, the jiggling of broadcast schedules, and the creation of Mayak were all accomplished without the customary public analyses and pronouncements of the Party. The suspension of jamming had been undertaken with little advance preparation. Mayak and the professional discussions that accompanied it constituted the beginning of a corrective for past neglect, but the popular press and the higher Party organs remained publicly silent. The silence was finally broken in July 1965 when the verdict that was pronounced was approval of what had been done, and, in practical effect, authorization to continue on the course begun with the creation of Mayak. It was probably not merely by chance that articles about foreign radio broadcasts gradually began to reappear in the mass media at about the same time.

The official pronouncement took the form of an unsigned editorial article in the main theoretical journal of the Central Committee.[27] The article discussed at some length general characteristics and methods of anti-Soviet themes in world propaganda and ideological competition. It then got down to particulars. Specific Russian-language broadcasts of VOA and BBC were described in a manner that depicted them as glorifying the material wealth of the West. Various techniques, such as the deceptive appearance of objectivity created by casual references to Western shortcomings, were stressed. The only other radio stations mentioned by name were RL, RIAS, RFE, and DW. However, it was said that the foreign broadcasting services of Italy, France, Spain, and Japan also echoed the Washington-Bonn anti-Soviet propaganda chorus. (France was never again referred to in this context, and Japan was mentioned only once.) The article then delineated the problem created in the Soviet Union and specified the remedy:

> Bourgeois propagandists are trying to use foreign radio, press, tourism, as channels of penetration of alien views into our midst. It would be rash on our part to be satisfied that these channels have not justified all the long-range hopes of the anti-Soviet propagandists. It is necessary to study the tactics of enemy propaganda and actively counteract them. And this demands the elimination of those shortcomings of ideological work which in contemporary conditions are becoming especially intolerable. Usually such shortcomings appear where the most important demands of the Leninist tradition of propaganda work are forgotten.
>
> In our time, when there is a radio receiver in almost every house, to be silent about this or that event, not to illuminate it from the position of socialist ideology—means to give "freedom of action" to the falsifications of bourgeois propagandists.
>
> More than that, it is important not only to explain correctly this or that fact, but it must be done promptly. It must be recognized that bourgeois information agencies

> have achieved a high operational efficiency, immediately responding to everything happening in the world, while we are sometimes late. This means that the false version flies around the world faster than the truthful and exact one. And the first report produces sometime the greater impression! In contemporary conditions the spread of information and its operational effect is becoming the most important sphere of ideological struggle, and in this, complacency is inadmissable.[28]

The article is a virtual recapitulation of the concepts presented at the "All-Union Creative Conference of Publicists" that had preceded the establishment of Mayak a year earlier. The challenge of foreign radio would be met by direct competition with it in the rapid distribution of news. Thus, by inference, the decision to suspend jamming was confirmed. And the competition in hard-news reporting was "becoming the most important sphere of ideological struggle." Not competition in ideas or theoretical polemics, but simply the ability to compete with the West in the rapid distribution of credible news was adjudged to be the key factor in holding the hearts and minds of the people. That did not mean that all censorship would be ended and the Soviet press given a free hand to react on its own authority, as some contemporary headlines implied.[29] A Party official had already noted that delays in news distribution were not a technical matter but fulfilled a political purpose, and the article itself cautioned that not all foreign distortions should be rebutted, because that would put the Soviets in a defensive position.

That delayed pronouncement had several purposes: It filled a gap between official doctrine and current practice; it confirmed the intention of the new Brezhnev-Kosygin leadership to continue on the course set by Khrushchev in that area of policy; most importantly in the long run, it placed the official imprimatur on a fundamentally new method of dealing with sensitive ideological and political problems. The statement contained a reference to the study of enemy tactics, but the very process of its formulation involved a more profound study than that: the study of social processes inside the Soviet Union. The statement itself was the product of almost a year of evaluation of the competition between Mayak and foreign radio. Instead of a pronouncement, ex cathedra as it were, to be carried out virtually in the dark by lower-level functionaries, preliminary research and testing were undertaken. The processes of this particular evaluation are not visible, but later research did receive some publicity, although only for a short time. The 1965 pronouncement was a step toward the direct use of social-science research and methodology in the formulation of political and ideological policy. As such, it was unprecedented in Soviet practice, at least since the early years of Stalin's rule. It opened the possibility of influence by social scientists and other formerly excluded groups in the closed world of political and ideological policy.

The Kommunist article received a curious handling that pointed up its sensitivity. It was distributed through the Soviet-controlled remnant of the Cominform organization in Prague for publication in the Communist press abroad. But the version that was published abroad was very different from the original. The section about the effects of foreign radio and the tactics for coping with it, including the entire passage quoted above, was deleted, and a completely new, upbeat, ending was added. And this was done without any indication that the foreign version differed from the original. Usually some vague, even if misleading, notation such as "with insignificant abbreviations" or "with abbreviations," is inserted in such cases. But all such notations were omitted from the article.[30] Vaguely noted, misleading, condensations are not uncommon in Soviet practice, but outright falsifications, as in this case, are rare. The fact that this was done to a statement on foreign radio was probably an indication of a fundamental insecurity about the consequences of the policy.

EARLY ATTEMPTS AT ASSESSMENT

Even while the new policy was being finalized, signs of nervousness were appearing. One such sign was the essentially negative comments about the ambiguous figures on listener mail that surfaced during this period. The central fact behind this dissatisfaction, although not the only cause, was a decrease in 1964 in the volume of listener mail received by the All-Union Radio.[31] The reasons for the negative interpretations were not clear. Although the downturn in the figures for 1964 was the first in several years, radio mail had not been in the past an index of response that was always on the upgrade (see Table 1). In 1961 the volume of mail was little more than half of what it had been in 1958. That striking decline did not elicit any known public comment. Yet the decline of 73,000 letters from 1963 to 1964, which amounted to 15 percent, was a subject of obvious concern. The article that recorded this fact did not offer any suggestions as to the possible cause of the decline. It did point to the need for more systematic study of audience desires. The decrease was said to have been mainly in letters to the music and children's departments, which may have been of some consolation. But it was pointed out with alarm that a major department, the one dealing with industry, had received only 43 letters during the month of October 1964, and 30 of these were from seamen requesting musical works.[32]

That was not the first time that concern had been expressed about trends in radio mail. Even while the overall volume was still rising, the opinion was expressed that radio needed to improve its

TABLE 1

Volume of Listener Mail
Received by All-Union Radio,
1949-64

Year	Letters
1949	246,210
1950	202,796
1951	194,063
1952	222,057
1953	256,625
1954	303,000
1955	390,700
1956	339,762
1957	350,973
1958	403,000
1961	226,000
1962	346,000
1963	498,000
1964	425,000

Sources: 1949-58: S. V. Kaftanov, ed., Radio i televideniye v SSSR (Radio and Television in the USSR), trans. Joint Publications Research Service, No. 4838 August 3, 1961, p. 105, cited by Gayle F. Durham, Radio and Television in the Soviet Union (Cambridge, Mass.: Center for International Studies, MIT, 1965), p. 78; 1961-62: "The Journalist at the Microphone," editorial, Sovetskaya Pechat' (September 1963):1-3; 1963-64: M. Aleskovskiy, "Applause and Whistles," Sovetskaya Pechat' (February 1965):38-41.

contact with the masses. It was pointed out that although radio mail exceeded 300,000 letters annually, Izvestia, with a circulation only one-thirtieth as large, was receiving 435,000 letters. The same editorial, perhaps meaning to infer a connection, also urged that the news broadcasts needed to be more timely, and said the various news programs had a disorderly format. The separate departments of the radio were said to be insufficiently specialized.[33] And a review of Mayak, after noting that Mayak's mail was lower than it should have been, went on to assert that, in general, radio mail, unlike newspaper mail, was not increasing in proportion to the number of listeners.[34]

On the surface, and on the basis of the fragmentary figures disclosed, the expressed alarm hardly seemed justified. It is true that the ratio of letters to the number of probable listeners was declining. In 1950 there had been one letter per year for each 56 radio receivers in the country. The ratio fell to 1:65 in 1955 and to 1:91 in 1958. (Those figures, unlike others used in this study, take into account the wired speakers as well as wave sets.) In the 1960s it was far lower: in 1961 it was 1:279; in 1962, 1:185; in 1963, 1:131; and in 1964, 1:170. Some of the relative decline in mail depicted by those ratios was almost certainly due to a shift from group listening to individual listening as the number of receivers increased. That is, the number of listeners did not increase in direct ratio to the number of receivers. But even though the majority of the mail was probably composed of simple requests for musical numbers or solicited complaints about general or personal matters unrelated to radio programming (much encouraged by Soviet press and broadcasting organizations), there was undoubtedly a real decline in listener response, and perhaps in listener interest, to Soviet radio.

After 1964 the broadcast organizations restricted access to information about listener mail, and only scattered references, overlooked by the censor, can be found. Radio mail for the year 1966 was reported to be 439,000.[35] This would indicate a slight falling off, compared to the years 1963-64, for the quantity of mail as a proportion of potential radio audience. But a passing remark in a 1967 article, the significance of which may have been unnoticed by both the writer and the censor, said that radio mail was currently arriving at the rate of about 6,000 letters per week.[36] That is equivalent to only a little more than 300,000 letters per year and works out to a ratio for annual mail per number of radio receivers of about 1:270. If those numbers held true for the entire year, it would mean that the mail-response rate of the Soviet radio audience had declined by almost one half during the first four years after the suspension of jamming, and that most of the decline had occurred between 1966 and 1967.

The obvious explanation for the decline in interest in Soviet radio would be the expansion of television. But serious Soviet analysts, to the extent that they could speak at all, carefully avoided that explanation. They could not say much because the television side of the State Committee was even more secretive than the radio side. According to an article published by the Union of Journalists, Central Television had a strict rule never to reply to criticism and not to allow the effects of critical articles to become known. It would allow no outside access to analyses of its mail or to its polls and research. It was, in fact, alleged to be basically hostile to the entire concept of studying audiences and principles of programming.[37]

What little those in authority said about Soviet television portrayed it in bleak terms. V. Chernishev, a deputy chairman of the State Committee, speaking to a conference of television executives in September 1963, noted the almost total lack of viewer response to some programs, citing particularly those for women and agriculture. The television magazine Iskusstvo could go a whole month without receiving a single letter.[38]

Television mail for the years 1961, 1962, and 1963—the last before secrecy was imposed on this statistic—totalled 46,000, 56,000, and 68,000 letters, respectively. Years later those figures were cited by one of the country's leading academic analysts as having led to the false conclusion that audience interest in television was rising. He asserted that that was not true, because no account was taken of the fact that the number of television sets in use was increasing. Additional information of which he was in possession was that the most popular television programs were those about youth, music, drama, and the Russian language. Political programs, except those about science, were much less popular. Programs for soldiers and women evoked little interest, and in absolutely last place was agriculture. During all of 1963 the agricultural programs brought in a response from the entire country of 10 letters.[39]

The television mail figures do not, in themselves, seem to justify the pessimistic conclusions drawn. While it was true that the number of television sets was rising, the rate of increase of viewer mail was twice as high. For 1961-63 the number of sets in use was up 23 percent, but viewer mail increased 48 percent. Even in comparison with radio mail, the situation did not look bad. The ratio of letters to radio receivers in those years ranged from 1:279 to 1:131; for television it was 1:141 in 1961 and 1:118 in 1963. Some of the difference could be accounted for by the fact that during these years group television viewing was almost certainly more common than group radio listening, but, nevertheless, the pessimism of the few available Soviet comments is striking.

The secrecy that was imposed on radio and television mail statistics after 1964 should be compared to what occurred in 1969, perhaps, when the Union of Journalists terminated its annual compilation and review of newspaper and magazine circulation figures. In that case the reasons were clear. The circulation of the political—but not nonpolitical—publications, after a long period of sustained increases, had almost universally begun to turn down. It was no longer possible to point to these figures, as had been customary every year, as an example of progress in political and ideological development. The silence about radio mail may well have been motivated by a suspicion that it was beginning to show undesirable trends in the relationship between Soviet broadcasting and the audience. The available radio mail figures are too fragmentary to say with any assurance that they were influenced by the growth in popularity of foreign radio.

The treatment of radio mail information was not the only sign of disquiet during this period of general confidence. Even while the experience of Mayak was being digested, and the Party's favorable pronouncement of July 1965 on the policy of meeting foreign radio with open competition in the field of news was being prepared, reservations were being expressed and precautions taken. In Leningrad, in particular, there were complaints about the lateness of Soviet radio and news services that gave enemy radio the first opportunity to become a source. The Leningrad Oblast and City Committees of the Party were reported to be conducting sociological research on the penetration of bourgeois influence and issuing regular recommendations on combating it. The matter was of such concern that in January 1965 the Leningrad City Committee held a special discussion on the subject, but no information on the substance of the discussion was given.[40]

The clearest semipublic warning that there were elements in the Party worried by the implications of the developing policy of unrestrained competition with foreign radio in rapidity and fullness of news reporting came in an address by a deputy director of the Central Committee's Ideological Department to the Executive Board of the Union of Journalists on February 5, 1965. The published version of the speech was "abbreviated," and it appears, as usual, that the deleted portions centered on references to foreign radio. The Party official repeated the by-now standard formulation that bourgeois propaganda masks itself in the guise of objective information and uses promptness to accustom people to get the "freshest information" from Western sources. He said that Soviet radio, TASS, and Novosti had improved their speed of reporting, but there were still situations where delay occurred: "This is not a technical, but a political question. The task is not simply to be quick, but to be sure that information fulfills a determined educational function."[41]

In speaking those lines the deputy director was voicing a traditional view. His may have been the first acknowledgment in the context of the debate over foreign radio that news delays were a deliberate political act and not simply a matter of transmission and distribution efficiency. In reminding his listeners that information—i. e. news—had to fulfill an educational function he was asserting the long-standing doctrine that promptness, and even the act of reporting itself, could not be the first-priority goal if it meant that it was not done by plan in a manner or context that furthered predetermined Party objectives. News had to wait until it could be determined how to fit it into the proper doctrinal or political framework, and if it could not be so fitted in, it should not be broadcast at all.

The restatement of those views, at that time, from that source, was of more than ordinary significance. The Ideological Department not only formulated or advised in the formulation of policy. It also controlled or had a hand in the appointments of the chief editors of the main press organs, and, more importantly, it exercised a substantial degree of direct management of current operations. At that time, for example, the Ideological Department called in the chief editors of all the central press organs every two weeks for instructional conferences. Those conferences had two purposes. General instructions were given for the treatment of the various issues of foreign and domestic policy likely to figure in the news in the current period, and those foreign statesmen to be given favorable or unfavorable treatment were identified. Specific mistakes of individual publications were discussed and criticized.[42] Under those circumstances the views held within the Ideological Department were as important as, or more important than, formal statements of policy.

Various commentators treated this crucial matter in different ways. The chief editor of Partiinaya Zhizn, delivering the 1965 Press Day speech in May, had no reservations about the importance of prompt news and commentary in combating foreign radio. He stated flatly: "This is one of the important spheres of ideological struggle, and it is forbidden to be complacent in this area."[43] On the other hand it was still possible—or, perhaps, prudent, prior to the formal statement of policy in July—to write long articles on the tasks of Soviet radio without mentioning foreign broadcasting and the associated problems of timeliness at all.[44]

At that time, also, the results of one of the first rudimentary surveys, devoted to international news coverage, appeared. It was not a true poll; rather, 5,000 questionnaires were distributed, and 800 returned. Among them were letters claiming that Soviet radio ought to, but did not, unmask and rebut foreign radio stations. The commentators added, "Many listeners and viewers agree." The figures were called "surprising." They showed that 37.3 percent preferred radio for international comment, compared to 35.3 percent for television. Dissatisfaction with radio on the subject was 12.1 percent and with television 15.8 percent.[45] More scientific polls later on were to show greater disparities in favor of radio on both counts.

By the time under discussion the formal Party statement endorsing the policy of meeting foreign radio on its own ground by competing with it in the area of prompt news and commentary had appeared in Kommunist. The mass media, before that statement silent, immediately began to implement it by discussing foreign radio and offering direct rebuttals to broadcasts. Such direct disputations, relatively rare before mid-1965, became more and more common, although they were not yet at the tempo they were to achieve in 1966. Those rebuttals were basically of two types. In one form they analyzed the general goals and techniques of foreign radio broadcasts, pointing out their nefarious purposes of sowing dissent and mistrust among and within the socialist countries, and the censorship and political manipulation to which they were allegedly subjected. The other form comprised direct discussion and rebuttal of specific broadcasts. The second was the more common form, especially prior to 1966, when an intensive campaign of denunciation was begun, and the results of Soviet research and analysis of Western broadcasting began to become available.

Such rebuttals eventually became so common that a survey of them would simply be tedious. The texts below are from early examples of each of the basic types. Later examples will be cited only if they show something new in the evolution of the policy of coping with foreign radio. The following passage illustrates the first type of public rebuttal:

> How objectively are international events reflected in the commentaries of the official U. S. radio station, the Voice of America? This question, writes TASS correspondent in New York, Oleg Onechkin, has again arisen following the appointment as Director of the Voice of America of John Chancellor, a former correspondent [words indistinct] in the White House.
>
> It is a secret to none that the Voice of America is one of the most active propaganda organs of the American government. At the same time it lays claim to complete objectivity. However, the New York Times, for example notes that the broadcasting of news and compilation of commentaries are subject to censorship by high-placed representatives of the State Department with the purpose of removing any criticism of government policy. Also subject to censorship are reports and commentaries by the Voice of America concerning U. S. policy in South Vietnam and the Dominican Republic.
>
> The New York Times says that the main purpose of the work of the Voice of America is [words indistinct] the policy of President Johnson in the station's broadcasts. The former Director of the Voice of America, on retiring, said himself that the broadcasts of the radio are oversaturated with propaganda.
>
> [Words indistinct] broadcasts of the Voice of America after the appointment of the new director, who is quite a graphic propagandist. He is close to the White House, and in the opinion of the press, he will pursue the Johnson line in the best manner. [Word indistinct] consider that the Voice of America from now on will try still harder to praise U. S. policy to the sky, as far as that is possible.[46]

The second type, during that early period, was used more frequently. The following may have been the first such broadcast under the new official policy, and it uses the phrase "as is well known" to refer to something that its Soviet listeners could have known only from listening to VOA. The euphemism, "Washington radio," soon disappeared in favor of more precise identifications of the targets of rebuttals:

> The barbarous bombing of North Vietnamese towns and villages, . . . these monstrous crimes, committed by the U. S. military under orders from Washington, lie on the conscience of the flock of hawks. This fact is indisputable and cannot be refuted. This is the reason the whole world met with evident skepticism the last statement by Dean Rusk, when he spoke on Washington radio. As is well known, in this extensive speech, the U. S. Secretary of State attempted to lay the responsibility for the bombing of North Vietnamese territory by the U. S. Air Force on the Democratic Republic of Vietnam. Listening to the Secretary of State, one would think that it is not the U. S. militarists who are sowing death on Vietnamese soil, but the Vietnamese, who have crossed the ocean and occupied the American state.
>
> On the same day that Rusk spoke on Washington radio, the New York Times published an article by its correspondent, Jack Raymond, which told readers about the program of the military government of South Vietnam, which is unprecedented in scope. . . .
>
> [. . .]
>
> No less clear is the notorious aim pursued by Dean Rusk in speaking over Washington radio with his pacifistic dissertations. This demagogic gesture was made by the U. S. Secretary of State in order to distract the attention of world public opinion from a series of new provocations against the Vietnamese people prepared by the U. S. military. By his slanderous attacks on the Democratic Republic of Vietnam, Dean Rusk attempted to stifle the powerful voice of the peoples of our planet, which is ever more resolutely and insistently demanding the immediate cessation of the aggressive actions of the United States in Vietnam.
>
> This oratorical trick, which Dean Rusk has resorted to, is nothing new in the history of U. S. diplomacy. However, its employment has never succeeded in deceiving public opinion. The deception has not succeeded this time either. The predatory hawk can be recognized by its flight.[47]

The last excerpt is presented because it comes from what was probably the most important Soviet forum for international commentary in the mass media: the regular Sunday-afternoon radio-panel discussion, "Observers' Roundtable," on which the best-known radio and press commentators rotated:

> Let us consider another aspect of this question. I mean this monstrous cynical campaign that the American propaganda is conducting at the moment. American racists, having been exposed to the whole world, could not think of anything better than to slander their victims. They pushed the responsibility for the events in Los Angeles on the shoulders of some agitators, who, they say, incited the Negroes of the Watts area in Los Angeles. This line is calculated for the U. S. people and is taken up by the American national press and radio. The Hearst papers of the Daily News type put the blame on the inhabitants of Watts area, although they were beaten up and suffocated with poisonous gases, and on the entire U. S. Negro population. Organs of U. S. foreign propaganda have joined in this chorus, especially the notorious Voice of America. During the first days of the riots it slandered the inhabitants of the Watts section quite maliciously. If you listened to the radio commentator last week, you might have got the idea that the racist terror in America is not directed against Negroes but against whites; that Negroes themselves are to blame for the difficult situation in which they find themselves.
>
> However, during the last days the tone of the American propaganda commentaries for abroad changed. The overwhelming majority of the world is not contaminated with the racial prejudices which the so-called average American imbibes with his mother's milk, and to try and sell the standard home propaganda on the foreign market is a difficult matter. This is why in the more recent commentaries the Washington foreign policy propagandists admit that the U. S. Negro population in general and in Southern California in particular is in a difficult economic and political situation. They admit that not only in the South, but also in many states where there is "officially" no racial discrimination, the Negroes are actually driven into poverty. Indeed, the Voice of America admits that the explosion in Los Angeles was caused by insufferable conditions for Negroes in that city.
>
> But what kind of a conclusion does the Voice of America commentator draw from this? It appears that the disturbances in that city had nothing to do with the fight for civil rights! On the contrary—I quote exactly—the commentator declares that the insurrection in Los

> Angeles was only harmful to the cause of civil rights. In other words, the commentator admits that the black population is entitled to legislation, but denies them the right to fight to realize it. Just like the mercenary writer from the Daily News, he places racists and their victims on the same level. He cites Mayor Brown and his policemen who spread terror in the Watts section. In the face of all the world he points at the corpses of women and children and says: "It is your own fault that you are dead. They," he says, "did not choose the weapons which Mayor Brown and his subordinates would have liked to see them use." Such cynicism is shocking. It reveals to the entire world the cynicism and mendacity of a society built on the subjugation and exploitation of people, the cynicism and mendacity of U. S. official propaganda.[48]

In 1965 that kind of comment was confined mostly to the radio; the central newspapers did not take it up in a systematic way until 1966. There were, however, occasional reports of local newspapers blaming VOA for inciting youths to passionate crimes of murder and rape.[49]

Along with the systematic organization of public rebuttals of foreign radio, there continued to be analyses of the problem and suggestions for further measures. One of these surfaced in Leningrad in the summer of 1965, where special research on the problem had been going on at least since the previous year. The Director of the Department of Propaganda and Agitation of Leningrad Oblast suggested that local propagandists be given access to the monitoring reports of foreign radio stations so that they would be better prepared to answer questions put to them by their audiences:

> But the main thing is that our propagandists are not always timely and well informed; they are weakly equipped with materials about the work of enterprises, of local party organizations, they are not acquainted with the surveys of foreign radio stations. Often they are supplied only by newspapers, radio, television. Here, they are at times on the same level as their audience. But the audience goes to the propagandist because they believe him to be a person knowing immeasurably more.[50]

That seems to have been the first public mention of monitoring reports. It was not adopted and subsequently appeared in print only rarely, mainly in connection with a major reform of the system of oral agitators. According to later reports of emigrants, finally, years later, the restricted bulletins of TASS were made available to local Party units, where local propagandists and lecturers, numbering perhaps several million, could come to read them. Evidently, the Party could not overcome its distaste of itself distributing undigested transcripts of foreign broadcasts even to its most active supporters. The restricted TASS bulletins would be a compromise, but also the Party by then had evidence that could give rise to suspicions about the use that the mass of lower level propagandists would make of transcripts.

At the end of the summer the highest Party organ, Pravda, finally got around to making radio broadcasting the subject of a formal editorial discussion. Since that was an infrequent event for Pravda, and since the lead editorial was not tied to any discernible anniversary, such as Radio Day (May 7), it probably represented a carefully thought-out position based on the experience gathered over the past two years. The editorial was, in space, carefully balanced between praise and criticism. Its first half described the tasks of Soviet radio, how it had improved since Khrushchev's ouster, and its growing popularity, evidenced by numerous favorable letters, and the good reception of its new programs. The second half was critical, but less so than the specialized, small-circulation journals. The main point of the criticism was that many programs ignored current and important themes, in fact, had no content and were of no interest to listeners. But this criticism was directed solely to local broadcasting, at the Union-Republic level and below. The organizations responsible for the All-Union Radio were notably absent from the list of those whose attention was called to this section. The central radio was, of course, the key to the competition with foreign radio, but it was not mentioned in the critical section of the editorial. The final section of the editorial brought up the question of foreign broadcasts:

> Our ideological enemies are waging on the air a fierce battle against the ideas of communism and against the truth, and are trying to disseminate all sorts of insinuations and inventions against the Soviet Union, the socialist countries, the communist, workers', and national liberation movements. These gentlemen will stoop to anything, and at the same time try to give the appearance of presenting objective information. The imperialists make wide use of radio for propaganda in favor of the rotten bourgeois ideology and morals. Soviet radio exposes, and in the future must expose with still greater force, the bestial ideology of imperialism, and foil the hostile schemes and traps of bourgeois propaganda, carrying the impassioned communist word to all peoples.[51]

Overall the editorial showed no feelings of alarm. In the opinion of Pravda all may not have been perfect, but Soviet radio was on the right track.

The year 1965 ended without signs of a sense of awareness of great problems on the broadcasting scene. A plenary session of the Union of Journalists on December 21 reviewed the situation. The director of TASS, in the keynote speech, noted the existence of a propaganda onslaught against the Soviet Union, citing the Penkovsky Papers, distortions of the Soviet economic reforms, and U. S. reports about a softer, more subtle line being taken by VOA.[52] In Goryunov's words, poisonous seeds were being sowed in the Soviet Union. But he expressed no real alarm. Likewise, the response of E. N. Mamedov, deputy chairman of the State Committee in charge of internal broadcasting and, therefore, the man most responsible for countering foreign broadcasts, was restrained. In the published version, he merely noted in the course of debate that the work of radio and television journalists must be original and deep, because the capitalists are spending huge sums on radio propaganda.[53] In the exchange there was no foreboding of the impending shocks of 1966.

SOVIET JOURNALISM

By the end of 1965 the machinery for promptly responding to foreign radio should have been operating smoothly. The political basis for the slowness of Soviet journalism is well known. No important news development can be reported until the highest levels of the government can formulate a position in relation to it. That condition applies not only to commentary, but also to the way, and even whether, an event is to be reported. It is what Yegorov, of the Ideological Department, meant when he spoke of a "determined educational function." The July policy statement left a loophole for continuing to handle news in that manner. The exhortation to compete with foreign radio in prompt reporting was followed by a caveat:

> It is necessary to conduct the struggle with antisovietism on a broad front, exposing the insidious examples of the enemy. This does not mean, of course, that one must respond to every concoction of the antisoviet propagandists. That would only play into their hands; we would be put into defensive positions, be concerned only with problems forced on us. Against antisovietism one must conduct an offensive battle in the whole panoply of communist ideas and communist affairs.[54]

But barriers to competing with foreign radio in speed and comprehensiveness were not only political. There were other barriers that might be termed procedural and psychological. Procedural refers to methods of processing and distributing the news. Processing involves passing material through Glavlit's censors. According to a former Soviet editor, in the mid-1960s Glavlit controlled radio and TV material as well as print. For purposes of speed, Glavlit censors worked in radio and newspaper offices, as well as in their own offices.[55] In the 1930s, according to the captured Smolensk archives, the rule was that radio material had to be submitted to the local censor at least one hour before air time. There was also a "Perechen," a list of forbidden topics. Whether that system could work well in the faster moving, more complex 1960s is problematical.

In any case, insofar as foreign news is concerned, radio stations received almost all of it from TASS, already predigested and precensored. The delays, then, took place at TASS, and here there was a more subtle consideration. TASS sorted out its news and distributed it in three categories, in separate, color-coded bulletins. The violet bulletin was for publication or broadcast; it could be shortened to fit available space or time, but otherwise it had to be used exactly as transmitted, without any changes or additions. The white bulletin went to those organizations that had their own commentators or writers; it contained fuller information and could not be published, but commentators could refer to it for background when they wrote their own commentary. The red bulletin contained the most sensitive news, and it was classified secret; only relatively high-level officials could see it.[56]

A former Czech newsman describes a similar system that, he says, was modeled along the lines of the TASS bulletin. The Czechoslovak news agency, CETEKA, sent out a bulletin in three parts, based mainly, it appears, on broadcast monitoring. One part contained only news about non-Communist countries; it went to a distribution list of about 200 persons. Sensitive information about Communist countries other than the Soviet Union and Czechoslovakia went only to a smaller list. And the most sensitive news of all, that about the Soviet Union and Czechoslovakia, could be seen by only about 30 top officials.[57]

That procedure of separate classes of bulletins can inhibit speed and comprehensiveness in several ways. There is the obvious delay simply in the time it takes to sort out the news between reception and transmission. More subtle, but perhaps more important, is the fact that not only is the permitted news being recorded, but simultaneously, a formal record of prohibited news is being produced. For those immediately responsible, if misjudgments are subsequently alleged, the bulletins represent a permanent and immediately available record of errors and omissions. Knowing that they can be so easily called to account, the news managers must be extra-cautious, consciously or subconsciously, more so than if they simply produced one bulletin, and the omitted news simply disappeared or ended up in obscure files, not easily retrieved or compared. Given Soviet traditions, that inevitably means that caution is weighted on the side of too little rather than too much news in the bulletin for publication. The penalty for mistakes in that direction is likely to be lighter than for mistakes in the opposite direction.

Inbuilt psychological inhibitions sometimes are the greatest deterrent to comprehensive or rapid reporting. A vivid demonstration of that fact is available. On April 26, 1966, an earthquake destroyed a large portion of the city of Tashkent. An earthquake is not a political or ideological event, and it would not appear necessary that coverage of it need be withheld or distorted. But in the Soviet Union, any event can be invested with such significance, if thought desirable, and so the news was distorted, initially, until higher authority stepped in. On the other hand, the fact that the earthquake was not truly political may account for the fact that the news editor of Pravda Vostoka, the chief organ of the Uzbek Communist Party, was allowed to publish an unusually revealing account of the journalistic reaction to the earthquake.[58]

On the first day after the earthquake struck only the correspondent of the All-Union Radio and the Pravda Vostoka editor succeeded in reaching the head of the seismic station and obtaining a full picture of what had happened. Thousands of houses had collapsed and every one of the more than 1.2 million population was seriously affected. "But," he wrote, "this was in a personal conversation. And after that, on the radio from Moscow we heard something completely different: In Tashkent everything is in order, here and there some plaster has crumbled." Back at the newspaper they were in a dilemma:

> The special correspondent of Selskaya Zhizn, A. Uzilevskii, dropped in on our department.
>
> "Well, fellows, what are you going to do?"
>
> But nothing was clear to us. In general, one ought to write something in the newspaper. . . .
>
> But now the special correspondent of a Moscow newspaper appeared.
>
> "I will not transmit anything. And I advise you not to either. One should not make an unhealthy sensation out of an earthquake."
>
> A special correspondent of a news agency came.
>
> "You are what? You are going to write about this? Tomorrow all the foreign countries will reprint it."[59]

Several of the correspondents who disagreed with this view set out around the city to gather a story. Everywhere they were met with the question from officials and Party workers: "Why inflame passions?"

This cautionary warning is apparently related to the frequent references in Soviet political discourse to the danger of panic arising in various circumstances. A notable example was the appeal of the government and Party at the time of Stalin's death, and other references that indicate what to an outsider might seem to be an exaggerated belief in the susceptibility of the public to panicky reactions when conditions become unsettled to an even relatively small degree. Those appeals implicitly portray the public as a sensitive, unstable, perhaps naive, creature that can erupt, or run amok at almost any moment of stress, if constant care is not taken to maintain control and keep it pacified. That idea may predate the Soviet era, and perhaps there are episodes in Russian history that could be used to justify it. But the tale from Tashkent makes clear that the attitude toward the public was deeply ingrained in the consciousness of virtually all authorities of the Soviet state and surfaced almost automatically. In the words of Pravda Vostoka's editor, the local journalists pushed themselves into action in the midst of the ruins, "when 'the authorities' advised us to occupy ourselves with other affairs."

While this was going on the central radio issued a governmental communique giving a more accurate account of the extent of the damage and announced that Brezhnev and Kosygin were flying to Tashkent to head a nationwide effort to aid the stricken city. That enabled the journalists on the spot to uncork their supplies of information: "Each of us had a 'store' of material; now everything was finally written and immediately transmitted to Moscow, or sent to press." "But what was more terrible than the underground tremors was the distrust toward people, the inertia of some."

But that was not the end of the matter. Brezhnev was apparently annoyed at the performance of the news media. At a meeting of the Republic Party activ, where Brezhnev spoke, "the question of full, prompt, and, if you like, sincere [zadushevnaya] information arose with special sharpness." The account does not precisely delineate Brezhnev's attitude, but it implies that Brezhnev stepped in personally to set matters straight. The correspondents present were so impressed that they spent a long time together afterward "polishing" every phrase. From that time on they pooled their information, and everyone shared with everyone else:

> The one who at first feared "unhealthy sensations" was soon brought to his senses by his editor from Moscow. After that he came to us, the whole day, collecting material like grains.
>
> [. . .]
>
> We drew a very important lesson for ourselves from the sleepless labor of these days.
>
> We saw how strong our own type of "information inertia" is, and how difficult it is to overcome it in

> others, and at times in ourselves! Apparently, to some it still seems that earthquakes can be everywhere else, but only not among us. Others suggest that one should write "not about destruction, but about creation;" a third does not want "to inflame passions." . . . But the reason for all this, apparently, is the same—distrust toward the reader.[60]

The picture presented is that of a news system so paralyzed by internal constraints that until it is prodded from above, it cannot even report an event bringing down its own buildings around its heads. The important point is that the restraints imposed by doctrinal principles had become so internalized by every individual trained to work in it that self-censorship had become an overriding factor. An organization brought up on those principles could not report quickly or comprehensively, even within the framework of a general policy that exhorted it to do so. It needed specific guidance in each case.

So unprecedented, even at that late date, almost a year after Kommunist had proclaimed the policy of full reporting, were the journalistic consequences of Brezhnev's intervention, that Soviet observers later reported that the stories were received with distrust. Such disasters, they said, had rarely been reported before, the figures were thought perhaps understated.[61]

Brezhnev was available at the time to take things in hand and perhaps knock some heads together. But even if Brezhnev was personally interested in making the news system work properly (and elsewhere at the time he also seemed concerned to do so), he could not be present to look over journalists' shoulders on a large number of occasions. The proclaimed policy of competing with foreign broadcasts in open competition of news coverage placed a burden on Soviet news organizations that they were psychologically unprepared to carry.

NOTES

1. N. Ivanovskaya, "About the Program 'Vremya,'" Sovetskoye Radio i Televideniye (May 1968):30-33; "On the Matter of 'Vremya,'" Zhurnalist (June 1968):15-17.

2. Rosemarie S. Rogers, "The Soviet Audience: How It Uses the Mass Media," Ph. D. dissertation (Massachusetts Institute of Technology, 1967), p. 132.

3. Erik Barnouw, The Image Empire: A History of Broadcasting in the United States, 3, From 1953 (New York: Oxford University Press, 1970), p. 107.

4. Sergei Ivanovich Tsybov and Nikolai Fedorovich Chistyakov, Front tainoi voiny (Front of the Secret War) (Moscow, 1965), pp. 112-13.

5. M. Kalashnik, "Ideological Work Is the Business of All Communists," Kommunist Vooruzhennykh Sil No. 21 (November 1966):14.

6. Oleg Kudenko, "The 108 Hour Day," Sovetskaya Pechat' (August 1963):28-31.

7. N. Skachko, "On New Frontiers," Sovetskoye Radio i Televideniye (August 1963):1-2

8. A. Zalutskiy, "It's Time to See the Birth-Certificate," Sovetskoye Radio i Televideniye (December 1963):23-25.

9. "Renewal," editorial, Sovetskoye Radio i Televideniye (December 1963):1-2.

10. F. Kaazik, "'Ekho Dnya': Prestige, Rights, Duties," Sovetskoye Radio i Televideniye (September 1968):33-36.

11. V. Snastin, "The Main Direction," editorial, Sovetskaya Pechat' (May 1964): 1-6.

12. D. Goryunov, "On a Great Campaign," Sovetskaya Pechat' (June 1964):1-7.

13. "Publicists of High Ideals," Sovetskaya Pechat' (July 1964): 1-17.

14. Ibid.

15. Ibid.

16. Resolution of the Central Committee, CPSU, June 24, 1964, "On the Improvement of Information on the Radio," Spravochnik partiinovo rabotnika (Handbook of the Party Worker), 6th ed. (Moscow, 1966), pp. 356-57.

17. Fed. Krutov, "Yesterday, Today, Tomorrow," Sovetskaya Pechat' (September 1965):35-36.

18. Benjamin Welles, "Voice of America Sends 'New Sound,'" New York Times, November 8, 1966.

19. "An Interview with the Deputy Chief Editor of Latest News and Mayak Leonid Vernerovich Gyune," Sovetskoye Radio i Televideniye (December 1967):5-6.

20. M. Barmankulov, "Battle on the Air," Prostor (Alma Ata) (August 1968):110-14.

21. A. Rapokhin, "Radio, Man, and His World," Sovetskoye Radio i Televideniye (May 1968):5-7.

22. A. Rapokhin, "The Tribune of the Millions," Selskaya Zhizn, May 7, 1970.

23. Gayle Durham Hollander, "Recent Developments in Soviet Radio and Television Reporting," Public Opinion Quarterly 31, 3 (1967): 359-65.

24. Sovetskaya Pechat' (September 1964):30.

25. Fed. Krutov, "We go to 'Mayak': 120 Days of Work of the New Radio Station," Sovetskaya Pechat' (December 1964):38-40.
26. Krutov, "Yesterday, Today, Tomorrow," pp. 35-36.
27. "Anti-Sovietism—One of the Main Trends in the Ideology of Modern Imperialism," Kommunist No. 10 (July 1965):64-77.
28. Ibid., pp. 76-77.
29. Stephen Rosenfeld, "Party's Journal Attacks Soviet News Censorship," Washington Post, July 11, 1965; Theodore Shabad, "Soviet Press Told to Report Fully," New York Times, July 12, 1965.
30. "Anti-Sovietism: One of the Main Trends in the Ideology of Imperialism Today," World Marxist Review, Information Bulletin, No. 57 (Toronto: Progress Books, October 25, 1965):5-20.
31. M. Aleskovskiy, "Applause and Whistles," Sovetskaya Pechat' (February 1965):38-41.
32. Ibid.
33. "The Journalist at the Microphone," editorial, Sovetskaya Pechat' (September 1963):1-3.
34. Krutov, "We Go to 'Mayak,'" pp. 38-40.
35. Zhurnalist (April 1967):23.
36. N. Kartseva, "Who, What, How?" RT No. 33 (August 1967):11.
37. Valentin Dyachenko, "The Desire to Learn Is a Sign of Strength," Zhurnalist (September 1967):38-40.
38. G. Sagal, "Life and the Silver Screen," Sovetskaya Pechat' (October 1963):25-26.
39. R. A. Boretskiy, "On Methods of Studying the Television Audience," Vestnik Moskovskovo Universiteta, Seriya XI, Zhurnalistika no. 3 (1967):18-29.
40. A. G. Yefimov and P. V. Pozdnyakov, Nauchniye osnovy partiinoi propagandy (Scientific Foundations of Party Propaganda) (Moscow, 1966), pp. 57-58.
41. A. G. Yegorov, "Strengthen and Develop Leninist Style in the Work of the Press," Sovetskaya Pechat' (March 1965):1-8.
42. Leonid Vladimirov, The Russians (New York: Praeger, 1968), pp. 86-88.
43. Ye. I. Bugayev, "Tribune of Millions," Sovetskaya Pechat' (May 1965):6.
44. A. Yakovlev, I. Chuprinin, and Yu. Orlov, "A Powerful Means of Propaganda," Sovetskaya Pechat' (June 1965):1-5.
45. N. Prokofieva and I. Gavrilova, "How the Tuning Fork Sounds," Sovetskaya Pechat' (July 1965):23-25.
46. Radio Moscow, Domestic Service, 1000 GMT, July 30, 1965.
47. Boris Vasiliyev, "The Washington Flock of Birds," Radio Moscow, Domestic Service, 0530 GMT, July 7, 1965.
48. Radio Moscow, Domestic Service, 1300 GMT, August 22, 1965.
49. "Seeds of Poison," Washington Post, September 20, 1965.

50. Ye. Zazerski, "The Force of Propaganda Is In Truthfulness," Pravda, August 18, 1965.
51. "Soviet Radio," editorial, Pravda, September 22, 1965.
52. John Osborne, "Speaking to the Russians in a New Voice," The New Republic, Nobember 6, 1965, pp. 9-10.
53. D. Goryunov, "The Main Theme," Sovetskaya Pechat' (January 1966):1-6, 18.
54. "Anti-Sovietism—One of the Main Trends in the Ideology of Modern Imperialism," Kommunist No. 10 (July 1965):77.
55. Vladimirov, The Russians, pp. 95-96.
56. Ibid., pp. 91-92.
57. Antony Buzek, How the Communist Press Works (London: Praeger, 1964), p. 204.
58. Yu. Kruzhilin, "Seven and a Half," Sovetskaya Pechat' (June 1966):38-39.
59. Ibid.
60. Ibid.
61. Viktor Veselovskiy, "Twelve Points of Courage," RT 12 (July 1966):4.

CHAPTER

4

FAILURE OF AN EXPERIMENT: 1966–68

THE NEW ATMOSPHERE OF 1966

The year 1966 opened with a series of shocks for the keepers of Soviet ideological law and order. In January Andrei Sinyavski and Yuli Daniel were put on trial for sending works abroad to be published. They had been arrested four months earlier, but the Soviet press had remained silent about the matter until the eve of the trial. Now, in a manner virtually unprecedented in Soviet history, the carefully prepared scenario for the trial fell apart. The courtroom, with its restricted admission, was pressed by crowds who learned of the time and place of the trial from foreign broadcasts. Smuggled accounts of the proceedings were broadcast back to the Soviet Union, revealing that for the first time in a political trial the defendants did not admit guilt. The Soviet press was forced into a defensive posture of trying to uphold its version of the trial. The outcome was a media and public-relations disaster. Even students who thought that Sinyavsky and Daniel were morally wrong in sending their works abroad and that the government was correct in refusing publication, because the masses were not yet ready for such materials, were opposed to the trial.[1]

Much worse, the Sinyavsky-Daniel trial set off a chain-reaction of similar events. The protests and smuggled transcripts led to more trials, which in turn resulted in more bootleg documents and more protests, all reported to the Soviet Union by Western radio broadcasts in a classic example of feedback. To the authorities, the process must have seemed to be a downward spiral of protests, trials, and samizdat, confronting them with the threatening prospect of losing control of public opinion. The multiplying samizdat, hitherto traditionally literary in character, became more and more overtly political. The possibility of distribution through foreign radio probably stimulated the output.

The sharp change in ability to control information is symbolized in the comparison of Press Day speeches separated by only two years. In 1964 the director of TASS had denounced bourgeois press and radio attacks on the Soviet Union, but mainly in the context of external propaganda, not in the context of radio broadcasts to the Soviet Union. He singled out as an example a controversy over the death of an African student in disputed circumstances near Moscow.[2] But the Soviets had seen the controversy as existing solely outside the boundaries of the Soviet Union; at the time the Soviet domestic press and radio did not see the necessity of mentioning the incident. The Press Day honors in May 1966 fell to the chief editor of Pravda. He found it necessary to speak not so much about the bourgeois press but about the reactions of the Soviet press. All its work, he said, had been complicated by foreign broadcasts. Now, he lamented, the Soviet press was becoming so tied up in refuting false reports and hostile commentaries from abroad that it was losing the opportunity to report directly on the events themselves.[3]

While the emphasis in this chapter is on the ways the Soviet ideological and media authorities managed this new situation, it should be mentioned that there was, of course, another aspect to the attempt to compete in the field of information; that of direct repression. How that appeared to participants on either side of the lines is illustrated by a conversation in the offices of the Leningrad Party Committee in a later phase of the period. On April 20, 1970, a well-known mathematician, Revolt Pimenov, was called in by V. A. Medvedev, the Party official then in charge of ideology in Leningrad, for explanations after "anti-Soviet literature" had been seized in Pimenov's apartment. A purportedly verbatim account later reached Western correspondents:

> I can try to explain to you. The reason for all this is that for some time we scientists have lost our sense of personal security. It has been roughly from the end of 1966. Until then somehow there was no fear. But we have been forced to experience fear. Why? It is necessary to examine the social reasons for this fear. . . . The threat to personal security explains the studying of politics. All this began with the trials of the writers. The most important element in the trials was how they were conducted. The violation of legal rights drew attention to them and aroused public concern.[4]

To that Medvedev replied with a remarkably candid exposition of the more heavy-handed school of thought within the Party bureaucracy. It was the line that was eventually predominant, but that came to prevail only slowly after 1966 and with evidence of considerable reluctance at the highest levels:

> What do you want? If you think that we ever will allow somebody to speak and write anything that comes into his head, then this will never be. We will not allow this. Do you want us to change the ideology? Of course, we don't have enough power to force all people to think the same, but we have still enough power not to let people do things that will be harmful to us. There never will be any compromise on the ideological question. Remember this once and for all. I can count for you on my fingers the eternal truths that cannot be violated. . . . But we will allow no one to hinder us. We will allow no one to harm us. . . .[5]

But the general Soviet approach to foreign broadcasting could still be more sophisticated than that suggested by Medvedev's attitude. As they had done with selective jamming, the Soviets could make use of foreign broadcasts to induce guilt feelings. One such accusation, by a noted religious writer who thought he had been victimized, was circulated in a samizdat document that reached the West. The BBC, the document said, had on July 30, 1966, broadcast some of his writings, as well as protests by two dissident Orthodox priests, Yeshliman and Yakunin. He wanted to emphasize that neither he nor the priests had ever seen a foreigner and that he suspected that the KGB might have delivered his articles abroad, so that a pretext for charges of illegal activity could be created.[6]

Foreign radio could also be used as a convenient alibi for awkward policies. Thus, in September 1967 the writer Aleksandr Korneichuk raised the question of how Aleksandr Solzhenitsyn's protest letter to the Congress of the Writers' Union in May 1967 came to be broadcast over Western radio. Solzhenitsyn avoided a direct answer but referred to the fact that his unpublished works generally received wide distribution through the hands of people whom he did not control. Konstantin Fedin, the chairman of the Union of Writers, entered into the discussion with the conclusion: "No, the letter should have been published right away. Now that foreign countries have beaten us to it, why should we publish it?"[7]

That comment could have applied, and may have been so intended, to all of Solzhenitsyn's unpublished works. It was an attempt to justify the ban on Solzhenitsyn and other writers by pointing to the outlet they had on foreign radio stations. However illogical the argument may have been, it was an embarrassment to the writers, and not something they could openly refute. In effect, the dissidents were being told that as long as they were interacting with foreign radio stations, they should take care on how far they go, lest they appear as traitors, not only to the regime, but to the masses as well. That theme was implicit also in some of the tactics applied at the trials, where the courtroom might be packed with "ordinary workers," who expressed vociferous disapproval of the conduct of defendants, there and in the press.

But after 1966 the regime seemed to lose interest in secondary manipulations of foreign broadcasts, which had become too much of a threat for such tactics to hold much attraction. The main direction of policy was to struggle directly against their influence, applying old techniques more intensively and seeking new techniques. The changes in official assessment of foreign broadcasting can best be seen by tracing the evolution of the struggle in strict chronological order. Some obscure relationships can then be placed in context. Four obscure aspects, however, are treated separately: the failure of the magazine RT; the confusion over a reform of the propaganda apparatus with the introduction of a new institution; the so-called "political information specialist"; and the systematic research on audiences and the underlying state of public opinion, which was undoubtedly the main influence on Soviet decisions in this area.

THE TWENTY-THIRD PARTY CONGRESS

At the moment when the storm broke over the Soviet news and opinion-making organizations the Twenty-third Party Congress, which was scheduled to meet during the first half of April 1966, was less than three months away. Major decisions, which tend to be made at the time of, if not at, Party congresses, waited for that event. Meanwhile, Soviet television, which should have been the most important means of attracting the audience from foreign radio, had become openly acknowledged to be a disaster area. Sovetskaya Kultura, which guided the rest of the press in matters of television criticism, published an article at the beginning of the year declaring that television was a failure. The reasons given were: a) It did not show real life; b) it was not original; and c) it did not respond to press and other criticism. To this article a response came that it let television off too easily because it was too simple. Those inadequacies, it was said, were already generally acknowledged, and Sovetskaya Kultura was not helping matters, because it confined its own criticism to plays and artistic matters, which constituted only two percent of television time.[8] But if the argument had any effect on television, it was not apparent. It took ten weeks just to get the rebuttal into print.

In the period leading up to the congress there were a few signs of new activity on the part of the press. A long article about RFE from the Hungarian press was reprinted in Izvestia "with some abbreviations."[9] It followed somewhat in the tradition of concentrating attention on RFE to the exclusion of RL, although RL was more relevant to Soviet listeners than RFE. A major point of the article, however, was the subtlety of the station, which was creating the appearance of objectivity for naive listeners by reporting Western scandals and praising achievements of the East. More interesting was the appearance, in the course of a two-part series on ideological warfare, of a fairly detailed account of some of the internal affairs of RL.[10] Nothing was said about subtle methods, but it did include remarks about RL's goals and techniques, called startling in their cynical frankness, made by a RL official at a symposium that, the author admitted, had been held "some time ago." It also described an internal document said to advise avoiding the term "Soviet people." The article may have been the first lengthy attack on RL intended for a mass readership to have appeared in the central press in several years. In that fact lies its main significance.

The Twenty-third Party Congress was preceded by party congresses held by the Union-republics. In many, if not all of those, the problem of foreign broadcasts was raised. That could hardly have been sheer coincidence, but must be taken as evidence of central coordination in preparation for some initiative to be put forth at the main congress in April. Among the congresses where those interventions were noted were those of the Ukraine, Byelorussia, Latvia, Georgia, and Armenia.[11] Pyotr Shelest, who was to get a reputation as one of the most hard-line members of the Politburo, told the Ukrainian Congress:

> The poisonous seeds of bourgeois ideology are hitting us through various channels. Every day tens of enemy radio stations broadcast for many hours against the Ukraine. There are individuals who become conductors of opinions alien to us. Our society cannot reconcile itself to these people who continue to spread the rumors, gossip, and inventions from hostile press and radio.[12]

The writer Aleksandr Korneichuk was so enthusiastic at the prospect of action being taken against foreign radio that he took the opportunity to recommend that those who repeated what they heard on foreign broadcasts be expelled from the Soviet Union:

> I mention this because we have individual young people whose ears have become swollen from listening at night to the sly and perfidious anti-Soviet radio propaganda. There are many rusty nationalist hooks with rotten bait cast all over the air by the bitter enemies—just in case there is a fool to swallow them. Unfortunately, there are such fools, and they gossip, repeating all sort of lies fabricated in West Germany for the dollars and marks paid by the German fascist remnants. Such young talents,

> losing both their face and conscience and not appreciating the greatest happiness possible in the world—belonging to the great family of Soviet peoples—we can address in only one manner: "Come to your senses, because if you are confronted with the people, they can deprive you of the Soviet passport and say: 'Leave the sacred soil!'"[13]

With the widespread preparation for this theme so evident, one would expect that the Twenty-third Congress would resound with denunciations of foreign radio and calls for strong action against it—and perhaps against listeners. But it was not to be. The one exposition of the subject reiterated the existing policy of moderation. The speaker was Nikolai N. Rodionov, who held the post of first secretary of Chelyabinsk Oblast, an industrial area in the Urals. Normally, an oblast secretary at a Party congress makes a rather cut-and-dried speech, giving general praise to the main proposals of the programmatic presentations and then relating the economic accomplishments of his district. Rodionov followed this pattern for the first two-thirds of his brief speech but then suddenly switched to a new subject—one that might be thought all the more unexpected for the fact that, because of weak reception, geographically remote Chelyabinsk probably had less concern with foreign radio than most places in the Soviet Union:

> How pleasant it was today, after the morning session, to see the latest Pravda issue with the communication of the first satellite of the moon and to read the reports on the Congress session! However, our press is often late in publishing information and commentaries on some important events in domestic and foreign affairs. Soviet people attentively follow all manifestations of life. When something has happened today, they wish to learn about it immediately and not two or three days or even a week later. Yesterday's news is of no use to anybody: It is no longer news. This fact is utilized with clearly evil intentions by the reactionary propaganda apparatus of the United States, the German Federal Republic, and other countries.
>
> Everybody knows very well that the "Voice of America," "Radio Free Europe," and other radio stations which regularly contaminate the airwaves broadcast distorted interpretations of many phenomena and facts. We must oppose them not only by our party truthfulness, but also by the high efficiency of the Soviet press. (applause) Our radio and press must virtually immediately respond to all events of life which deserve interest. This will

> increase even more their authority in the eyes of the people and their role as militant assistants of the party.[14]

The speech was nothing more than a measured restatement of the existing policy of competing with foreign broadcasts by providing better news service through the Soviet press. It did not even contain the usual amount of invective and denunciation of Western radio stations but restrained itself to what was probably the minimum of obligatory criticism when their names are mentioned in public. The thrust of the criticism that the presentation did contain was directed at the Soviet press for its backwardness. No one else at the congress alluded to the subject. Given the angry buildup in the weeks preceding the congress, it appears that, probably after a sharp internal debate, a decision had been reached to continue along basically the same path as before and give the Soviet press more time to demonstrate that it could handle the competition. Additional measures were taken to supplement that approach, but attention was not drawn to them in the congress itself; they appeared later and did not alter the basic policy of relying on improvement of the press as the main means of countering foreign radio.

Additional light on what may have happened to bring about that outcome can be seen in an examination of the background of the speaker. Rodionov was an unlikely choice to be the enunciator of the liberal policy, not only because of the remote locale of his assignment but because of his past record as a security official and supporter of hard-line repressive measures. At the Twenty-second Party Congress in 1961 he had shown an inclination for repression when he was one of the minority who supported Khrushchev's demand for criminal punishment of members of the "anti-Party group" for their deeds in Stalin's time. He was then the second secretary in Kazakhstan, the post reserved in non-Russian areas for Russians responsible for enforcing security and suppressing nationalistic tendencies. Rodionov was also one of the very few personalities who had been purged during the factional struggles of the Khrushchev era and had then made a comeback after Khrushchev's overthrow. Almost all the losers of that period were left out in the cold by Khrushchev's successors. Rodionov had been appointed second secretary in Kazakhstan in January 1960, at a session attended by Brezhnev. He was removed in December 1962 in a purge directed by Frol Kozlov. His comeback occurred in October 1965, when he was appointed first secretary of Chelyabinsk Oblast. All this suggests that he was closely associated with Brezhnev and had been caught in the rivalry between Brezhnev and Kozlov under Khrushchev.[15] Rodionov was promoted again in 1970 when he was brought to Moscow and made a deputy minister of Foreign Affairs.

With those connections it is reasonable to conclude that Rodionov was speaking for Brezhnev. Brezhnev, then, would have stepped into the argument about foreign radio in early 1966 and squelched those who wanted to reverse the relatively liberal policy of tolerating foreign radio broadcasting. Further indication that Brezhnev was holding out for a continuation of a relatively moderate policy toward foreign broadcasting, aimed at an improvement of Soviet capability, came less than two months after the congress, when, in an election speech, Brezhnev listed as one of the tasks still to be solved, "the supply of fuller information to the people about what is occurring inside the country and in the international arena, and greater publicity for the work of Soviet organs."[16] Up to 1968 Brezhnev and the hard-lining Shelest appear to have been the only members of the post-Khrushchev Politburo to speak out on problems raised by foreign radio broadcasts. Brezhnev at that time also showed his concern to strengthen the implementation of a moderate approach by intervening personally to break down the restraints on reporting the Tashkent earthquake.

In journalistic circles the response to the almost offhand reaffirmation of policy from the forum of the congress was immediate—and relieved. Even before the congress had adjourned, the organ of the Journalists' Union had quoted Rodionov in its lead editorial.[17] Soon the journalists let go their breath, and it was admitted that these thoughts had long worried the profession but had been repressed.

The editor of Pravda, delivering the Press Day speech on May 5, was franker than ever before:

> Take, further, the problem of fullness and timeliness of information. In conditions when the channels of penetration of antagonistic ideological propaganda from the capitalist countries under the mask of "objective" information have become much broader, delay in the publication and explanation of reports about the most important events complicate all our work. It so happens that our concern turns out not to be with reporting the event itself in its true light, but with the refutation of false reports and hostile commentaries already broadcast by the bourgeois press, which we could exclude with greater timeliness. We ought to significantly broaden and speed up our reporting, so that our reader and listener will learn all interesting and important news first of all from his own newspapers and radio.[18]

The Union of Journalists organized a symposium to discuss the results of the congress. The editor of Leningradskaya Pravda dealt with Rodionov's remarks:

> There is still another question. I was glad that the First Secretary of the Chelyabinsk Oblast Committee of the CPSU Comrade Rodionov raised the question of the timeliness of our information. I was glad that from the high tribune of the congress in full voice they addressed that which has already for a long time professionally disturbed us journalists. But simultaneously this circumstance has evoked feelings of deep distress: to what degree has the matter of information in the press, on the radio and television, been neglected, to the point that the need arose to speak about this at the congress! And we have long felt this, long spoken about this within the editorial boards. And here at zonal and all-Union conferences and seminars, at plenums of the Board of the Union of Journalists, the view has been expressed, that nothing was happening. And, unfortunately, our journal was also silent. And if suddenly they address the subject, it is only as if it were in the form of an accusation of the journalists. Here, they say, what kind of clumsy people are you, friends, you don't care about promptness.
>
> Of course, sometimes it is important to report about the fact that the Volga flows into the Caspian Sea. . . But it is more important to assume that the majority of journalists know all these truisms. And we should have investigated the reasons for the paralysis of our timeliness long ago. In general, it seems to me that the journal Sovetskaya Pechat' will become still more popular if it more bravely and sharply will respond to the most important problems of Soviet journalism, if didacticism will completely disappear from its pages, if in its columns we will more often meet, in particular, brave polemics on the most important problems of our difficult, but honorable profession of the party journalist.[19] [Ellipsis in original.]

Thus, it was finally admitted that nothing was being done. It was six years since TASS had been ordered to service radio stations, three years since jamming had been suspended, and almost a year since the policy of open news competition had been formally instated. Yet it is obvious from those remarks that little had been done to carry out the policy seriously. It had not even been possible to discuss the problem openly. Now, the congress had at least opened up the possibility of dealing with the problem and had given the media more time to show results. But the congress had provided no open guidance on practical measures.

Probably as a result of that criticism, the organ of the Union of Journalists, Sovetskaya Pechat', was suppressed, as of the beginning of 1967, for what was described as its deficiencies and low level of content.[20] It was given a new title, Zhurnalist, a new staff, and a new format, and it was ordered to engage in more profound analysis of Soviet media. Whether by intent, or from the coincidence that the results of social-science-type research were just then becoming available for the new magazine to feature, the change appeared to be more than just cosmetic. The circulation of Zhurnalist quickly rose to about 130,000, four times that of its predecessor.

Despite the meager rhetoric of the congress, at least three important actions of an operational nature to counter the effects of foreign radio were soon initiated. The press campaign of general criticism and specific rebuttals to foreign broadcasts, aimed at the general public, was greatly intensified. A lavish new magazine, RT, was inaugurated with the dual aim of exposing foreign radio and building audience interest in Soviet broadcasting. And the time-honored system of oral agitators, a fundamental link in the Party's means of communication with the masses, was deemphasized, and a new category of operative, the "political information specialist" (politinformator), was introduced, in part, it was made clear, because the agitators were unable to cope with the questions put to them by listeners to foreign broadcasts. The reorganization did not occur until six months after the congress, but it was then claimed, perhaps with some exaggeration, that it had been decided at the congress.

The first two of those actions, however, were closely timed to the closing of the Party congress. The new press campaign was kicked off with an article on April 14 under the specially authoritative byline "Observer," in effect introducing RL to the general public.[21] The article was designed to guide the press on a subject that had for a number of years been treated with a marked reticence, if not quite a total silence. Observer described RL, quoted some of its instructions and goals, and noted in particular its airing of the writings of Sinyavsky and Daniel. It named some of the Americans on the staff, connecting them with intelligence services, and some of the Russians on the staff, emphasizing former service with Vlasov and the Germans. The instruction circular "Guiding Principles of Broadcasts" was cited as calling for undermining the Soviet system and telling how to spread provocational rumors and sow disbelief and pessimism. In conclusion, it asked whether it was proper for the United States and the Federal Republic of Germany to support such broadcasts when they maintained diplomatic relations with the Soviet Union. It also questioned the use of wavelengths granted by NATO members and others that were said to have been piratically seized. Its final comment was that the Soviet people had to assess the broadcasts as provocational and aimed at spoiling U. S.-Soviet relations.

The content of that article can be considered fairly routine. Its main significance was its timing, after years of relative silence, and its purpose of stimulating systematic treatment of the subject in the Soviet press, which had not been considered advantageous before. Long afterwards, local organs were repeating it almost verbatim, without crediting it as the source.

RT was suddenly unveiled, without previous notice, on April 16, only six days before its first issue. The first issue, on April 22, bore a press date of April 13. A weekly, published by the State Committee for Broadcasting, its chief editor, Boris Voitekhov, said it would "speak about everything which interests the Soviet people and that is what we shall write about." There would be articles of general interest and articles about Soviet broadcasting, along with a complete broadcast schedule. But the feature that attracted the most attention was that it was to carry a regular column—or rubric, as it was called—titled "Caution, Falsehoods in the Air!" that would rebut foreign radio programs.[22]

THE 1966 PRESS CAMPAIGN

The press campaign of rebuttals and denunciations, except for RT, picked up momentum slowly, at least in the central newspapers. At first there were articles analyzing general Western propaganda tactics and methods.[23] One of them reported on Hungarian experience in dealing with foreign radio. It recommended what it said was the successful Hungarian tactic of going on the offensive and replying by pointing out shortcomings in the West relating to the topics in foreign broadcasts. Referring to "sharp questions," an expression coming more and more to mean exclusively matters brought up on foreign programs, the article concluded: "They have developed a feeling for the new, that is, I would say, a taste for sharp questions. And they are more and more often driving imperialist propaganda into a corner."[24]

It was apparently not until August that the main newspapers began replying to specific radio programs. The first occasion was a reply to a "recent" VOA statement that the United States had no territorial ambitions in South Vietnam. The article listed various unlimited forms of U. S. military action in South Vietnam and added sarcastically that in view of continued military beatings suffered by U. S. forces whenever they ventured outside their fortified bases, the United States was in the position of the fox in the fable who renounced the grapes that it was unable to reach.[25] Meanwhile, the Soviet radio was providing a lengthy reply to an August 15 VOA broadcast on historical examples showing the apparent impossibility of forming coalition governments with Communists,[26] and to VOA broadcasts alleging Soviet responsibility for the lack of progress of the Geneva disarmament talks.[27]

But the clearest sign that the policy of rebuttal had become regularized was when Izvestia instituted a continuing feature under the title "Muddy Waves of the Ether." Its first appearance was on September 15, and it compared VOA to the fabled liar, Baron Munchausen. The reference was to a VOA broadcast of September 13 that described a calm, peaceful opening of the school year. This was contrasted to reports of racial clashes at schools in Granada, Mississippi.[28]

"Muddy Waves of the Ether" appeared in Izvestia a total of 11 times, until the end of 1967. Nine articles were used to attack VOA and two to attack the West German radio, DW. After Izvestia took on the task of replying to individual programs, Pravda seemed to confine itself to relatively few articles of a more general nature about foreign radio stations. The total for the two newspapers in this period was 15 articles. Since that was a total, a quantitative breakdown might be of some interest as a gauge of Soviet concern in respect to the different stations and to different subjects. Of the 15 articles, 11 attacked VOA, three were directed at DW, and one at RFE. Concerning subject matter, the distribution was as follows: four articles on economic conditions in the United States; three on racial conflict in the United States; three on Vietnam; two on Soviet economic conditions; two on internal affairs of foreign stations; one on economic conditions in Germany. Notably absent from this list are anything connected with ideology and any aspect of international affairs except for the war in Vietnam. Soviet radio, however, was much wider ranging. No quantitative summary is possible, but it dealt with foreign programs much more often than did the press and in the process covered ideological and theoretical arguments and wider aspects of international affairs.

Only VOA and DW appear prominently on the list above, but the press did not neglect RL and the BBC, although other stations of the more than 30 said to be broadcasting to the Soviet Union were rarely mentioned. With RL the previous tendency to concentrate treatment of it in the local and nationality press apparently continued.[29] There was an admission in a publication of general circulation that RL was having some success, and its listeners were requested not to spread its wicked propaganda.[30] The case of the BBC is more complicated. It may seem strange that in spite of its established reputation the major newspapers appeared to ignore it and concentrate attention on VOA and DW. In fact, however, the BBC was not ignored: The Soviets had decided that it worked according to different principles and therefore should be handled in a more specialized manner.

Soviet analysis adjudged the BBC to have a narrower, although not less influential, appeal. Its key was said to be a subtle, insinuating flattery. It restrained itself from advertising capitalism or open anti-Soviet acts, using instead a formula of 60-40, for and against. Most importantly, it selected its audiences very carefully, and was particularly aimed at a narrow circle of the enlightened, regarding all the rest as "natives," while the youth supposedly had no social-political ideas or interests. With what one suspects was great respect, it was noted that "the well-experienced British ruling classes are behind all this."[31]

Given the Soviet assessment of the appeal of the BBC, it is perhaps not surprising that the main burden of replying to it was assigned to Literaturnaya Gazeta, a newspaper supposedly designed for an intellectual readership. By 1968 Literaturnaya Gazeta was carrying on what sometimes amounted to a running dialogue with the BBC, with much greater continuity of subjects from program to program than was customary in the treatment of other foreign radio stations by other press organs.

Since the major Soviet press organs evidently had specialized assignments in replying to different foreign stations in accordance with various categories of appeal and purpose in which Soviet analysis placed them, one cannot estimate the relative seriousness with which the different stations were regarded by counting the number of attacks on them either within or between the different press organs. There was one exception, however: The new magazine RT had as its target the radio audience itself, and one of its overtly stated purposes was to carry warnings about foreign broadcasts. Therefore, a measurement of how its editors carried out its assignment presumably has a relation to the Soviet assessment of the popularity or the relative extent of the influence of the various stations.

During the 20-month life of its first incarnation, RT attacked or rebutted the 30 or so foreign radio stations the following number of times: VOA, 15; BBC, 9; DW, 8; RFE, 2; others, 2. Leaving aside the reasons for the paucity of those numbers over a span of more than 80 issues of the magazine, the main omission was any mention of RL. RT apparently followed the standard policy that RL was not to be described in the general circulation central press, except on occasions when policy guidance or a general line was being distributed. RFE may be considered to have been included, in part, as a surrogate for RL. The special treatment of RL, with its rebuttals confined to the local press, is an indication of its great sensitivity.

Taking that into account, in addition the fact that RL continued to be jammed and that its broadcast hours to the Soviet Union were greater in volume than VOA's, it is reasonable to assume that in Soviet eyes it was at least as important as VOA. Using that assumption as a starting point, RT's choice of foreign radio targets yields the following table of relative importance assigned to the stations by the Soviets: VOA, 30 percent; RL, 30 percent; BBC, 15 percent; DW, 15 percent; all others, 10 percent. The possible sources from which the Soviets drew their assessment are discussed in the section on polls and in the epilogue.

In concluding discussion of the mass press campaign against foreign broadcasts it may be fitting to quote from a Soviet radio commentary that, almost on the eve of the decision to resume jamming, acknowledged, with more than usual frankness, the problems involved in counteracting foreign broadcasts:

> In VOA broadcasts considerable time is devoted to music, sports, events, and extensive and at first glance varied information. All is reported, unemployment, Negro disturbances, and even demonstrations against the Vietnam war. One might think: What objectivity! Anyone, however, accepting all this at face value would be mistaken.
>
> The news of various problems and difficulties merely serves as very carefully calculated, psychological bait. An American specialist in propaganda, Professor of Psychology Choukas specifically points out in his book, "Propaganda Comes of Age," that at times practical reasons may cause a propagandist to speak the purest truth, in order to make people swallow the big lie later. One must accept a slight setback to obtain subsequently the conditions needed for a big conquest.
>
> These are the tactics adopted by the directors of the VOA in their approach to listeners in socialist countries. It cannot be denied that a considerable part of news of sports, jazz, or certain international events does indeed correspond to reality. But food of another kind is added to this in the transatlantic propaganda kitchen: such as talk of alleged difficulties of socialist construction and of some advantages of the way of life in countries of the capitalist world. By a tendentious comparison of the two social systems the gullible listener is supposed to be persuaded that capitalism is supposedly no longer actually capitalism and that it is really progressing toward a merger with socialism. Therefore, there is no need for a class struggle nor for any revolutionary theory.[32]

WORRIES IN OFFICIAL CIRCLES

In step with the intensification of the public campaign against foreign broadcasts Soviet ideological officials gradually expanded open intramural discussions of the subject. The foreign radio problem was seen as part of a broader problem of a general spread of bourgeois ideology. Thus, a Party secretary of Volgograd Oblast added to a point about the increase of foreign tourists there a more general warning of the broadening of channels of penetration of bourgeois influence and called for special vigilance.[33]

The general dimensions of the problem were particularly broad at Moscow University, where the effects of radio broadcasts were multiplied by the presence of many foreign students. There, according to a Party official of the university, they had constantly to conduct indoctrination lectures to combat those influences, and special conversations and question-and-answer sessions to deal with a plague of "meticulous, hair-splitting" (dotoshniye) students. There was even a problem with the faculty, which was apparently unable to cope with the situation, unless it was also constantly reindoctrinated in what was described as a "many-sided and complex process." The teachers had to be able to show "sincerity" in handling the now-familiar "sharp" questions.[34]

The university official emphasized the presence of foreign students as the source of the ferment, but an American student there at the time reported that the test of a radio receiver at Moscow University was whether it could pick up VOA, a quality that had been even more emphasized during the period of jamming. However, he considered the student dissent as not being deep but rather as directed more at the cant and bombastic style of presentation of official policy, during which students took pleasure in putting forth annoying questions. At another point, however, he described the ferment and dissent as being deeper and more serious.[35]

As if taking heed of Kurtinin's criticism of its silence on important issues, Sovetskaya Pechat' in its waning days hesitantly ventured into the subject of foreign competition to Soviet media. The matter of Finland's television's being receivable in Estonia was mentioned briefly at the end of an article on Estonian television. The only comment made, however, was that the majority of Estonians watch their own programs. That was immediately followed by the cryptic, unelaborated statement that the most popular programs of Estonian television were not the entertainment programs, but social-political programs.[36] That that was hardly a frank treatment of the subject was apparent two years later, when a propaganda official of the Komsomol described at some length the competition between Estonian and Finnish television in Estonia. Finnish television, he said, was "freely" watched, and the trouble was that it was far from being simply entertainment.[37]

Another venture in that area was more revealing of the views held in journalistic circles. An interview with the famous writer and journalist Ilya Ehrenburg ranged widely over some of the shortcomings of Soviet press practice. Ehrenburg praised the coverage of sports in the Soviet press and then slyly backed into his topic by noting that the Soviet press might be more interesting and substantive if it covered the rest of the news as well. As for himself, he got his news from Le Monde; he would prefer to use the Soviet press, but he couldn't find out what was happening inside the Soviet Union from it. The fault, he thought, was in the quality of the editorial staffs. (If he was inclined to place any responsibility at a higher level he could hardly expect it to be published.) Ranging over various forms of superficiality in the work of foreign correspondents, he suddenly commented on the quality of U. S. radio broadcasts, which he called naive.

All its boasting about U. S. wealth, he said, would convince no one. "But," he said, "you will agree, that photographs [in the Soviet press] of slums in Europe and America do not convince. There are still shortcomings, unfortunately, in the socialist countries. The talent of the journalist consists of convincingly revealing tendencies in society."[38]

Despite many nonsequiturs, which may have been the result of very heavy editing, the overall effect of the interview was a severe indictment of the Soviet press, with the inference that it could not yet compete with foreign sources of information. That, at least, is particularly striking in the revelation of the preference for Le Monde. Ehrenburg seemed to be saying that Soviet reporting was no better than that of VOA, or even implying that the accusations leveled against VOA in the Soviet Union (by then very frequent), could be directed at the Soviet Press.

The main significance of the article is not that Ehrenburg or anyone else held these views but that they could now be published. That was certainly a consequence of the more liberal mood endorsed by Brezhnev (by proxy) at the Twenty-third Congress, and a necessary, if delayed, step toward a serious reform of Soviet information practice as formulated by the 1965 policy statement. The upsurge of dissidence and criticism had not yet disturbed the intention to continue the policy of open competition in news and information; rather, it had spurred a determination to implement it in a serious manner. That intention is better confirmed by statements of that time that showed that direct broadcast television by satellite across international boundaries was to be accepted as a matter-of-fact development. Later, when the policy of open radio competition was reversed, the acceptance of the permissibility of direct-broadcast television was also reversed.

The continued existence of opposing views in influential quarters was testified to by the appearance at the time of a statement by the deputy director of the Political Department of the Armed Forces that attacked not the foreign radio stations but those who permitted people to listen to them:

> On all sectors of work with people one must fence off personnel from the pernicious influence of bourgeois propaganda.

> Meanwhile, as life shows, this is not everywhere and not always being done. At times the necessary measures are not being considered for closing all the channels of penetration of bourgeois ideology into the consciousness of some unstable people. Liberalism is being allowed in relation to those who listen to foreign hostile radio broadcasts. In a number of places they have not eliminated cases of a tolerant attitude towards those who "sing from an alien voice," carry on unhealthy conversations.[39]

There is no direct evidence that those views had any influence at the time on the general policy of open competition. They had no counterpart outside the armed services. Even after the policy was reversed and jamming resumed, there was little evidence of the kind of direct pressure on individual radio listeners that might be implied by the above statement.

In late 1966 efforts to improve the Soviet press were stepped up—or at least there was more open discussion of them. A mammoth conference of the heads of all press and broadcast organs down to the oblast level was called by the Central Committee from October 3-7, 1966. P. N. Demichev, the Central Committee secretary in charge of ideological affairs, spoke to the conference as did most of the subdepartment and section heads of the Central Committee's Propaganda Department. The conference was then broken up into sections according to functions, each section headed by the relevant section head of the Propaganda Department. The head of the radio and television section was P. V. Moskovskiy.[40] As was the usual practice on such occasions, the contents of the work of the conference were not reported, although there were more than 100 speakers. It was perhaps not unrelated that while the conference was in session Pravda printed a solicited response of an ordinary worker on the subject of improving the supply of information for answering questions prompted by foreign radio broadcasts:

> I should like to take advantage of this opportunity to express a wish. Our ideological enemy is not asleep. Shrinking neither from slander nor juggling of the facts, he is trying to shake the convictions of Soviet people and to sow seeds of doubt in their hearts. The air waves are filled with broadcasts of this sort, and one cannot always distinguish what is truth from what is lies. People come up with various questions. Who if not the propagandists, the agitators, the students in the system of Party education should be the first to give correct answers to these questions? I think it would be useful to combine the study of Marxist-Leninist theory in schools

> and seminars with aggressive and effective counter-propaganda and to better the fund of information possessed by propagandists, agitators, and all Communists.[41]

That could have been a prod to the assembled journalists, stating as it did, in effect, that the press was not being effective in helping people "distinguish what is truth from what is lies," and suggesting that the primary burden be shifted to propagandists, agitators, and Communist activists. No doubt that was an important topic at the conference, but the intervention may have been directed more at an even higher-powered conference of ideological workers that opened just four days after the end of the journalists' conference. It was at that ideological workers' conference that the concept of the political information specialist definitively surfaced.

The journalists' conference was followed up at the end of the year by more specialized meetings of radio and TV news personnel. A report on one of them by the head of the central television network showed that the liberal policy of open news competition was still in the ascendance. He merely mentioned in passing that direct-broadcast television, or "Worldvision" as he styled it, would soon be a reality.[42] Not long after that there was a very positive reference to direct-broadcast television. It was stated that world television was coming direct to the home, and that viewers, presumably Soviet viewers, would have a choice. For that reason, a study of audience interests was necessary. Scientific research in communications in general was necessary because of, among other things, the permanent struggle with bourgeois ideology.[43] Serious research on broadcast audiences was in fact already well under way.

It is inconceivable that those comments would have been allowed to appear had not the intention to continue not to jam Western radio broadcasts been firmly maintained through the intensive conferences of late 1966. The Soviet attitude toward direct broadcast television moved precisely in step with the attitude on short-wave radio broadcasting. After jamming had been resumed, the Soviet Union became very hostile to direct-broadcast television and adopted the position that it must be ruled absolutely impermissible without the consent of the receiving country. The defensiveness or vulnerability of Soviet feelings was apparent when a U. N. working group on direct-broadcast television began work in 1969. Most of the participating countries sent international experts or technical specialists to represent themselves in these discussions. The Soviet Union sent E. N. Mamedov, a deputy chairman of the State Committee who was responsible for internal broadcasting.

The uses of jamming as a sensitive political indicator had not been forgotten by the Soviet Union, nor by its former associates, now ideological competitors. Near the end of 1966 the Albanians put into operation new radio transmitter facilities, built with Chinese aid. At the dedication ceremony Albania took the opportunity to needle the Soviets for having ceased jamming of Western broadcasts, especially of VOA, and for using the jamming stations instead to jam Radio Tirana. The Soviets, they said, were panicking, having been unmasked by the Albanian radio, which was being listened to by thousands in the countries ruled by the "modern revisionists."[44]

The Albanians were prone to exaggeration, but the Soviets did resume jamming of Radio Peking on January 5, 1967, for the first time since the ouster of Khrushchev more than two years earlier. The context of that act was the violent phase of the Cultural Revolution in China and the beginning of the strong Soviet reaction to it. A plenum of the Central Committee of the CPSU had been held in December, and the proceedings of the session, which have never been disclosed, were disseminated to restricted groups of Party members in January by means of journeys around the country by members of the Politburo. The Chinese may well have feared that that was a prelude to strong Soviet action against them, even more so when on January 16 the Soviet press ceased altogether to report on China. In relation to that the massive three-week siege of the Soviet embassy in Peking that soon began might have been a preemptive action by the Chinese.[45]

The resumption of jamming of Radio Peking, in connection with the other Soviet activities, was seen as an ominous development by the Albanians, who, either speaking for themselves or on behalf of the Chinese, were quick to point out the connection.[46] Just as the changes in jamming patterns of Western radio stations had earlier been closely attuned to the highest-level political decisions, the reaction by the Albanians showed that they also believed that jamming was a sensitive indicator of major political decisions, and since they had once participated in those decisions, they presumably had reason to know.

The Albanians continued to draw attention to Soviet jamming policies as evidence of basic political attitudes. When the Soviets entered into an arrangement to participate in an international television program on June 25, 1967, the Albanians again attacked Soviet jamming policies. They claimed, exaggeratedly, that jamming of VOA began to decrease immediately after the Twentieth CPSU Congress in 1956 and that beginning in 1960 the Soviets transmitted VOA programs on their own radio system.[47] (The Soviet Union withdrew from the international television program shortly before it was held, using the Arab-Israeli War as a pretext.)

The problem of handling the so-called "sharp questions," which were brought up by listeners to foreign broadcasts, was receiving extensive discussion in the open press by 1967. Much of the discussion was in connection with the establishment of the new institution of the political information specialists, but the matter had broader import. It was now officially admitted that, contrary to desired practice, the term "sharp questions" had come to be synonymous with the content of foreign radio broadcasts. The admission was made by the director of an unidentified section of the Central Committee's Propaganda Department who commented on it in an article about various concepts of bourgeois ideology, in the course of which he included some practical advice on how to handle them. He believed that the opinion that any sharp question in a letter to the editor or at a lecture was the result of uncritical listening to foreign broadcasts should be considered stereotyped; in any case, he added, conceding that that was the popular understanding of the term, one had to be able to answer any question. Using as an example the question of whether U. S. workers are paid more than Soviet workers, he said that one should not try to conceal that that is so; instead, one should point out that the higher wages are due to greater productivity of labor and better organization in the United States, and then this question can be used as the starting point to talk about the importance of raising labor productivity and the future of economic reform.[48] A major audience poll based on equating of sharp questions with foreign radio broadcasts was being drawn up just about the time this article appeared.

A perfect example of the difficulty of coping with sharp questions had recently been provided by a Sevastopol propagandist. A lecture on international events of the week had just been completed in a factory. The talk had been well prepared and well presented, "correctly" and "profoundly." However, the propagandist continued:

> But now the talk was finished. "Are there any questions?" One worker gets up: "I heard that . . ." And there followed one of the multitudinous rumors spread by the voices of some foreign radio stations. The politinformator clearly lost his head. This question was not foreseen by his plan, he simply does not know how to answer it. However, instead of directly saying this and coming to an arrangement that the answer will be given next time, he throws a retort: "It would be better to collect and set afloat less of these various rumors. . ."
>
> The fellow sits down. An awkward, tense silence sets in. There are no more questions.

Pointing out that the silence did not mean that the people did not have questions, the propagandist said that the trust of the listeners had been violated and they would no longer be fully open with him. And without this full openness and mutual trust, it was impossible to conduct mass-political work with the people. The qualification was that the politinformator could not indulge the lovers of various rumors, of course; he must not operate by shouting, however, but argumentatively unmask rumors.

But the problem was broader than that of simply information received from foreign broadcasts. The propagandist went on to give another example that in some ways was even more significant. In that case a group of construction workers on a lunch break were reading a Soviet newspaper that contained an item about the criticism of the president by a U. S. senator. That set off a spontaneous discussion about the nature of the U. S. political system and the concept of democracy. It attracted the attention of a passing politinformator, who intervened and competently steered the conversation into a discussion of the "ostentatious essence of bourgeois democracy." The point that stands out is that even the simplest strictures of the mass press were now evoking uncomfortable questions from broad segments of the general public. The main cause of the phenomenon was probably the growing level of education and sophistication of the society, but it is possible that such spontaneous comparisons were also facilitated by the existence of a general background of information derived from foreign radio.

The propagandist's prescriptions for the prime requirements of successful politinformator work imply that foreign radio broadcasts were really uppermost in his mind. First, there was the necessity for specialization in fields of expertise, (that had been part of the original rationale for creating the specialists); second, there was the need for each of them to have the freshest and broadest current information in their "specialty," in particular the latest news. The second qualification would hardly have been necessary except to handle matters raised on foreign broadcasts; otherwise, they could have relied on conventional Soviet sources of information.

But the tip-off to the evaluation of foreign radio as the most important problem was the recommendation to orient the work on the "sharp" questions: "It seems to me that the main attention in our mass-political work today must be to ensure that people are not left with any uncertainty on the so-called sharp questions. In my opinion the very characterization—'sharp'—exists only because we at times depart from such questions. And they must not be left out!"[49]

The upsurge of concern over the significance of "sharp" questions can be connected to the receipt by the Central Committee of results of the first serious survey of public attitudes toward the media. The figures on the popularity of foreign radio are unknown because it was classified "for official use," "not intended for the open press." Only the section on film audiences has been leaked to the West,[50] but that, together with an account of a discussion of another part, shows that a major concern of the research was the influence of foreign broadcasts. The Central Committee's Department of Culture—and probably also the Department of Propaganda—had commissioned a sociologist, Aleksandr Krasilov, to do the studies, which were based on large-scale polling. The film study was based on answers to a 77-point questionnaire put to 3,571 people, consisting 28 percent each of factory workers and professional-technical employees and 22 percent each of farm workers and university students. Probably the same sample was used for the other parts of the study.

At a seminar in Leningrad from February 28 to March 2, 1967, attended by journalists, academicians, and Party officials, Krasilov gave a presentation, probably based on his survey report, "Sociological Characteristics of Readers of Central Newspapers." The published account of the seminar indicates that the characteristic of newspaper readers that Krasilov thought most significant concerned their interest in foreign radio broadcasts.[51] Krasilov reported that listeners to foreign radio (delicately termed "supplementary sources") were socially less active and ideologically immature compared to those who did not listen to foreign radio.

Krasilov was subjected to criticism, and perhaps even ridicule, by E. P. Prokhorov, a Moscow University scholar, and Boris Gusev, an Izvestia correspondent. His analysis, they said, led in effect to the conclusion that a good Soviet citizen was one who was less informed and kept to his own business. It was well-known, they said, carefully citing a Central Committee resolution, that the Soviet press was late in reporting internal and international news, and Krasilov was attempting to dismiss the problem by placing guilt on those who listened to foreign radio. Their criticism was shared by "many" participants in the seminar.

Perhaps hinting that they considered Krasilov's scientific project a politically biased attempt to discredit the policy of open competition with foreign radio, they went on to criticize Krasilov's entire methodology as faulty. Particularly singled out was Krasilov's use of Yevtushenko's poetry as an indicator. Krasilov had analyzed his sample in terms of its attitude toward Yevtushenko and concluded that those who disliked Yevtushenko's poetry were preferred over those who liked it. One can only guess whether there was laughter in the hall. Sitting through the criticism was Vasiliy Sitnikov, sector head in the Propaganda Department of the Central Committee, who wrote in the same issue of the journal an article pointing out the critical connection between "sharp" questions and foreign radio, and advocating dealing with them openly and frankly. Sitnikov's remarks at the seminar were not reported.

Other officials also prodded on the subject through 1967. The head of the International Department of the Central Committee wrote: "It would be wrong to disregard the public's unprecedented need for news, the enormous possibilities of obtaining this news from various sources and the influence on the mind of the news that comes first. . . . The task is to achieve a situation wherein the audience we are addressing would receive from us first the most complete, rounded, and authentic news."[52] The chief editor of Izvestia emphasized the need for promptness: "Promptness of information in today's world has become a factor of exceptional importance. . . . To reconvince readers and listeners is more difficult than to convince them."[53] The press editor of Pravda issued advice on how to arrange radio news items: Internal news, he said, is still particularly boring and trivial. He concluded by placing his advice within the framework of combating foreign radio, because that is why the ability to "do the news" is so important.[54]

But signs of opposition, apparently squelched after the Twenty-third Congress, to the policy of open competition with foreign radio began to appear again toward the end of 1967. In December a long article on the distinctions between socialist democracy and bourgeois democracy contained the following passage:

> The Communist Party and the Soviet state are performing tremendous work to inculcate the Soviet people with qualities of high ideological content and noble moral principles. One may ask: Why should we, by our own will, simultaneously upset these efforts and destroy these qualities? When the world is publishing countless books, journals, and papers, when the air is literally filled with all kinds of broadcasts, the urgent problem of selecting information inevitably arises. It is at the same time a problem of politics and a problem of morality.
>
> Why should our state give free access to subversive propaganda against the regime which corresponds to the interests of the people and for which generations of Soviet people fought and died?![55]

The passage is couched in theoretical and rhetorical form, but it may well be regarded as a veiled call for a resumption of jamming. It was not absolutely necessary in the context of the argument to pull in a reference to "all kinds of broadcasts" in the air. Even more to the point was the fact that early in the new year attacks on foreign radio stations and references to their baleful effects mushroomed.

At the end of 1967 plans for the transformation of television news came to fruition. A new television news program in prime time, "Vremya" (Time), went on the air on January 1, 1968. It was the first serious attempt to make television an important factor in the dissemination of news. One can only wonder why it was not until that late date that the Soviets woke up to the potential of television in that field, when the primacy of television as the main source of news for the mass audience in the West had been long established. The inertia in this respect is even more surprising when one considers the importance that had long been emphasized in attracting away the audience of foreign radio. Television news offered the obvious advantage of visual coverage that foreign radio could not duplicate, yet it continued to be neglected.

Probably the best explanation is the inertia engendered by entrenched doctrines and procedures in one of the oldest and tradition-encrusted fields of Soviet statecraft. Propaganda and ideological management was one of the earliest areas of specialization and expertise of the Communist Party, and it may be that any change in this well-established area of practice was naturally slow and retarded by resistance of those who had always done things in time-tested ways. That would seem, for example, to explain the immense effort that went into maintaining the systems of oral agitation and wall newspapers long after those devices had lost much of their usefulness in an era of greatly increased educational sophistication and more efficient mass media.

Certainly, the backwardness in making use of television was not the result of a lack of knowledge of the low esteem in which television news was held. Television news before 1968, insofar as it did not consist of "talking heads," was, it seems, mainly illustrated lectures about undated developments, using visual material that was likely not to be that of any identifiable event. There was little on-the-scene, updated coverage. The COMCOM survey of former Soviet citizens showed that they preferred radio over television news for speed, fullness, and significance, by margins ranging from five to 50 times. The sample was over-urbanized and over-educated compared to a representative cross-section, but even ordinary workers, presumably much less sophisticated and less discriminating, knew the difference, as the Soviet authorities were aware. As early as 1965 a survey of the workers of 14 Moscow enterprises, 90 percent of whom had television sets, showed that they preferred radio news to television news by a margin of two to one (32 percent to 15.7 percent).[56] At the same time they preferred television over radio, usually by a wide margin, for every other category of program except music. Other Soviet polls showed the same relative results, although usually with a higher absolute interest in news.

It was perhaps significant that the results of the 1965 poll were not published until 1968, after television news had been reorganized. Whatever had been the early inhibitions about such revelations, frank studies of the contents of television news were discussed even in advance of the 1968 changes. In one case, a perusal of an entire week of TV news evoked a flat and uncompromising conclusion that television could neither show the day's events nor react to them.[57] It was also noted in the first review of the new program that the requests of viewers had influenced its planning. The requests were: more on-the-scene reportage, more facts, more promptness, more international news, and shorter items.[58] Those requests could have applied to a much broader sphere of Soviet journalism than television alone. And, indeed, "Vremya" was later to be criticized as showing faults typical of all news services.

The initial review of "Vremya" was friendly, although it may not be without relevance that the review was in the organ of the State Committee. The program was described as being a fast-paced presentation of pure facts, with details and commentary left to radio and the newspapers. There was some criticism of the holdover of the type of short, standard item on leading workers that served no informational function other than showing a good social example. It was also noted that the cliche items about conferences (showing views of applauding workers that offered nothing about the content of the conference) still existed. But the outside journal, with an anonymous reviewer, was much more critical.[59] "Vremya" was said to have the same old troubles of lateness, narrowness, and poverty of content. The program of March 26, 1968, was taken as an example: Of 26 items, 12 were simply views of meetings and conferences, people applauding, and so on. The program was judged to be dominated by machines and uninformative statistics; the majority of the items were undated. Most tellingly, the program was depicted as a general illustration of the faults of all news services.

After jamming was resumed, the State Committee's journal subjected "Vremya" to very sharp criticism, citing especially its use of people as symbols of labor achievement, rather than as subjects of news reporting.[60] But _Zhurnalist_, formerly critical, now partially praised the program, citing its ability to compress a large number of items into a short period, and said that it had won great popularity. But it also noted that the TV producers had not responded to its previous criticism. (_Zhurnalist_'s editor had been purged in the interim.) However, the most interesting aspect of that postjamming review was its advocacy of a new approach to the selection of news items, one that would subordinate the objective of providing viewers with the best news service to that of giving the program a propagandistic impact as a whole. That was, of course, a reversal of the idea of using news as a competitive instrument against foreign radio and may have been another reflection of a decision to substantially abandon the struggle as being unwinnable—a decision implied by the resumption of jamming the previous year. As if in confirmation of that possibility, the reviewer went even further and attacked the whole concept of orienting news programming according to the desires of the audience, suggesting that there was something wrong with people who were very interested in news.[61] That outburst, however, is more relevant to the broader controversy over the relationship of the state of public opinion to foreign broadcasts, as it was discussed after jamming was resumed.

POLITICAL INFORMATION SPECIALISTS

The political information specialist (politinformator) was created to replace—or, as it finally worked out, to supplement—the long-established system of oral agitators. The agitator was the lowest link in the chain of contacts between the Party leadership and the masses. In traditional Party parlance agitation was distinguished from propaganda in that agitation was considered to be the exhortatory transmission of relatively simple ideas and appeals to the broadest masses, while propaganda operated at a higher intellectual level, being the explanation of more reasoned and specialized concepts to differentiated audiences. In practice the agitator was usually a part-time, unpaid functionary, supervised by the lowest levels of his primary Party organization, who was assigned to circulate among his fellow workers, providing them with political guidance and explanations of the current Party policies and campaigns, perhaps giving a weekly lecture in his shop on some topic of current interest and answering questions. He may have been given some type of brief training for his role, but his main source of current guidance was more likely to be one or more of the special biweekly or monthly journals, such as Agitator, that contained both methodological-pedagogical advice and instructions on current themes to emphasize.

On general principles the modernization of Soviet society should tend to make the agitator system obsolete, at least in the eyes of those who did not have a personal stake in its operation. In the earlier Soviet society, with a generally low level of education prevailing, widespread illiteracy, and a lack of technical means for the mass distribution of information, the system of agitators could have a high utilitarian value. Greater sophistication and education, the availability of the mass media and other sources of information were probably not the only reasons for the decline of interest in the agitators. A desire for personal privacy and better use of increased leisure time may have created psychological desires for more personal means of acquiring information than attendance at meetings and even subtle barriers between the agitators and their "clientele." The general factors tending toward the decline of the agitators need not be discussed, however, but rather the extensive indications that a major factor in the arguments for their replacement was their inability to handle a rising tide of questions relating to information learned from foreign radio broadcasts.

The politinformator, who came into existence in late 1966, was supposed to differ from the agitator in at least three significant respects. First, he was more carefully selected from higher-level personnel and professions than the agitator, so he was likely to be more intelligent and more educated than the average agitator. Second, instead of being a generalist, expected to discourse on any subject, the politinformator was to specialize in one of four areas: domestic policy, international affairs, economic matters, or cultural-social topics. Third, he was organized and supervised at a higher level than the agitator, either a major primary Party organization or the raion (district) Party committee, so he was likely to have access to more authoritative sources of information and could be moved around to wider circles of contacts, even to different enterprises.

The first indications of high-level dissatisfaction with the agitator system came in early 1965 in some critical remarks by obscure functionaries in Agitator and in omissions of any mention of agitator work in the early articles of V. I. Stepakov after he became head of the Central Committee's Department of Propaganda and Agitation in mid-1965.[62] (The phrase "and Agitation" was dropped from the department's name in May 1966.) It is possible that Stepakov and those who supported his desire to reform the agitator system had in mind the results of a remarkable study (for that time) performed in early 1965. Developed from a survey of 250 attendees of Party propaganda courses, apparently people in training to become propagandists and agitators, it was a fairly widespread sampling, from the "Borets" hard alloy factory and the "Trekhgornaya Manufactura" of Moscow, the Chita railroad repair and machine building plants in Siberia, and the Polotsk glass fiber plant in the western region of the country.[63] Among the questions in the survey was one asking to whom respondents turned for help when seeking information. The responses were: friends, 51.2 percent; propagandists, 42.4 percent; party secretary, 36 percent; leader or superior at work, 10 percent; agitator, 6.4 percent. That result certainly showed the low status of the agitator's competence in the eyes of his compatriots but probably surprised no one in view of the changes in Soviet society already mentioned. But if it was a factor in the decision to create the politinformators, it may have been one of the first instances in which social-science type research was used as a basis for an important political-ideological action.

If that part of the survey results was predictable, other parts were surprising, perhaps even shocking by the standards of the uniformity-of-thought ideal to the Propaganda Department. The would-be propagandists were asked whether they believed what they heard from their propagandist instructors. Only 62 percent answered that question affirmatively. A negative response was given by 13.2 percent, and the remaining 24.8 percent did not answer this question. Actually, the true negative opinion of the credibility of the propagandists was probably higher than 13.2 percent. A breakdown of the answers according to education, age, and Party membership that was provided showed that the refusals to answer increased among the more highly educated. The responses for "believe," "disbelieve," and "no answer" among those with less than high school education were 71 percent, 8 percent, and 21 percent, respectively. For those with high school and higher education the equivalent figures were 55 percent, 17 percent, and 28 percent. The "no answer" responses were also proportionately higher among those who were younger and not members of the Communist Party.

If the "no answer" choices represented true "do not know" responses, the proportion responding that way would decrease as the educational level rose, not increase as it did. Many of those refusals to answer must have been prompted by a prudent desire to avoid expressing an opinion, probably in fear of unfavorable consequences if they were identified, despite the anonymity of the questionnaires. Only those who had a negative opinion of the propagandists' credibility would evade responding. If we assume that half the "no answer" respondents were actually disbelievers in the propagandists' credibility—and, as later data indicates, that is probably a conservative assumption—then the disbelievers would amount to about 25 percent.

That figure becomes even more impressive when one considers that the group surveyed was one that would have been more favorably disposed toward the regime than an average cross-section of the population. More than half were members of the Party, compared with about 10 percent of the total population, and presumably they were volunteers for propaganda work, implying a greater-than-average attachment to the goals of the regime. Some volunteers were less than totally willing, perhaps, and some had careerist motivations, perhaps, but since even careerism requires some faith in the system from which advantages are sought, that factor hardly lessens the import of the figures. And later polls on attitudes toward the media of more representative groups, had similar results.

Even the lower 13.2 percent figure was large enough, however, to indicate to the authors of the work in which it was reported that it required explanation, despite the "subjectivism of opinion." That explanation began by ruling out the possibility that there could exist Party propagandists who would consciously distort reality. Instead, the negative reactions to the propagandists had to develop either because they were not able to argue convincingly or because they created distrust by avoiding the sharp questions. Those situations most often were attributed to the discomforts of daily life or to bureaucratism and misuse of authority. There was no hint in that of problems with other sources of information, but, in commenting on the low proportion of respondents who said that they would turn to agitators for information, the need for promptness in the face of enemy efforts was brought up. And while in his initial proposals for politinformators Stepakov, too, did not mention foreign radio as a factor, in the controversy that followed others did.

The Soviet press attributed to the Twenty-third Congress the decision to create the politinformators. In fact, there is nothing about them in the Congress resolutions, nor did any of the speakers there attack the work of the agitators. The proposal to establish the politinformators was brought forth by Stepakov, apparently without previous warning, at a high-level conference of ideological workers that met in Moscow from October 11-25, 1966. After declaring that the agitators were incapable of conveying information in a systematic and qualified manner, he made his proposal for a higher-level informator, to be selected and trained on the same basis as propagandists. As for the agitators, experience would show whether they could continue to exist. But Stepakov apparently intended that they should fade away, if not be officially abolished.

The idea was unusually controversial, so much so that no consistent follow-through was ever enforced. Even the initial reporting of the measure was inconsistent. Only Agitator printed Stepakov's remarks on this subject. Partiinaya Zhizn deleted them from its accounts of the conference, and Pravda, which had published lengthy accounts of the last previous conference of ideological workers, never printed anything at all about this one, other than the fact that it had been held. Subsequent press discussions and methodological materials varied greatly in their emphasis on politinformators and agitators, but by early 1967 the press had reported the establishment of politinformator groups all around the country. Inasmuch as it has not been established how the main power centers of the Party divided on this subject, and the top leaders never spoke on it at all, it is not worthwhile to pursue the general controversy here. What does seem significant is that that was the first time in the history of Agitprop that an important issue was allowed to drift indecisively.[64]

The discussion here will be limited to the evidence that at least some of those involved considered the influence of foreign radio broadcasts to be an important, if not the most important, reason for creating the informators, so that the controversy mirrored, or tied into, the disputes over foreign radio and what to do about it. Thus, the outcome, or lack of one, would be an indication of how the struggle with foreign radio was faring—and all the more so in that among those who called attention to this relationship were fairly high-ranking Party officials.

The most comprehensive account of how the politinformators struggled to cope with the effects of foreign radio broadcasts was given by the Sevastopol propagandist in early 1967. That particular correspondent left no doubt that he considered foreign radio broadcasts the primary target for the work of the politinformators and propagandists. Others were more circumspect but referred to the connection almost immediately. Within a day of the conclusion of the ideological conference the first secretary of the city of Omsk had ready an article that contained the following passage:

> It is well known that the air is now flooded with false information of bourgeois propaganda. Not to take this into account, not to conduct counterpropaganda, would be a mistake. That circumstance that our people have become more literate, subscribe to many newspapers and magazines, listen to the radio, watch television programs, regularly go to the movies, does not exclude, but, on the contrary, increases the need for the heart-to-heart talk of a comrade, speaking with political information.[65]

He went on to assert that leading workers (i. e., executives and officials) used as politinformators could oppose rumors with information on the true state of affairs and "quickly catch the mood."

As time went on the sensitivity of the subject apparently increased and the references to it were more often couched in code words or general formulations, but the meaning was unmistakable. Of course, the most common formulations were "promptly" (operativno) and the well known "sharp questions." Thus, one commentator wrote on how the local Party committee could keep the politinformators up to date on local matters and then added: "But what a need makes itself felt for additional material (promptly!) on for example, international, questions." He added later: "The informator is considered as a link of a system, the goal of which, in accordance with the decisions of the 23rd Congress, is to profoundly and intelligibly explain the policy of the Party, not evading sharp problems, sensitively taking into account the requirements and spiritual needs of the people, their growing cultural and educational level."[66] Another approached it through references to the penetration of alien ideology: "It follows that one must also take into account the sharpening struggle of the two ideologies, demanding a decisive intensification of political work." He concluded: "One must judge the work of the politinformators on how they are able to convince people, how they help the party organizations in the struggle with the penetration of alien ideology, in the upbringing of the masses, in the mobilization of them for the fulfillment of the five-year plan and an honorable meeting with the fiftieth anniversary of October."[67]

One of the highest-level advocates of the importance of using politinformators to combat the influence of foreign radio was the first secretary of Sverdlovsk Oblast, a post-Khrushchev appointee who was probably quite close to the top leaders of the Party. It was the end of 1967, and the problem of continuing to tolerate foreign radio had probably been reopened. Yet without once mentioning foreign radio directly, he sprinkled references to promptness through a whole article and even worked it into the title, "Promptness and Depth." Beginning by noting that interest in events abroad was exceptionally great, he said that that interest impelled party organizations to make political information more prompt. Conversations and talks were becoming so complicated and various that events could not be explained with a few phrases: "Often they concern the ideological struggle of the two systems, and this struggle acquires many types of forms." A high ideological level was the main, but not the only demand on oral information. The other very important demand was promptness. The politinformator did not have the right to lag behind life. When an event occurred it had to be responded to and explained immediately. But unfortunately it happened that an event had occurred, was being discussed, and the politinformators remained silent, awaiting "instructions." And here the oblast secretary went back to the old problem, hinting that it had never been solved at the central level. Measures by local Party organizations alone were necessarily insufficient: "Sometimes the informator is silent, not speaking out because he does not know what to say, does not have the material for a reliable talk. And the local, yes, even the central newspapers and magazines provide such material sometimes with great delay, its volume and quality do not always correspond to the growing demands.[68]

The article was nothing less than an accusation that the original policy of providing news quickly enough to compete with foreign radio stations, dating back to 1965 and earlier, had never been satisfactorily implemented. If that was still the situation at the end of 1967, one might ask what hope there was of ever doing so. The question would certainly be more than rhetorical, as attacks on foreign radio stations by proponents of a hard-line approach soon began to escalate.

And perhaps it was more than merely a coincidence of dates that the retreat from the emphasis on politinformators stepped up at just the time of the article. All along there had been an undercurrent of articles that gave relatively less emphasis to the primacy of politinformators over agitators than those quoted here. The attention paid to their coping with the problems created by foreign radio seemed to correlate with their emphasis on the work of the politinformators as opposed to the agitators. The turning point may have come at the end of 1967 with a response in Pravda to a question from Kamchatka on whether agitators were being phased out. The answer was absolutely that they were not, and in 1968 "remarks critical of the work of politinformators and sympathetic towards agitators increasingly found their way into the central press."[69]

The reputed "turning point" article did make a passing bow in one sentence toward the problem of foreign radio: "And our agitators clashed daily with such difficulty: today it is necessary to speak about the situation in Africa, tomorrow—about the economic reform, after that—about the norms of communist morals. . . ."[70] But that was no more than a ceremonial bow compared to the attention paid foreign radio by the advocates of the politinformator. So probably it was no accident that the politinformator, though never repudiated, drifted toward the background as the decision to resume jamming took shape. The question, whether to rely on the politinformator or on the agitator, continued to drift after jamming resumed, but by about April 1969 it was firmly decreed that both institutions should continue to exist side by side, and their work should be combined, not kept separate from each other. That was the unequivocal pronouncement by the editor of Agitator, who, with the silence of Stepakov on the subject after 1967, acted as the chief spokesman and troubleshooter in explaining the twists and turns of the Party line on this convoluted matter.[71]

Stepakov himself was dismissed as head of the Department of Propaganda in 1970, perhaps in connection with the bombastic pretentiousness of the campaign leading up to the observance of Lenin's hundredth anniversary that had cast an aura of absurdity over it and created apathy. The Soviets then tried to name Stepakov to the long vacant post of ambassador in Peking, but the Chinese refused to accept him. The Chinese, it is thought, regarded him as discredited and without influence.[72] He ultimately became ambassador to Yugoslavia.

Stepakov's downfall certainly should not be ascribed solely to the politinformator-versus-agitator issue. But it was surely related to the failure of the Propaganda Department and related agencies to halt a continued deterioration in the receptivity of the general public to the regime's ideological and information output. A number of the major officials of the media, including the head of the Committee for Radiobroadcasting and Television, were dismissed at about the same time. It was an admission of a general failure in the whole field of propaganda and information. The influence of foreign radio broadcasts was only part of that general problem, but it was a major part. The correlation between the uncertainties of direction in the politinformator affair and the handling of the foreign-radio problem suggests that one was closely connected with the other; and the effort and importance attached to it are evidence that foreign radio broadcasts were regarded as being close to the center of the general crisis in propaganda.

THE RISE AND FALL OF *RT*

The connection between the politinformator initiative and foreign radio is largely, although not entirely, one of inference, since the politinformators had to deal with other matters besides the questions raised by foreign broadcasts. It is not possible, in addition, to measure the results of politinformator efforts directly. But the other major innovation of the period bears directly on radio broadcasting, and its fate reveals much about the nature of the situation that had developed by 1966. That innovation was the magazine *RT*, which began publication in April of that year.

RT had as one of its assignments the exposure of the falsehoods and distortions of foreign radio broadcasts. That was part of its overall purpose, which was to increase the popularity of Soviet broadcasting. Soviet broadcasting had serious problems in satisfying its audience, even apart from competition with foreign broadcasts. Its general dullness and ideological didacticism was shared with most other cultural and media operations under the imposition of the Party's doctrinal requirements. Thus, the success of *RT* as a magazine was in large part related to, even dependent on, the popularity of Soviet broadcasting as a whole. That the presumed Central Committee resolution authorizing the establishment of *RT* was not published was an indication of the sensitivity of its purpose.

Both the lavish expenditure on *RT* and the uniqueness of its format testify to the importance that was attached to making it a success. It was a 16-page weekly and came out with an initial press run of 100,000. In striking contrast to the typical Soviet magazine printed on a grayish low-grade stock, *RT* used a bright, semiglossy paper in an immense page size, with large quantities of full-page color illustrations and art work.

RT's production cost, among the highest of any magazine in the Soviet Union, would have been justified if the magazine enhanced the effectiveness of Soviet broadcasting. But the critics—and the public—quickly found its contents to be simple-minded and formless. In addition to a weekly listing of the central radio and TV schedules, *RT* carried descriptive articles about programs or on the production of and a miscellany of articles on topics of presumed general interest. Very few were serious analytical or sociological discussions of the problems of radio and television. And, surprisingly, its most advertised feature, regular rebuttals of foreign broadcasts, appeared irregularly.

The introductory column in the first issue said that *RT* would teach its readers how to listen to foreign radio and to distinguish the half-lies and half-truths of the broadcasts, naming, in order, only VOA, BBC, DW, and RFE. After the first two issues, which had articles about a VOA broadcast on Vietnam and a DW program on economic affairs, there was an 11-week gap and then occasional articles, adding up to 32 in RT's 82-issue life before its reorganization into a new format. It appears that RT had trouble finding suitable material to satirize or refute. The borderline between the trivial and the relevant was very fine. To be relevant in criticizing the specific content of foreign broadcasts was to risk creating interest in them, and RT's editors, despite open prodding from the Party's journals, took refuge in often letting six or more weeks go by without touching the topic. Some of the choices showed considerable strain in finding suitable subjects.[73]

A few months after RT's inauguration, the Union of Journalists published its first evaluation. It was preceded by a series of letters, some from prominent personalities, complaining that RT contained nothing of interest and cheapened and attenuated every subject it wrote about. The reviewer agreed with that criticism, assessing RT as having little interesting information and a low intellectual level. RT's most important task, its "superproblem," was to find a new approach to the advertising of radio and television, it was reminded. But RT's descriptions of programs decreased interest in them: "If everything is already known, then why listen to it? The modern reader and listener understands everything from a hint."[74] In other words, Soviet radio and TV was so stereotyped that it was completely predictable. A few words would describe everything and remove any reason to see or hear a program itself.

A few months later, Pravda issued its one and only assessment of RT and found that the editors had "allowed serious defects in both the ideological content and the format of the journal." Pravda's review was similar to that of the Union of Journalists, but in more categorical terms. It also reminded RT that its "direct obligation" was to give a "decisive rebuff" to foreign radio broadcasts.[75] A count of RT's rebuttals of foreign radio, however, shows only a slight increase after the date of the article, compared to the period preceding it.

A week after Pravda's pronouncement, RT's first editor, Boris Voitekhov, was fired. The replacement, V. A. Mezentsev, was not found for seven months. By then RT's circulation (tirazh) had declined from 100,000 to 73,500. Mezentsev lasted only five weeks. He could not stem the decline in readers, but he did try to shift the blame. He published letters accusing Soyuzpechat, the agency responsible for all magazine and newspaper subscription and newsstand sales, of being responsible for RT's declining sales. Soyuzpechat replied that it was filling all orders, leaving Mezentsev nothing to say except that distribution of new magazines was too subtle and complex to be entrusted to kiosk tenders.[76]

After Mezentsev was fired, no one could be found who would take the job. Perhaps it had already been decided to convert the magazine to a new format instead of trying to find someone who could make it work. Circulation declined steadily through the second half of 1967, until it reached 47,500, less than half the initial circulation. The conversion of RT began in September 1967, with a change of title to Programmy RT. In November, half the glossy pages were replaced with the standard coarse paper of Soviet periodicals, and the textual content was cut back to make space for a greatly expanded annotated program schedule. The new orientation of the magazine was made more explicit at the beginning of 1968, when its title became Programmy Radio i Televideniya. Political and ideologically-oriented articles were not completely discarded, but the magazine was now primarily a utilitarian service bulletin. The expectations of 1966 that RT could reverse the public's increasing apathy toward the output of Soviet broadcasting had been abandoned.

In fairness to RT, it should be noted that it was not alone in losing circulation in 1967. Almost all Soviet mass-circulation periodicals that were heavily political in content began to lose readership at the time, while the less ideologically-oriented publications continued to gain or held their own. RT's decline was greater than most, however. Simply explained, RT was just badly edited. But RT's special problem was that it had to orient almost its entire content on radio and television programming. Perhaps, then, the public's lack of interest was a reflection of its attitude toward radio and television. And this, possibly, could be related to popularity of foreign broadcasts.

THE RESUMPTION OF JAMMING

December 1967 saw the demise of RT and the de-emphasis of the political information specialists. It was also the time when the Soviet polls, not yet disclosed, brought in specific new information on the interest in foreign radio. January 1968 saw the surfacing of a strong campaign to resume jamming of foreign radio.

The month began with a classic illustration of the influence of foreign broadcasts. Another of the series of trials of dissident writers and protesters, the Galanskov-Ginsburg trial, took place. The trial was not reported in the Soviet press at the time it was held, but the street outside the courthouse was filled with people who said they knew of its time and place from Western broadcasts. During the week after the trial there was a series of articles about it, first in the local Moscow evening paper, then in Izvestia, and finally in Komsomolskaya Pravda, each article more disclosing than the previous one. The last of them said that it was in response to the "fussing" of foreign radio broadcasts and the protests that they had reported of noted writers abroad. A week after the end of the trial, Komsomolskaya Pravda conceded for the first time that the chief defendants had not admitted guilt but had defended themselves.

That was after part of the transcript had been smuggled out and broadcast back by foreign radio stations. But as a Western correspondent on the scene commented: "Although the broadcasts have clearly influenced Soviet media to be somewhat more explicit, the Soviet citizen still could not form an intelligent picture of the case even after today's Komsomolskaya Pravda account."[77]

The dilemma was perfectly clear: Foreign radio made it impossible to manage the news about important events in accordance with the ideological planning for them, yet at the same time, even after the most blatant evidence of the breakdown in those plans (the crowds outside the courthouse, the smuggled transcripts), the regime was flatly unwilling to provide full reporting that could in any way satisfy those who turned to foreign radio. The ideological requirements of news management were apparently still considered irreconcilable with the conditions necessary for effective competition with foreign radio. The gap must have engendered frustration, and it opened an opportunity for the advocates of the simple shortcut to a solution: the resumption of jamming.

Insofar as it is possible to date the public emergence of a campaign for a reconsideration of the tolerant policy toward foreign radio, January 27, 1968, seems to be significant. On that date Aleksandr Chakovsky, chief editor of Literaturnaya Gazeta, the organ of the writers' union, published the substance of a lecture he had given earlier to an "All-Russian Conference of Cultural Workers," attacking "writers" and others who sought the attention and protection of foreign radio stations and foreign public opinion. Castigating them as seeking glory and false bravery, he generalized: "In solving the concrete tasks of Communist education, we do not have the right to forget that our foreign enemies are conducting a struggle for the souls of people, especially youth, and with enormous cunningness and hypocrisy, every day are bringing to bear on them their muddy radio waves."[78]

Had Chakovsky published that in his own weekly newspaper, it would not have been so noticeable. But instead of its natural place there, the lecture was in the much more important daily Sovetskaya Rossiya, the organ of the Russian Federation.* Sovetskaya Rossiya soon took the lead in the frequency and vehemence of warnings about the deleterious effects of foreign radio, and after the resumption of jamming in the Soviet Union went so far as to put pressure on the

---

*Unlike the Union-Republics with their separately organized Communist parties, the RSFSR had been run by a special bureau within the central party apparatus. Thus, Sovetskaya Rossiya's leadership of the campaign against foreign radio in 1968 suggests a possible location of the main source of opposition to the policy of nonjamming.

East European countries to resume their jamming. Chakovsky's own paper began on February 7 a running dispute with the BBC,[79] and over the next year averaged about one such feature a month. It even took on RL, concerning its programs on Belorussian literature, despite the policy of keeping specifics on RL's programs out of the central press.[80]

A plenum of the Central Committee to be devoted to ideology was scheduled for April 1968. It was to be the first plenary session to concentrate on the subject since the one of June 1963, which had been accompanied by the end of jamming. Now there were increasing signs that foreign radio was in the forefront of problems demanding action. One of the most important was an election speech of Alexei Kosygin at Minsk in February, which included the following passage:

> It must be remembered that our ideological adversaries are experienced and cunning. At times they may confuse some who are unsophisticated in politics and lack tempering in the school of life. This of course applies only to a handful, but each person is dear to us. A number of European radio stations broadcast in the Russian language. Some of them operate very cunningly and subtly, proffering slander in sweetened and camouflaged guise.[81]

The significance was not in what was said, which was rather mild and noncommittal compared to what others were saying at this time, but in the fact that it was Kosygin who said it. Kosygin, as far as can be determined, had never before deigned publicly to take notice of foreign radio. For him to do so at the time probably meant that the subject had newly become one of active discussion at the Politburo level.

The extent to which foreign radio had become a dominant, if not the predominant, area of concern was demonstrated at the specialist level that same month. At the first session of what was intended to be an annual conference on scientific-theoretical questions connected with radio the discussion was quickly diverted from its advertised theoretical plane when the head of the news department of the Estonian radio reported that a poll had shown that only 27 percent of the people considered that Estonian radio reported the news promptly. He then by inference extended the responsibility for this situation to the central authorities. Having lost hope that TASS would speed up its services, Estonian radio was getting its news by recording Mayak and the central radio's "Latest News" and translating it for use on Estonian radio. Hence, the slowness for which the public was indicting Estonian radio was really that of the central news services. The anonymous correspondent who reported on the conference then added that the sharpness of the question for all the participants turned the discussion into a purely practical matter.

What this meant to the participants was that it was foreign radio broadcasts with which they were mainly concerned. V. Zorin, the central radio's political commentator, asked why people listened to foreign radio and then gave the answer himself: "Because we still keep the audience on short rations of news. It is the slowness, the insufficient news, and inept preparation of some materials." Zorin was saying openly—and this may have been one of the first times that it was thus acknowledged—that the trouble with Soviet news was not only that it was slow but that much of it was censored out completely. A Ukrainian official, V. Zhigilis, added that the problem with Soviet radio was that it reported only about successes.

Reportage of further details of the discussion was sharply curtailed. Much of the discussion revolved around the prospects for radio: whether it should try to compete with television or seek specialized audiences. As a representative of Armenian radio put it, radio should consist simply of prompt news and music. Many of the participants concluded that interest in radio was falling with the rise in education and the decrease of the rural population. In the face of television the future of radio depended on a better understanding of the role of news.[82]

As was often the case, the practical results of the April plenum did not become apparent immediately. At the June 1963 plenum the major decisions were not made at the plenum itself but privately, at the time of or in the period preceding the plenum. The same was true for the April plenum. Its published materials predictably called for a greater offensive struggle against bourgeois propaganda, but the all important means were not spelled out. However, postplenum comments and instructions made clear that combating foreign radio was one of the areas to which particular attention was being paid.

Sovetskaya Rossiya was first to interpret the meaning of the plenum. Its lead on the plenum pointed out that special attention should be given to exposing the lying broadcasts of bourgeois radio stations, "which attempt to start provocational rumors and propagandize the bourgeois, especially the American, way of life as supposedly 'fun,' 'easy,' and 'problem-free' in character. It is imperative to show, by using all forms of our truthful, communist propaganda, the reactionary and anti-popular essence of imperialism's domestic and foreign policies. . . ."; it went on to deplore the fact that some of the intelligentsia were falling for the bourgeois bait.[83]

Other leading papers, not choosing to connect the plenum resolutions specifically to foreign radio, implied that an area of uncertainty about the policy towards foreign broadcasters may have still existed. But the sketchy accounts of the private meetings for the working levels of the ideological apparatus and the articles directed at them showed that foreign radio was at the center of attention. The organ of the Union of Journalists editorialized that the plenum had made especially important the prompt and broad reporting of news, internal and foreign: Its exhortation was one that had come to have a single meaning.[84]

The State Committee's response was not so direct as to refer to foreign radio in a format so prominent as an editorial. However, in the first issue of its journal and after the plenum, it did publish an article by a deputy chairman on methods of combating foreign radio, without relating it to the plenum. VOA, BBC, and DW were named as more and more unifying their programming efforts. VOA was more effectively masking itself with apparent objectivity and loyalty to the Soviet Union. Greater counterefforts were demanded. At that point the order of precedence was given for different types of counterefforts, showing, that the Soviets' most important area of concern was that the faster and more complete news provided by foreign stations was undermining the credibility of the Soviet media, and, thereby, trust in the regime itself.* He then went on to describe different types of Soviet programs and methods of programming. For his purpose he approved scientific, sociological research but then, significantly, attacked polling. He mentioned "campaigns" of polling, calling them "noisy" and "muddled."[85]

The annoyance with polls was probably inspired more by their results than by defects in their methodology. Attacks on polls were becoming more explicit as their results came in. At the time one of the most important—on sources of international news—had been completed already, but the broadcast organization never publicly acknowledged its results, even though some of its contents were disclosed elsewhere. Eventually, five months after the partial disclosure of the results by another organization, it issued a curt statement that it had received the results and sent them on to various editorial councils for their consideration in improving programs, but it never said what those results were.[86] In this respect the State Committee was acting in its typically secretive and aloof manner.

Another consequence of the April plenum was a closer supervision of the press by the Party. A deputy director of the Propaganda Department, T. Kuprikov, personally instructed the heads of the Party organizations of at least those press and broadcast organizations in Moscow on the matter. He told them that the April plenum meant that there would be firmer Party guidance and interest in the press—that being all that the few sentences announcing the meeting said.[87] But that general phrase had some significant consequences that pointed toward an increasingly negative attitude about the policy of

---

*See above, pp. 33-34.

open competition with foreign radio. It meant a purge of editors and media officials, and among the changes were at least two that were not consonant with an effective implementation of the policy of open competition. One of the victims was E. V. Yakovlev, the chief editor of Zhurnalist since its reorganization in 1967. He was removed sometime between April 9 and May 21, 1968. The new editor was V. N. Golubev, who began the first issue under his direction with an editorial criticizing his predecessor. Zhurnalist, it said, had not satisfactorily explained the party leadership of the press, was weak and poorly oriented to press worker materials, and had too many illustrations, which error it compounded by making them too modernistic and naturalistic in character. Those conclusions had been drawn from the justified Party criticism of the journal.[88]

Golubev proceeded to squeeze out much of what had made the new Zhurnalist so interesting and popular. Most important for the matter of radio competition was the gradual elimination of the reporting of research results on the media, especially the opinion polls. That of course, was probably part of a policy decided at higher levels, but it meant that one of the main props of the means of competition with foreign radio had been removed. This research was valuable both as a spur to action and a source of basic information on what was needed to compete. If its dissemination was now to be restricted, it would almost certainly be because of a loss of interest in continuing the competition along those lines. The drying up of substantive content in Zhurnalist could be quantitatively measured in a loss of circulation, which amounted to between 10 and 20 percent over the next year and a half. That did not bother Golubev's superiors, who showed their esteem for the job he did by promoting him in 1969 to the prestigious position of chief editor of the newly-established central daily newspaper, Sotsialisticheskaya Industriya.

A second personnel change of mid-1968 was even more indicative of a reduction of emphasis in making Soviet broadcasting qualitatively better than foreign broadcasts. The change involved the director of the central television network, the hapless Anatolii Bogomolov, who lost his position on some unspecified date prior to August 12. The Department of Propaganda had held a special meeting to review the situation of radio and television news. It formally reported that Mayak was not always prompt, especially during the night and morning hours (i. e., the time when foreign stations were on the air). Television news was still at a low and misleading level. Practical suggestions (undisclosed) were made.[89]

The Union of Journalists followed up with an editorial urging the improvement of television news and other aspects of television.[90] But the new head of central television, P. I. Shabanov, was not a professional from the field of broadcasting: He was a Party official whose previous assignment had been that of a raion secretary in the city of Moscow. While that was certainly a faithful implementation of the call for stronger Party leadership of the press, it was not the kind of move that would be made if the professional quality of broadcasting and its ability to draw listeners away from foreign radio stations was uppermost in the planning for future operations. The movement away from professionalism was reemphasized when Shabanov brought in as his deputy still another Party official, V. I. Orlov, who had been in the People's Control section of his raion.[91] Characteristically, those moves, primarily affecting broadcasting, passed without public notice by the State Committee, while they were reported, even if only cursorily, by others.

While those structural changes were being made, attacks on foreign radio broadcasts were being stepped up in the public press and also within Party circles. On May 21, for example, the Moscow Writers' Organization was called together to be briefed on the April plenum. The account of the meeting was made available only in curtailed form, but it was revealed that part of the meeting was given over to a discussion of foreign radio broadcasts. A warning was given about the broadcasting back to the Soviet Union of harmful works by Soviet writers.[92] That was not the first time that this subject had been raised at writers' meetings, but bringing it within the framework of the April plenum added to its weight. Moreover, the publicizing of the affair of Grigori Yablonsky at almost the same moment by Sovetskaya Rossiya did add a new element.

Yablonsky, who was called a highly-regarded figure at the Novosibirsk Institute of Catalysis and was a member of the Party to boot, had signed a letter of protest about the trials that had been published in the New York Times and later broadcast by VOA. Sovetskaya Rossiya's investigation turned up the fact that even earlier Yablonsky had sung a song at an amateur-night performance at the Institute that included a line that a shipment of Spidola radio receivers had arrived at GUM. (The Spidola, a seven-band transistorized portable, was considered the best domestically-sold receiver for listening to foreign broadcasts. It was always in short supply.) Yablonsky attempted to pass off his signature as a careless accident. But the newspaper concluded from a long conversation with him that he had been misled by Western radio broadcasts about the trials. Yablonsky, it said, had not turned to his seniors to learn the reasons for the Western radio agitation about the trials; and who would have told him that the broadcasts had clearly anti-communist goals. Yablonsky, it said, stayed within a closed circle of friends who most often discussed rumors and gossip of a doubtful character.[93]

A point in the matter that seemed particularly worrisome was the fact that Yablonsky was in a privileged position and had, or could have had, access to superior sources of information. The implication was that if foreign radio could deceive someone like Yablonsky, there was not much prospect in combating it through existing procedures. And Sovetskaya Rossiya seemed to reinforce that implication by quickly coming back with another lead editorial urging the raising of the level of ideological struggle and connecting the need with "tens of radio stations pouring out their various categories of disinformation and hypocrisy."[94]

A different but equally worrisome, because broader, type of influence of foreign radio was also aired for what may have been the first time. Writers and publications were said to be receiving anonymous "letters" containing ideas derived from broadcasts of VOA and DW. That was used as a starting point for a denunciation of these ideas, accompanied by long quotations from VOA commentaries on the obsolescence of Marxism, its treatment of the Columbia University demonstrations, and the status of the NDP in Germany. Presumably, monitoring reports were provided for this purpose.[95]

Whether those particular "letters" were real was not so important as the public allegation of the existence of mail being sent to Soviet institutions as the result of foreign broadcasts. Even if such mail had always existed, it had not previously been subject to public comment. Thus, the attack was in effect another stage of escalation in the new campaign against foreign radio. Mail of that sort could be considered a form of pressure on the Soviet system, and by blaming it on foreign radio an additional argument was created for taking more drastic action against the broadcasts.

The overall level of attacks on foreign broadcasts increased sharply in the first half of 1968. By mid-summer they had attracted the notice of foreign correspondents, who reported that one of their themes was the attribution to foreign broadcasts of much of the trouble with dissident intellectuals. The correspondents hypothesized that Soviet leaders were regretting the abolition of jamming. Nevertheless, the Associated Press correspondent concluded that the resumption of jamming was unlikely because it would be "retrogressive" and too damaging an admission of fear.[96] Blaming the dissent on foreign broadcasts did not necessarily mean that the primary responsibility for the dissent was placed on them or even that the Soviet leaders saw such responsibility as the source of the major objection to the broadcasts. Less ephemeral effects of the broadcasts might be more important, but the propagation of that line could be useful in more than one way. It was a convenient shifting of the blame for the dissent, and it was a good justification for a change in policy, especially among the lower ranks of the Party apparat, who daily had to face the consequences of the ferment and explain it.

Some of the explanations, more explicit than any that had appeared before, came out in the last days before the resumption of jamming. Kommunist, the Central Committee's main theoretical journal, had a series of articles that might be described as setting the general framework. Pavel Demichev, the Central Committee secretary responsible for ideological work, went over at length all the "dogmatic," "revisionist," "pseudo-leftist," and "nationalist" contemporary trends and in the light of the April plenum called for stepped up work against them.[97] The next issue carried a detailed survey on the means and methods of the propaganda, including the foreign radio stations, that had to be combated.[98]

In getting down to details, two explanations—perhaps they should be called alibis—stand out. In one, P. Tkachenko, a Party official of the Elektrosila plant in Leningrad, deplored a tendency of Communists who remained silent in the face of praise of foreign life. He was referring to spreading influence of foreign broadcasts, and mentioned an engineer in the plant who went around quoting foreign news broadcasts, as an example of becoming "a sort of extended communications line for a foreign radio station."[99] Kommunist, in its last issue that went to press (on August 12) before the resumption of jamming, had a more eloquent expression of the problem:

> An interesting thought was told to me by Yu. A. Matsal: "Now, everyone has radio receivers—you listen to whom you want and as much as you can stand. Only some, although very few such, listen and are off: to somewhere 'there'—that other, beautiful, life. . . . Of course," continued Yulyan Antonovich—"this certainly does not mean that a bad man is in front of us. Simply sometimes he believes the tales, or else, even when not believing them, begins to wag his tongue. Some only 'wag,' but some take it seriously. And after that, from the alien voice, he goes off to convince others, to tell all sorts of fables. So one must clear up all this at the very beginning. Here no one will replace the Communists."[100]

What was being described was no more than what might be considered the normal tendency to gossip and chat on the job. Such public alarm about it had rarely or never been aired before. The politinformators and others had been set the task of counteracting just that kind of talk. Here, again, it was being said that they were unwilling or unable—or both—to do so. Also, it did not matter whether the broadcasts were taken seriously or believed. It was simply the existence of the unwanted information, whose spreading by word-of-mouth could not be prevented, that was undermining the work of the ideological cadres. Or so the cadres wanted their superiors to believe.

Those explanations read like excuses for the propaganda workers' difficulties, although they must have had broader roots than foreign broadcasts alone. Between the lines the propaganda functionaries were saying, in effect, "Look, we cannot satisfactorily conduct our ideological work among the masses if we have to contend with the unchecked spread of information from foreign broadcasts. It must be more effectively checked at the source or handled at a higher level." The appearance of a few such complaints in prominent publications was probably evidence of considerable pressure from the lower levels of the Party's propaganda apparatus to do something about foreign broadcasting. The pressure would not be less effective for the fact that those people might exaggerate the extent of the broadcasts' influence, in order to blame as much of their own shortcomings as possible on "outside agitators." In fact, they could be expected to do so.

In what was, perhaps, a coincidence an analytic reflection of the argument appeared at almost the precise moment that jamming was resumed. A prominent academic commentator who often wrote on the tactics of foreign radio broadcasting summed up its general technique. It was, he said, the selection of facts, a balancing of negative and positive sides, a montage of those balances, the use of music breaks, and praise of listeners' achievements, resulting in the creation of an emotional attitude. He discussed whether agitation by "naked facts" had to be a Western specialty and took issue with a school of Soviet thought that asserted that objective information was incompatible with the presentation of reality. (Here the argument was running up against a more sophisticated version of the propagandists' view that all outside information was harmful, regardless of its inherent content.)

But, he went on, arguing against those who were opposed to the whole idea of news reporting in the conventional sense, Communist information could be used to reflect reality in the manner that they desired. The Communist press had found it necessary to meet the foreign radio competition, although sometimes it was going too far and harming its propaganda function by giving too much space or time to news. Earlier, Soviet radio had just imitated the newspapers, but now it was trying to catch its listeners' interest at the beginning and not bore them before the end. This was not (as some say) a principle suitable only for foreign radio but a general principle. In conclusion, he maintained that Soviet radio must hold to this position, "the more so, because now almost all stations are heard freely, and the owner of a receiver, with a turn of the wrist, can 'catch' any wave."[101]

This article went to press August 21, 1968, the day jamming resumed. Obviously, there had been no time to coordinate or inform in advance the writers and editors responsible for those discussions. The rapid development of events in Czechoslovakia would have prevented that.

The jamming began about two hours after the world news agencies first transmitted the news of the Soviet invasion of Czechoslovakia.[102] Jamming was resumed against the VOA, the BBC, DW, and the Canadian Broadcasting Corporation (CBC), thus restoring the line-up to what it had been in 1963. The United States waited one month and then, noting that the jamming was virtually continuous, on September 19 delivered a diplomatic protest about it to the Soviet Union. The Soviet Union, perhaps calculating that the best defense was an offense, had already delivered a protest about the U. S. publication of some samizdat literature and documents, most of which had been previously published elsewhere.[103] Nothing came of those pro forma expostulations, of course. The United States went on periodically to attempt to raise the subject, and the Soviet Union either refused to acknowledge the existence of the subject or claimed that it was an internal matter not open to discussion. After exactly one year had passed, the United States resumed use of the long-wave frequency it had relinquished under the 1963 tacit agreement, bringing in turn protests from the Soviet Union.

When the jamming was first resumed, it was at a lower level than it had been during the early 1960s. It remained that way for six months. Then in March 1969 its intensity began to increase, and in May it was reported to have reached the peak levels of early 1963. (That would be the post-Cuban-missile-crisis rate of 70 to 80 percent.) There was no discernible political event or change in U. S.-Soviet relations to explain the increase. U. S. officials thought that it was the result of increased technical skill or new equipment.[104] That suggests that the Soviets were not quite prepared in August 1968 for the demands on the system of the increased jamming schedule. Even had the 1963 jamming network been maintained at its full scale, the total load on it in 1968 could have been excessive. There were now a larger number of stations to be jammed, including the Chinese, and the Western radio stations had increased their schedules, especially during the Czechoslovakian crisis.

The organizational and technical unpreparedness in 1968 for a general resumption of jamming suggests that the decision developed approximately according to the following timetable. Advocates of the resumption of jamming accumulated additional materials in support of their views around the end of 1967 and the beginning of 1968. The April 1968 plenum strengthened their position, and either then, or during the next few months, a tentative decision was taken to resume jamming. The timing, and perhaps even the finality of its implementation, was still in doubt when the Czechoslovakian crisis came to a head. But, judging from the delay in bringing jamming back to its 1963 level, if it had not been for Czechoslovakia jamming would have more likely resumed in 1969 instead of 1968.

The invasion of Czechoslovakia certainly determined the timing of the resumption, even though the state of the Soviet domestic situation seemed about to force it anyway. Czechoslovakia provided at least two additional reasons to hasten the resumption of jamming. First, the Soviets would have better control of information about its reaching their own public. They did not expect to have too much to worry about in that respect, since it was planned to be a smooth operation at the "invitation" of Czech leaders. It did not quite work out that way, but in advance planning there was one very important and undesirable information aspect that they could anticipate. That was the sure knowledge that many foreign Communist parties would criticize the intervention, a feature that they would be most anxious to conceal from the public.

A second and more basic reason for making the jamming resumption coincide with the Czech events would be to minimize the long-term propaganda and image damage to the Soviet Union. The resumption of jamming was bound to reflect unfavorably on the Soviet Union, both on its image in world public opinion, since it was an admission of weakness, and on the relations between the Soviet public and government. Therefore, it is not surprising that the jamming resumption was to be carried out in a manner that would call the least attention to it, both at home and abroad. In the drama of the intervention the new jamming would be overshadowed to the maximum possible extent. That alone would be sufficient to justify whatever difficulties were created by the lack of time for thorough preparations.

An indication of the lack of advance preparation was the relative constancy in tone and content of professional and Party comment on information policy before, and for some time after, the resumption of jamming. Of course, neither the suspension nor the resumption of jamming was ever subject to open discussion, but one would expect indirect acknowledgment of the new situation in analyses and in domestic information policies. It may have been that the jamming was not expected to be totally effective, and, therefore, the same prophylactic measures connected with the policy of open competition had to be continued. But, eventually, some signs of adjustment did appear, so it is possible that the delay was a catching-up of analysis with events, rather than a deliberate policy of noncoordination between different levels of the apparat (which would not be illogical if a high level of secrecy was being maintained) or a sign of continuing conflict over the direction of the new, more repressive approach.

In any case, the earliest example that could be found of even an implied explanation after the renewal of jamming was in a year-end editorial of the Union of Journalists on the strengthening of Party control of the press. The editorial noted that the growth of means of information also leads to the growth of the danger of disinformation, and, therefore, no consideration could be given to any lessening of controls.[105] But that was so vague that if jamming had not already been resumed, it would have been difficult to assume a connection. For at the same time statements were still appearing that referred to foreign broadcasting as if nothing had changed. One such was in an article by an official of the Propaganda Department on methods of handling intellectual elements of the population:

> Sometimes comments are made that news in the West, while deliberately false, is quicker than ours and places the lecturer, speaker, or propagandist in a difficult situation. This worry is understandable, and all measures should be taken so that our news, which is always distinguished by objective coverage of events and facts, is made more efficient.[106]

That was substantially identical to many warnings about the problems of operating in open competition with unjammed foreign broadcasts. While the writer may have considered the jamming of the moment to be ineffective, or may have been unsure of its permanence, his position was also conditioned by his responsibility for the more highly educated sectors of society, and he could plausibly assume that no matter what repressive or obstructive measures might be decreed, there were some groups that would always find methods for keeping themselves informed.

As of December 1968 the Soviets tacitly assumed the technical ineffectuality of jamming by ascribing to foreign radio an extremely influential role in causing unease in the society. They claimed that Minister of Trade Struyev had to go on television to counter Western reports of possible price increases in the Soviet Union.[107] That was not a good advertisement for the efficacy of jamming, and it may have contributed to pressure for more intensive measures in the following year.

A remarkable expression of the anti-foreign-news school of thought got into print shortly after that. A reviewer of the year-old television news program "Vremya" criticized it for giving too much attention, even the "lion's share," to foreign news: "They say that sociological research shows a rise in interest in foreign news. . . but the creators of the program exploit this interest too much." The reviewer asserted that the quality and attention given to foreign news was lowering the quality of internal news. His final comment on the subject was, "The Soviets have their own pride (poet's deep thought)."[108] In other words, foreign news per se is harmful, and an interest in it is unhealthy. The public, no matter how much it wants it, should be kept on short rations of foreign news.

That isolationist philosophy seems to derive directly from the views of Mikhail Suslov as he expressed them to Svetlana Alliluyeva. When Stalin's daughter was seeking permission to travel outside the country Suslov, then the fourth-ranking member of the Politburo, asked her why she wanted to do that. He himself almost never left the country, he said, and paid little attention to the affairs of others. In his opinion there was nothing interesting outside the Soviet Union. Given this attitude at the top, it may be readily surmised that there had always been substantial opposition to the policy of enlarging news coverage and improving the quality of information disseminated to the public—a policy most graphically symbolized in the suspension of jamming from 1963 to 1968. But before the resumption of jamming, it would have been awkward, if not ridiculous, to promulgate that viewpoint openly. So its appearance in early 1969 was a signal that the proponents of jamming and of the general intensification of efforts to isolate potential sources of dissent and freer public opinion had strengthened their position and were more confident of prevailing over the long run.

The determination to clamp down on news was not so one-sided that it could forbid the expression of opposing viewpoints. The editor of Za Rubezhom, the most important Soviet publication for distributing detailed international news (through the device of reprinting articles from the Western press), without referring directly to Yakovlev's article, took issue with it. He criticized Soviet international reporting and, in so doing, picked out its low volume and monotonous similarity for emphasis. That similarity did not allow for the nature of particular audiences. He concluded that more, not less, foreign news was needed.[109] Thus, one can see that the reimposition of jamming did not mean a return to the enforcement of a monolithic front of approval for the whole philosophy it represented. To some extent the increased freedom of opinion and research about the direction of information policies, which had grown up during the period of open competition, continued. More restrictive policies may have been decreed for an indefinite duration, but the occasional manifestations of disagreement were probably signs of a continuing vigorous behind-the-scenes dispute about the proper course to follow.

Sovetskaya Rossiya, which had led the drive in 1968 for the renewal of jamming in the Soviet Union, was able seven months later to turn its attentions to Eastern Europe. With the approach of Lenin's hundredth anniversary, its lead editorial said, Western radio stations were more and more discrediting Lenin's thought. VOA, the Voice of Israel, RFE, RL, and Radio Peking had particularly joined together in a common front. Then, in an extremely rare open mention of jamming, it called on the East European countries to resume jamming. It did so by quoting a passage from an American book on the cessation of jamming in East Europe: "Contacts, it says in it, will widen. At the present time, jamming stations have stopped work in Rumania, Poland, Hungary, Czechoslovakia, and partially in Bulgaria. At a certain stage the whole population of East Europe will have access to Western radio broadcasts." The editorial then went so far as to recommend a cutback in the admission of tourists to Eastern Europe, a very important source of foreign currency, in order to prevent the introduction of alien ideas.[110] The newspaper could hardly have taken up this advanced position if it was not by then sure that jamming had been firmly installed as a long-term policy in the Soviet Union. It may also have been a sign of a hardening of attitude that Pravda featured a direct attack (by a secretary of the Belorussian Communist Party) on specific RL programs at that time, despite the general policy of avoiding detailed references to RL in the central press.[111]

Another indication of more repressive measures being instituted at this time was the arrest of a person who had been trying to keep in touch with VOA. His letters to VOA, all apparently intercepted and not delivered, had been known to the authorities since 1966. He also wrote to the U. S. embassy after the invasion of Czechoslovakia. On June 24, 1969, his apartment was searched, but nothing was found except for copies of his VOA correspondence and tape recordings of broadcasts. He was arrested the next day.[112] His activities had been known since 1966, but not until 1969 was action taken against him. It is not known whether the case is unique, and, thus, how significant a change in policy it might represent, since it was reported only in the samizdat literature. Had it been reported in the Soviet press, it would certainly have been a signal of a firmer policy against listening to foreign broadcasts, even if the arrest itself was not the first of its kind. So far as can be determined, the Soviet press never reported the arrest of anyone solely on the basis of evidence of interest in foreign broadcasts. Nevertheless, what had been tolerated since 1966 apparently was no longer so tolerable in 1969.

An intended finality in the resumption of jamming was assumed more directly in two articles that appeared in 1969. In a discussion of the way that ostensibly innocent tactics of foreign broadcasts are really clever traps the special importance that foreign stations put on being first in reporting internal events in the socialist countries was mentioned. That observation in the past had always been followed by an exhortation, even if only ritualistic, that Soviet information services should work faster, but now there was no mention whatsoever that Soviet news services should be faster.[113] The omission has greater significance because its author was a deputy chairman of the KGB and its resident expert on penetration of alien ideas. He had published a book on the subject while still a local official in Azerbaijan and continued to write on it in the major journals of the Party. Whether or not his expertise was responsible for his rise in the hierarchy, his continued public attention to the subject showed the increasing importance being given to the struggle against the penetration of uncontrolled information. If he now omitted a call for better competition with Western news broadcasts from the Soviet news services, it was probably a consequence of his knowledge that greater efforts were being made to cut off those sources before they reached the Soviet public and that these efforts, most notably the jamming, would continue.

A second article that seemed to assume that the resumption of jamming was deemed permanent was written towards the end of 1969 by the chief editor of Zhurnalist. The article included a discussion on methods of counterpropaganda and took up the argument about how much detail could be permitted in quoting examples of Western propaganda in the Soviet press. Some said that if, in the course of rebutting it, Western propaganda was repeated, it only played into the propagandists' hands. The editor of Zhurnalist opposed that view, saying that concrete examples should be given, and not general reproaches that would leave the reader mystified. The reason for his approach was the fact that the "overwhelming majority" of Soviet people learn about bourgeois propaganda only from Soviet articles.[114] That would seem to be a rather optimistic assumption in light of the fact that less than a year before, the minister of Trade had to go on television to refute rumors alleged to have arisen from Western broadcasts. But this statement could be considered justified if it was thought that jamming was now effective and permanent.

It would be appropriate to conclude with an official explanation of the abandonment of the attempt to compete openly with Western broadcasts, but, of course, none was given. Among the sometimes conflicting analyses in the journalists' publications, the following seems to correspond most closely with the general trend of Soviet theories about the effects of Western broadcasting that had developed over the years of the experiment. A higher degree of authoritativeness can be ascribed to it, because it was selected to appear in the yearbook Problemy televideniya i radio rather than only in the more ephemeral monthly journals.

According to the account,[115] U. S. radio propaganda could be understood to be based theoretically on seven axioms: the use of labels and stereotypes; "sparking enrichment" (that is, beautiful words); acting like simple folks, or pretending to be a friend of the listener (the BBC's Anatol Goldberg was cited as an outstanding example); quoting from authorities; using axiomatic evidence (that is, presenting propositions as if they do not need demonstration); promoting the herd instinct and conformity; using false or partial data and coverage. The increasing subtlety of bourgeois propaganda, the account finds, "renders influence on separate unstable elements in the socialist countries." These axioms were coupled with the "law of precedence," which refers to the theory that the first report has a stronger effect than subsequent correctives. The "law" has several modifiers. It is weakened if the audience's educational level is higher or if the audience has a higher level of confidence in its principles, if the prestige of the source is low or if the audience is forewarned about that source. On the other hand, it is strengthened if there is only one source or if other sources are late, if an event is successfully forecast, and especially if the audience has time to discuss it on its own. Therefore, the quickness of enemy news reporting was not simply a striving for "sensation," as some Soviet analysts had contended, but a calculated stratagem. From that consequence the account derived the conclusion that Western broadcasts' interpretations of events and ideas may not be as important as the effort to build distrust toward domestic sources, which is the outcome of the operation of the "law of precedence."

It was because Western broadcasters consider the value of that "law" high that they were willing to report objectively even events that were unfavorable to them. Being first enhanced their opportunity to interpret events in their own way. The analysis then went on to make the appropriate recommendations, basically repeating the well-known suggestions that the Soviet press work faster and adding the refinement that the morning broadcasts were especially important because they provide the first news, on which the listener orients his working day. Therefore, the time had come to do special research on increasing the quality of morning news presentations, so that when private discussions began and the alien news was heard there was already the Soviet version present in their minds.

The analysis stated in theoretical terms the point already made by the State Committee and others that the harm caused by foreign broadcasts derived not so much from the substantive content of what they said as from the fact that they were so often faster than the Soviet media. The distrust toward the Soviet media thus created inevitably would affect attitudes toward the government and Party, of which the media are an integral part. The same concern was implicitly shown by the sequence of priorities endorsed in revamping Soviet news broadcasting as laid down by the deputy chairman of the State Committee, A. Rapokhin: the omission, at the time jamming was resumed, of any accusation that the United States had broken agreements made at the time jamming was suspended in 1963; the pattern of selective jamming before 1963; the apparent reluctance, after jamming resumed, to discuss broadcasting matters as freely as had been done before 1963. The information then being developed by Soviet research made the point explicitly.

By 1968 the Soviet Union had gone from total jamming to selective jamming to the suspension of most jamming, through five years of relatively unhampered foreign broadcasting, and then to the resumption of jamming. But the resumption of jamming was certainly not a return to conditions that had existed before jamming was suspended. No one was more aware of this than the Soviets themselves. During the interval they had developed a substantial research and analysis capacity applied to public attitudes toward the media, which in Soviet conditions could not avoid touching on sensitive matters affecting the relationship between society and the political regime. The results of that survey research, insofar as it was disclosed, can be used to make a crude independent evaluation of trends in the relationship between foreign broadcasting, Soviet media, and the public's attitude toward both. Given the virtual identity between Soviet media and the regime, the public's attitude should reveal something of the underlying factors conditioning political life in the Soviet Union.

NOTES

1. William Taubman, The View from Lenin Hills (London: Hamish Hamilton, 1968), pp. 186-99.
2. D. Goryunov, "On a Great Campaign," Sovetskaya Pechat' (June 1964):1-7
3. M. Zimyanin, "An Affair of Our Honor," Sovetskaya Pechat' (May 1966):3.
4. Bernard Gwertzman, "Soviet Scientist and Party Aide Clash on the Freedom of Ideas," New York Times, October 8, 1970.
5. Ibid.
6. A. E. Levitin, "Listening to the Radio," document 51, Problems of Communism 17 (1968):107-9.
7. Document 63, Problems of Communism 17 (1968):40-47.
8. N. Vasilenko, "The Press and the Small Screen," Sovetskaya Pechat' (March 1966):36-39.
9. Ishtvan Pinter, "A Den of Poisoners of the Ether," Izvestia, March 6, 1966.
10. S. Golyakov, "An Alliance of Dirty Hands," Komsomolskaya Pravda, March 17-18, 1966.
11. Peter Grose, "Leaders in Soviet Fear West's Radio Is Ensnaring Youth," New York Times, March 25, 1966.
12. Ibid.
13. Radio Kiev, Domestic Service, 0600 GMT, March 17, 1966.
14. Nikolai N. Rodionov, "Speech to the 23rd Congress of the CPSU," Pravda, April 5, 1966.
15. Michel Tatu, Power in the Kremlin (New York: Viking Press, 1969), pp. 152, 155, 515.
16. Radio Moscow, Domestic Service, 1300 GMT, June 10, 1966.
17. "The Great March Towards Communism," editorial, Sovetskaya Pechat' (April 1966):1-3.
18. Zimyanin, "An Affair of Our Honor," p. 3.

19. M. Kurtinin, "This Has Long Agitated Us," Sovetskaya Pechat' (May 1966):10-11.
20. Resolution of the Central Committee, CPSU, November 22, 1966, "On the Publication of the Magazine Zhurnalist," Spravochnik partiinovo rabotnika (Handbook of the Party Worker), 7th ed. (Moscow, 1967), pp. 287-88.
21. Observer, "Slanderers on the Air Waves," Izvestia, April 14, 1966.
22. Pravda, April 16, 1966; "Soviet Magazine Rebuts U. S. Radio," New York Times, May 1, 1966.
23. B. Yakovlev and A. Leonov, "Disinformation—A Weapon of 'Psychological Warfare,'" Pravda, June 25, 1966.
24. B. Rodionov, "Meeting Battle," Izvestia, June 28, 1966.
25. E. Alekseyev, "Read, Misters, Krylov," Pravda, August 21, 1966.
26. Yuliy Aleksandrov, "Political Ragmen at Work," Radio Moscow, Domestic Service, 0800 GMT, August 21, 1966.
27. Radio Moscow, Domestic Service, 1630 GMT, August 29, 1966.
28. "The Disgraced Baron," Izvestia, September 15, 1966.
29. Cf. for example, Nikolay Rozhkov-Ruzhitskiy, "For Whose Money?" Radio Minsk, in Belorussian, 1830 GMT, January 2, 1967; Nikolay Rozhkov-Ruzhitskiy, "Service Is Service," ibid., 1830 GMT, October 30, 1967.
30. V. Chernyavsky, "Filthy Loudspeaker," Druzhba Narodov, (February 1967):212-19.
31. Vladimir Osipov, "The Keys of the BBC,"Zhurnalist (May 1968): 56-59.
32. Radio Moscow, Domestic Service, 1620 GMT, January 3, 1968.
33. A. Nebenzya, "Political Upbringing of the Masses," Kommunist No. 10 (July 1966):21.
34. B. Mochalov, "Party Work in the Institute," Kommunist No. 10 (July 1966):39-40.
35. Taubman, The View from Lenin Hills, pp. 67-71, 186-99, 238-49.
36. A. Khazanov, "Experiment? No! Practice," Sovetskaya Pechat' (October 1966):20-22.
37. G. Gusev, "Silhouettes and Call-Signs," Sovetskoye Radio i Televideniye (October 1968):5-8.
38. G. Sagal, "The Most Difficult Is to Guide the Pen Along the Paper," Sovetskaya Pechat' (October 1966):39-41.
39. M. Kalashnik, "Ideological Work Is the Business of All Communists," Kommunist Vooruzhennykh Sil (November 1966):14.
40. "The Present Day and Our Tasks," Sovetskaya Pechat' (November 1966):3.
41. "Our Knowledge, Strength, and Weapons," Pravda, October 4, 1966.

42. Anatoliy Bogomolov, "News Comes to You," Zhurnalist (January 1967):45-47.
43. Boris Firsov, "Mass Communications," Zhurnalist (February 1967):50-52.
44. Radio Tirana, Domestic Service, 1900 GMT, November 27, 1966.
45. See Maury Lisann, "Moscow and the Chinese Power Struggle," Problems of Communism 18, No. 6 (1969):32-41.
46. Radio Tirana, 0900 GMT, February 9, 1967 (in French).
47. Radio Tirana, Domestic Service, 1900 GMT, May 14, 1967.
48. Vasiliy Sitnikov, "Leninism in the Battle of Ideas," Zhurnalist (April 1967):8-10.
49. I. Dzhus', "Around the Sharp Questions," Pravda, January 26, 1967.
50. Felice D. Gaer, "The Soviet Film Audience: A Confidential View," Problems of Communism 23, No. 1 (1974):56-70.
51. "Meeting of Historians of the Present Day," Zhurnalist (April 1967):11, 14.
52. D. Shevlyagin, "The Invincible Power of Marxist-Leninist Ideas," Pravda, June 14, 1967.
53. Lev Tolkunov, "The Word Is the Deed," Zhurnalist (July 1967):2-5.
54. N. Kolesov, "Stop, Instantly," Sovetskoye Radio i Televideniye (August 1967):2-5.
55. G. Smirnov, "Democracy, Freedom, and the Responsibility of the Individual," Pravda, December 4, 1967.
56. A. Shumakov, "Intellectual Vertical," Sovetskoye Radio i Televideniye (February 1968):18-20.
57. Yuri Budantsev and Vladimir Derevitskiy, "On This Day and Hour: The Telescreen and the Event," Zhurnalist (March 1967):46-47.
58. N. Ivanovskaya, "About the Program 'Vremya,'" Sovetskoye Radio i Televideniye (May 1968):30-33.
59. "On the Matter of 'Vremya,'" Zhurnalist (June 1968):15-17.
60. V. Mikhailov, "The Publicism of Fact on the Central Television Program 'Vremya,'" Sovetskoye Radio i Televideniye (January 1969):40-41.
61. Boris Yakovlev, "Yet Again About 'Vremya,'" Zhurnalist (February 1969):27-28.
62. Aryeh L. Unger, "Politinformator or Agitator: A Decision Blocked," Problems of Communism 19, No. 5 (1970):30-43. Citations on politinformators not otherwise attributed are taken from this article.
63. Yefimov and Pozdnyakov, Nauchniye osnovy partiinoi propagandy, pp. 97-109.
64. Unger, "Politinformator or Agitator," p. 43.
65. V. Demchenko, "Political Information: Our Experience," Pravda, October 27, 1966.

66. V. Kozhemyako, "A Word for Each," Pravda, May 31, 1967.
67. V. Danilov, "Political Information. How to Conduct It?" Pravda, August 3, 1967.
68. K. Nikolayev, "Promptness and Depth," Pravda, December 14, 1967.
69. Unger, "Politinformator or Agitator," p. 41.
70. E. Latysh and P. Chernyshev, "About the Agitator and the Politinformator," Pravda, December 25, 1967.
71. M. Kuryanov, "Information Is the Base of Political Agitation," Pravda, May 28, 1969.
72. Harold C. Hinton, The Bear at the Gate: Chinese Policy-making Under Soviet Pressure (Washington, D. C.: American Enterprise Institute for Public Policy Research; Stanford, Calif.: Hoover Institution on War, Revolution, and Peace, 1971), p. 47.
73. Cf., for example, V. Tsvetov, "How Many Pairs of Pants Does a Japanese Have?" RT No. 12 (March 1967):12.
74. "Intrigues, Forms, and Contents," Sovetskaya Pechat' (September 1966):28-30.
75. V. Kosin, "Twenty-six Issues of 'RT'" Pravda, November 20, 1966.
76. "Why Is the Magazine Becoming a Rarity?" RT No. 29 (July 1967): p. 4.
77. Anatole Shub, "Western Radio Forces Soviets' Hand," Washington Post, January 19, 1968.
78. A. Chakovksy, "On Audacity Real and Feigned," Sovetskaya Rossiya, January 27, 1968.
79. "Britain Through the Eyes of Soviet People?" Literaturnaya Gazeta (February 7, 1968):9.
80. A. Stuk, "On the Wave of Slander," Literaturnaya Gazeta (July 31, 1968):2.
81. Sovetskaya Belorussia, February 15, 1968, cited in Current Digest of the Soviet Press 20, No. 7 (1968):15.
82. "A Beginning in Kyaariku: The First All-Union Scientific Theoretical Conference of Radio Journalists 'The Present, Man, and Radio,'" Zhurnalist (May 1968):28-29. A collection of the proceedings was promised, but it has not been located.
83. "The Sharpest Front of the Class Struggle," editorial, Sovetskaya Rossiya, April 13, 1968.
84. "The Reporter," editorial, Zhurnalist (June 1968):5-7.
85. A. Rapokhin, "Radio, Man, and His World," Sovetskoye Radio i Televideniye (May 1968):5-7.
86. "From the Session of the Committee," Sovetskoye Radio i Televideniye (January 1969):15.
87. Official Department, "In the Department of Propaganda of the CC, CPSU," Zhurnalist (July 1968):78.
88. "The Whole Heart with the Party," editorial, Zhurnalist (August 1968):2.

89. Official Department, "In the Department of Propaganda of the CC, CPSU," Zhurnalist (August 1968):78.
90. "The Screen of Millions," editorial, Zhurnalist (September 1968):2-3.
91. Zhurnalist (September 1968):79; ibid. (November 1968):79.
92. Literaturnaya Gazeta May 29, 1968.
93. Yu. Shpakov, "The Logic of the Fall," Sovetskaya Rossiya, May 28, 1968.
94. "To Be an Ideological Fighter," editorial, Sovetskaya Rossiya, June 5, 1968.
95. N. Gribachev, "What a Day to Come . . . , "Komsomolskaya Pravda, July 25, 1968.
96. "Broadcasts Breed Dissent in Soviet," New York Times, July 14, 1968.
97. P. Demichev, "The Construction of Communism and the Tasks of the Social Sciences," Kommunist No. 10 (July 1968):14-35.
98. A. Nikolayev and K. Ushakov, "High Vigilance Is the Armament Against the Probes of Imperialism," Kommunist No. 11 (July 1968):93-102.
99. "Not on Instructions, but by Conviction—Readers' Dialog," Pravda, July 31, 1968.
100. I. Laptev, "Soldiers of the Party: A Tale About the Communists of One Shop," Kommunist No. 12 (August 1968):46-55.
101. M. Barmankulov, "Battle in the Air," Prostor (Alma Ata) (August 1968):110-14.
102. Nan Robertson, "Soviet Resumes Jamming of the Voice of America," New York Times, August 22, 1968.
103. Peter Grose, "U. S. and Soviet Exchange Charges over Propaganda," New York Times, September 25, 1968.
104. Robert H. Phelps, "U. S. Says Russians Step Up Jamming," New York Times, July 9, 1969.
105. "The Strength of the Press Is in Partymindedness," editorial, Zhurnalist (December 1968):2-3.
106. N. Sviridov, "Party Concern for the Upbringing of the Scientific-Technical Intelligentsia," Kommunist No. 18 (December 1968):36-45.
107. Ye. Nozhin, "The Law of Precedence," Sovetskoye Radio i Televideniye (May 1969):34-36.
108. Boris Yakovlev, "Yet Again About 'Vremya,'" Zhurnalist (February 1969):27-28.
109. Daniel Kraminov, "The Battle for Minds and Hearts," Zhurnalist (August 1969):34-37.
110. "Revolutionary Vigilance," editorial, Sovetskaya Rossiya, March 11, 1969, quoting Robert F. Byrnes, ed., The United States and Eastern Europe (New York: Prentice-Hall, 1967), p. 99.
111. S. Pilotovich, "Party Life: Knowledge and Consciousness," Pravda, March 26, 1969.

112. "The Case of Yuri Levin," *Khronika Tekushchikh Sobytii*, August 31, 1969, reprinted in *Problems of Communism* 19, No. 2 (1970):50.

113. S. Tsvigun, "To Struggle with the Ideological Diversions of the Enemies of Socialism," *Kommunist* No. 11 (July 1969):102-12.

114. Vladimir Zhidkov, "In Order to Persuade . . .," *Zhurnalist* (November 1969):30-32.

115. Nozhin, "The Law of Precedence," pp. 34-36.

CHAPTER 5
OPINIONS AND TRENDS

MEDIA AND PUBLIC OPINION

The preceding survey of Soviet activities has concentrated on the observed reactions of Soviet officialdom to foreign radio broadcasting—primarily that portion of it that they wished to present to public view—in order to seek an explanation for the cessation of jamming and its subsequent resumption five years later. The picture that developed was that by 1963 the Soviet ideological authorities felt that Western radio stations (with the exception of RL) had moderated their programming practices to the extent that when the informal guarantees that Western stations would exercise care in their programming, and the projected improvement of the Soviet media, were taken into account, it was thought that the Soviet media would then be sufficiently competitive to minimize adverse effects of the Western broadcasts.

Those calculations did not work out. The most important reason for the resumption of jamming was the continued superiority of foreign radio over Soviet media as a source of hard news, especially in comprehensiveness of coverage and speed. That superiority tended to undermine the public's respect for the Soviet media and was certainly a contributing influence, if not the prime cause, for the increasingly overt signs of dissent after 1966. Since the Soviets were well aware of the relationship between the efficiency of their own media and the popularity of foreign broadcasts and in 1965 made it official policy to compete for the audience, one wonders why they did not do more to upgrade the quality of their own press. And if they would not or could not do more in that direction, why was the decision to resume jamming postponed so long?

One reason for the failure to do more to improve the quality of their own news coverage was the inbuilt structure and traditions of Soviet journalism, which were such that it could not be changed simply by issuing general orders from above. But there may have been more profound, political reasons for the refusal to carry the policy of open competition to its logical conclusion. They relate to the ongoing changes in Soviet society and the changing role of the mass media, which was becoming an ever more important link between the political structure and the public.

Until the 1960s the mass media had a relatively minor role in the Soviet Union, compared to their place in other industrialized societies. Before 1960 the right to subscribe freely to magazines and newspapers was frequently restricted, because of an insufficient supply of paper. After 1960 circulation figures soared. It was not until after 1960 that the number of television sets exceeded one for every 50 people. Even radio did not exceed this relative density until the 1950s. In place of the mass media, persuasive communications were the function of a more personal system of contacts, largely face-to-face. Those included propagandists' lectures, agitators, wall newspapers, Party meetings, the work of Party members as activists, and activists of other organizations. As the mass media increased in importance, all these systems continued in operation but with decreasing efficiency. The agonized controversy over the institution of the agitators and the attempt to replace or supplement them with politinformators was the consequence of the reluctance of traditional institutions to acknowledge evidence of their obsolescence.

Since the mass media were fully controlled by the Party, it would seem that a switchover of emphasis to them would be primarily a technical question. But the matter is not so simple. Mass media are less personal but at the same time are received more privately, and the different public response to them can affect the way it forms its attitudes toward the leading institutions of society. How this interaction is affected can be subject to various theoretical interpretations, but the following excerpt gives an example of how the interaction might be applied to the particular conditions of Soviet society:

> In general, modernization substitutes mass media influence for certain forms of traditional control and indoctrination within the family and other primary groups. While it loosens the grip of these primary institutions, however, it does not destroy them, and it also impels the growth, not the decline, of various forms of civic, commercial and social organizations.
>
> It is this complex double-barrelled process that is taking place in the Soviet Union too. On the one hand, as the Soviet Union becomes a more complex industrial society the number and variety of organizations that it needs to create to carry out its myriad economic, social

and scientific programs grows and grows. On the other hand, as the mass media become an increasingly important mobilizing, homogenizing and value-setting institution, many of the functions performed previously by the most primary and most personally controlling organizations, particularly the family and the local party organizations, are taken over by the media.

In a non-Communist society the most natural outcome of the mixed relationship in the process of development between the mass media and organization, is pluralism. A complex society which mobilizes itself partly by the essentially noncoercive but unindividualized means of mass media persuasion on the one hand, and partly by a myriad of specialized organizations on the other, tends most naturally to a pluralistic pattern of partial and overlapping loyalties and affiliations. This pattern is in sharp contrast to the kind of pre-modern society that socializes and controls each person within a single all-embracing primary group, be it a family, caste or clan, or be it a guild or party organization.

In short, the Soviet conception of organization of society, via an encompassing structure of activities arranged at the place of work under the full direction of the local party organization was appropriate for mobilizing an underdeveloped country without an effective mass media system. It is an incubus in the complex society of today and is inevitably eroded to the degree that there are effective mass media. . . .

No issue in Soviet life will be more important over the coming years than the struggle over the role of the party. The conservatives will continue to insist on effective control via party organization even at the inevitable cost of inefficiency and backwardness. The struggle will center to some degree on the role and character of the mass media, for, to the extent that the mass media are allowed to become lively and appealing, they must escape party control and indeed will tend to undermine party control. To the extent that the mass media are, on the contrary, held to the limited role of loudspeakers for party policies and resolutions, their potential for effectively mobilizing society are partially sacrificed. Without the debaters being fully aware of it, the debate over the mass media is also a debate over the party.

It is in the light of these issues about the domestic Soviet media that the importance of international media must be evaluated. Foreign radio and other foreign media have a profound influence on the course of Soviet develop-

> ment over and above their influence as direct sources of ideas. As competitors for the audience they force the Soviet media to become more candid, more lively, more varied. (In that respect, incidentally, foreign media succeed precisely as they lose their audience.) To the extent that these things happen the role of the party is changed and diminished.
>
> What will happen to Soviet society as a result of the new influence of the mass media is difficult to say. Change is not necessarily gradual and continuous. All sorts of things may happen. . . .[1]

That was written in 1965, before the outbreak of dissent, before the controversy over the role of the agitators, before other events that tend to confirm the growing importance of mass communication in the Soviet political system. Most striking in the account is the suggestion that the mass media can perform the role ascribed to them in the modernization of society only at the expense of loosening the control of the Party on development. In that may lie the fundamental conflict that prevented full implementation of the policy of open competition with foreign radio by means of an efficient Soviet press.

However, the Soviets were not aware of that possibility at the time they set out to show that their information and ideological control systems could work without the aid of jamming. They did not begin to do serious research on public attitudes toward the media and information policies until the mid-1960s. When they did, they quickly turned up disquieting results—results that may have been the final determinant in the decision to resume jamming. More than that, the research may have been the key to explaining the severity of the repressive measures against the small groups of dissenters who emerged after 1966—measures so severe that most Western observers have considered them out of proportion to the threat from the visible disaffection, and an indication of an unexplained insecurity among the Soviet leadership. The origins of the research effort, the Soviets have made clear, stems from concern about foreign radio broadcasts.

AUDIENCE RESEARCH

Applied sociology—sociological research in general—was one of the fields of activity forbidden in the Soviet Union from the 1930s, after Stalin's clampdown. The ban remained in effect until the late 1950s, when, after the Twentieth Party Congress, sociology slowly began to revive.[2] It could naturally be expected that among the last of the topics subjected to sociological research would be anything so sensitive as popular reactions to the official media or attitudes toward ideological and political issues. In fact, foreign radio was such a touchy matter that even the most basic step, the monitoring and transcribing of the broadcasts themselves, was not done until 1953.[3] It is possible that this was because of economic and technical obstacles during the period of postwar reconstruction, but it is more likely that Stalin, in his characteristic suspicious frame of mind, forbade recordings to be made; if any were made, they were restricted to a few high officials and were quickly destroyed. In any case, Soviet scholars cannot study them, because there are no pre-1953 records in the Soviet Union.

Thus, it is not surprising that the application of social science or scientific study to propaganda was slower than the revival of social science and sociology generally. One student of the subject has concluded that the first recorded reference to scientific study of propaganda was not until the June 1963 plenum on ideology, the event that coincided with the suspension of jamming.[4] The first Soviet radio poll was in 1960—in the United States. It was a poll of listeners of Radio Moscow's American programs.[5] The State Committee conducted a poll in the United States before it dared do so in its own country. The reinstitution of polling in the Soviet Union had to be approached gradually and slowly. It would take several years to master a methodology that could obtain reliable data. It has not been stated exactly when Soviet radio polling started inside the country, but the Estonians were conducting voluntary mail polls by 1962.[6] The first poll of newspaper readers was in 1962. Very few results of that early polling activity have been reported, probably because they were considered of doubtful reliability. In April and May 1963 the State Committee tried to conduct a poll to determine how television was affecting radio listening, but it was reported that it was not worked out satisfactorily.[7] Perhaps it was an effort to back up with some hard data the decision to suspend jamming. It has been stated that in practice the study of the television audience began about the end of 1962 or the beginning of 1963.[8]

The methodology of reliable polling had to be relearned. Particularly difficult problems were finding ways to obtain representative samples (relying on voluntary returns of questionnaires, as in Komsomolskaya Pravda's Institute of Public Opinion, begun in 1960, was unsatisfactory) and honest answers to questions on sensitive subjects. By 1966 a book on methodology had been written.[9]

While the development of methodology was proceeding, a systematic program of research was being put together. It was decided at the beginning that radio audience research would take precedence over television audience research, despite the fact that the greater expense of television programming and the projected rapid increase in number of television sets would nominally indicate television as the subject of greater interest. Significantly, the reason given for this reversal of priorities was that the existence of foreign stations gave radio listeners an option that television watchers did not have. Because it was acknowledged that the research program was oriented around the problems of competing with foreign radio, it is plausible to attempt to interpret the fragmentary results that were reported in the light of what they reveal about the influence of foreign broadcasting.

The research was said to be designed to proceed in four stages. The first stage was to determine the size of the potential audience for the central Soviet broadcasting networks. That presumably meant investigation of basic listening habits, different categories of listeners, and so on. For that there was already a solid groundwork in the studies of one of the earliest subjects of applied research: the use of leisure time. The second stage was to determine the countries and stations that could be received by the audience. The third stage was to measure the relative popularity of different stations, including the foreign stations, and to find out the amount to which each was listened. Apparently those three stages could at least partially overlap each other, but the fourth stage was to be done only after the first three stages. The final phase of the research program was to measure the popularity and effects of separate programs.[10]

The research effort got under way rather slowly. Ideally, it should have been in full gear by the time jamming was suspended. But even in Estonia, which appears to have been a model for the rest of the Soviet Union, there was only episodic polling in 1963 and 1964. A permanent study group was not created there until the beginning of 1965.[11] As late as mid-1966 no less a personage than the chairman of the Committee on Public Opinion Research of the Soviet Sociological Association could assert that no meaningful research had been done on the relationship between the mass media and public opinion. He suggested, however, that there had been a good deal of self-deception on this subject.[12] The one set of data that he considered firmly based were the overall figures for radio listening and TV viewing. The returns from Komsomolskaya Pravda's Institute of Public Opinion showed that 71 percent of the population listened to the radio daily and 16 percent watched television daily (intellectuals and students somewhat less, pensioners and housewives much more.)

The assertion that serious research had hardly gotten under way by 1966 seems confirmed by the timing of the appearance of results. Little that was really interesting was published about research results until 1967. For about 18 months after that there were reports on a series of polls, and then publication apparently stopped. Research had not ended, but censorship had tightened. Poll results were never fully published in any case. The research program, as it was outlined had provided for polling on listenership of foreign radio stations, but, with one intriguing exception, none of that data was ever reported. The cutting off of publication probably was motivated mainly by discomfort about the results. Attacks on polls increased as the picture became clearer. The attack on polling by the deputy chairman of the State Committee, three months before the resumption of jamming, has already been described (see pp. 94-95). Also notable was the outburst about polling's revelations of the immense interest in international news, which was characterized (not without rebuttal) as shameful, and something that had to be disregarded.

Those were probably signs of a deeper ambivalence about the purpose of research and polling, and about the whole concept of objective inquiry into the desires and thoughts of the general public. The slowness in gearing up the research effort was not caused solely by methodological problems and inexperience. There were signs of continual debate about the basic concept and purpose of the effort. Any use of research to enhance the ability of Soviet media to compete with foreign radio would demand the utmost flexibility and open-mindedness in relating the results to policy formation. Some idea of the philosophical, and political, problems presented can be gained from the following description of its purpose:

> Investigation of opinions, positions, and tastes of radio listeners and TV viewers (film goers or readers) are not carried out to comply with them blindly, to make the contents of "information" disseminated by way of "mass media" fully dependent on the wishes of the public. In fact, our aim is just the opposite. These investigations are carried out in order to achieve control over the processes of changes in the ideological superstructure both in the sense of direction and development. Instructions for the preparation of radio and television programs are not formulated by listeners, but by the Party. The investigation of public opinion must help in the implementation of the instructions.[13]

That interpretation was written in Poland; nothing so blatant seems to have been allowed to appear in the Soviet Union. But, judging from some of the antagonism to polling that did appear in the Soviet press, it must have reflected the views of significant circles among those involved in dealing with the problem there. Since the Soviet polling effort was undertaken as an adjunct of the policy of open competition with foreign radio, officially proclaimed in 1965, there had to be an element of conflict between the various ways in which audience research might be directed and used. That conflict could not only slow down the research but affect its structure and the way it was reported, in ways that are not readily determinable.

Before total censorship was imposed data were reported from eight or nine polls. Almost all those reports appeared in 1967 and 1968. The beginning of the period was apparently the earliest time that reliable results were obtained. The latter date apparently reflects a decision to cut off reporting of the polls, probably because of the disturbing picture that was developing. The use of the polls to derive information about sensitive areas of internal opinion requires some consideration of conditions affecting their interpretation. Those conditions involve both the reliability and the validity of the polls. Reliability involves mainly questions of whether the polls accurately measure even what the Soviets intended them to measure. Validity, in this case, means the plausibility of reinterpreting the results in ways different than reported by the Soviets.

Judgments of reliability can comprise both deliberate and unintentional falsification of results. There are grounds, however, for excluding deliberate falsification. In the first place, such falsification would presumably be undertaken for propaganda reasons, and there are few signs of interest in propagandistic exploitation of the polls. They were reported and discussed mostly in publications designed for professionally-oriented readers and in a generally straightforward tone. It would certainly have been counterproductive to their purpose to mislead this audience, some of whom could probably recognize deliberate deception. And had deliberately false reporting been undertaken, the results presented would almost certainly have been more favorable than they were.

Questions of unintentional inaccuracies, as a consequence of methodological problems, are more difficult. The two most important influences in that area are difficulties in obtaining representative cross-sections in the samples surveyed and in getting honest answers from a populace unaccustomed to polling and fearful of possible personal consequences of negative expressions of opinion. That the groups surveyed were representative samples of the larger population generally must be accepted on the basis of Soviet assurances. The published reports usually included such claims, and although details were usually omitted on how the groups were selected, there do not seem to be any substantial reasons to doubt the claims. When there were qualifications on that score, the reports were scrupulous in saying so. Early polls were discounted on the basis of methodological shortcomings, and by 1966 the Soviets were sufficiently skilled to recognize the conditions that were necessary to constitute representative samples. In at least one case difficulties were admitted in reconciling a conflict in selecting the sample and assuring those selected that the interview had no personal consequences. As a result, the highly favorable nature of the responses was discounted. Nor were there any problems with the size of the samples: They were as large as 4,000 to 5,000 interviews. In the United States, polls of public opinion on the national scale are often based on groups of about 1,500 interviews.

The matter of responsiveness of those polled is much more difficult to assess. It is clear that the polls are less precise in that respect than what would be considered standard in the West. The public was well aware that when it was asked for its opinions on the quality of Soviet information services and media it was in a sense expressing judgments on basic policies of the Party and state. Inhibitions and reticence in responding openly can be assumed, even when anonymity was apparently assured. In many cases the requirement of face-to-face interviews or the nonrandom selection of specified individuals for the purpose of obtaining a representative cross-section made the assurances of anonymity even more tenuous. In the 1965 poll of propagandist trainees already described, the proportion of "no opinion" responses increased with the educational level of the respondents—a result that can almost certainly be ascribed to a deliberate withholding of opinion.

A dramatic example of distortions introduced by the technique of nonrandom selection turned up in a poll of readers of *Izvestia*. The responses were overwhelmingly favorable to questions about the quality of news coverage in *Izvestia*—much more so than had been predicted. Rather than succumb to the temptation to accept the results at face value, analysts went back over the methods used in conducting the poll and concluded that the answers given were misleading. What they thought had happened was that in some cases, when a subscriber of the newspaper was selected for an interview, the interviewers had gone to his place of work, a factory for example, called him off the production line, brought him to his foreman's or superior's office, and sat him down for the interview or questionnaire. In those circumstances, naturally, the subject might be intimidated or overawed and therefore fear to give negative or unfavorable responses. Hence, it was concluded that the deviation between the expected and actual responses could probably be explained in part by the effects of those procedures.[14]

The frank report of this occurrence confirms what one would intuitively suspect about poll taking in Soviet conditions. But while the fact of the conditions requires that the polls must be received with some reservations, it also strengthens the case for accepting the accuracy of the polls up to certain limits. The Soviets, having run into those difficulties in such concrete form in a relatively early (October 1966) poll, could take steps to minimize them in subsequent efforts. It is clear that a good deal of attention was given to the problem. The director of research in Estonia described some of the lessons learned about the problem: Among the factors that had to be carefully controlled in order to gain the confidence of the people questioned, for example, was the selection of personnel who actually conducted the interviews, and the atmosphere and scene in which they were carried out. It was learned early on that the interviewers should not be people who held any kind of official position or who were associated with organizations of authority, such as Party or Komsomol activists.[15]

The care taken by the Soviets to compensate for those effects, while not able to ensure total frankness and responsiveness, was still sufficient to produce interesting results. There is also direct evidence that Soviet citizens sometimes could be sufficiently outspoken or confident to disregard cautionary thoughts about expressing themselves. In the one reported result of a question about foreign-radio listening, despite the absence of anonymity, a substantial number answered affirmatively.

There is a compensating relationship between the direction of the bias introduced by inhibitions and an extended interpretation of the statistics. The bias would generally tend to reduce the percentage of responses that could be interpreted as being critical of some aspect of Soviet information practices or media. Since the polls are examined here for evidence of dissent or dissatisfaction, especially as indications of a larger potential in that respect than has been generally assumed, the effect of the bias is to introduce an element of conservatism in the interpretations. The conservatism results from using Soviet figures as a starting point and then accepting the inevitable ambiguities and uncertainties arising from imprecisely reported questions and a high proportion of "don't know" and "no opinion" responses. The unknown or overlooked influences are much more likely to operate in the direction of greater dissent than lesser.

AUDIENCE ATTITUDES AND POLITICAL OPINION

The basic purpose of examing the polls is not simply to report what the Soviets discovered about the performance of their media but to interpret the polls in a fashion not done by the Soviets (at least not publicly) with a different juxtaposition of some of the figures and the making of comparisons that the Soviet reports avoided. More abstractly, it also infers a relationship between opinions on information practices and attitudes toward basic political values of the system governing the lives of those who expressed the opinions. What derives from that inference is not a direct measure of the effects of foreign radio broadcasting on the system but, perhaps, an indication of the minimum level of interest or potential interest of the public for foreign broadcasts. It is also a measure of the potential attitudes toward the very small numbers of visible dissenters.

The question that arises is whether it is valid to make the connection between the rather pedestrian polls about media and the attitudes toward the political system. In most societies the connection would at best be subtle and indirect. The difference in the Soviet Union, of course, is that all media are controlled by the government, and the public is very conscious of that fact. The Soviet press is very sensitive in responding to nuances of policy, and large numbers, no less than Western specialists, are accustomed to reading "between the lines." That explains the visible hesitance in responding to the polls.

An implication that the Soviets considered attitudes toward the media to have a broader and sensitive significance may be perceived in the fact that the polling effort was largely inspired by the competition from foreign radio broadcasts, and the extreme caution, reaching finally to virtual complete suppression, in releasing the results of the polls.

It is not necessary, however, to rely entirely on indirect evidence from Soviet sources and generalized assumptions about effects of Soviet conditions to posit a relationship between opinions about the media and attitudes toward the political system. At least two non-Soviet studies have produced information supporting the relationship: the Harvard study of Soviet refugees, done mainly in the 1950s, and the COMCOM project at the Massachusetts Institute of Technology in the 1960s. Their samples did not duplicate the Soviet population as a whole, being more highly educated and more urban, but they were not all emigrants for political reasons, and in the nonpolitical aspects of media habits that were tabulated (and where Soviet polls covered the same ground) the results were generally comparable.

The relationship does not derive from the attention given to the mass media or the amount of interest in news in general. According to the COMCOM survey, which found that it was in agreement with the Harvard study: "Occupation, education, and social class are the more powerful predictors of media exposure than anti-Soviet sentiment or the various factors of media exposure."[16] That is probably especially true in regard to listening to foreign radio. One Soviet poll indirectly suggests that the greatest interest in news reports from foreign radio is found, between classes, among government officials.

The situation changes when one speaks not of use of the media but of opinions about it. The COMCOM study, summing up the Harvard work as well as its own experience, said:

> Because of the role that is officially assigned to the mass media in the Soviet Union, and the consequent official control of their content (as well of their form, of their distribution, etc.), attitude to the mass media is an

> indicator of attitude to the political regime or system in general. The Harvard Project on the Soviet Social System found, within educational or occupational groups, a significant positive association between amount of exposure to the mass media and favorable attitude to the regime. The observed relationship was so clear that the authors chose to include into their index of "anti-Soviet sentiment" the results of a question concerning the reliability of the mass media.[17]

Amount of exposure to the media in that case referred solely to Soviet media—and that at a time when there was very little opportunity to evaluate it against outside sources compared to the situation that existed later. But even when access to foreign radio was still low, those who were critical of the Soviet media also tended to be critical of the political system. The term used by the Harvard Project, "anti-Soviet sentiment," is imprecise and can have different meanings at different times. Dissent in the late 1960s was more diversified in form, and the term, if it is to represent something measurable, should not be interpreted in a narrow ideological sense. Instead, the critical attitudes that emerge in the Soviet polls should be regarded as a reflection of a generalized sense of dissatisfaction, including not only those who are overtly anti-Soviet but also the groups and individuals who have sought reform within the legal or ideological framework of the Soviet system. This, of course, is a Western view. To those in authority amorphous—and therefore unknown but possibly widespread—feelings of dissatisfaction may well be considered much more dangerous than small-scale, manifestations of open protest, and less easy to cope with. The Soviet system, for its political and moral legitimacy, relies more than most on the acceptability of its ideology, supplemented by economic progress, and gives its citizens few explicit means, such as elections, to express their approval. Thus, credibility of authorities becomes particularly important, especially when the same authority is responsible for both the ideology and the press. The apparent overreaction to the seemingly ineffectual dissent after 1966 would be partially explainable by official acceptance of that view.

Whatever the link between the media polls and dissent, their figures are still of interest. There is some consistency in them that can be correlated with other indicators of the state of public opinion and interests in the Soviet Union. Since so little is known quantitatively about political attitudes among the public in the Soviet Union, any figures that can be obtained may be useful in other studies.

SIZE OF THE FOREIGN RADIO AUDIENCE

An important background to the opinions reported in the media polls is the quantity of listening to foreign radio. Yaroshenko specifically included it in his outline of the research program, but, with one exception, the figures were never published. Foreign-radio listening cannot be equated directly with the expressions of dissatisfaction that appear in the polls. As even one of the polls indicates, it is clear that officials, presumably for professional reasons, are among the most interested listeners. And as the propaganda and ideological establishment was quick to claim, the influence of foreign broadcasts spreads far beyond original listeners. But whatever magnitude of listening can be imputed from the fragmentary reports is useful as a reference point in assessing the meaning of the polls in regard to Soviet media.

Altogether, three independent indications of foreign-radio listening during the mid-1960s period were located. One of them has been mentioned previously. A Soviet work of 1964 reported that "if their owners [of radio receivers] are asked if they listen to broadcasts from the so-called 'free world,'" the "absolute majority" are completely uninterested in such broadcasts.[18] That is a curiously modest claim in that it leaves the possibility of up to 49 percent being interested in such broadcasts. In that more relaxed era, the implication may have simply been overlooked, because the statement was clearly meant to disparage the significance of foreign broadcasts, asserting that the imperialists were wasting their money on them. However, in view of the history of audience polling, which appears to have started only in 1966, it may be questioned whether this assertion was pulled out of thin air, rather than being based on any serious research. But it remains plausible that the statement was based on something resembling a true poll, as the work was published under military auspices, and the military and security organs of the state may have secretly engaged in such activities unknown to the academic-scientific and operational organizations that conducted and reported the later polling efforts.

From the USIA during that period there are two separate estimates of the audience for VOA. For 1966 VOA estimated that in Eastern Europe as a whole it was listened to by 23 percent of the total potential audience.[19] There was no explanation of how this estimate was derived, but "potential audience" apparently meant owners of radio receivers, and listeners were those who listened at least once a week. Listenership of VOA (but not necessarily of all foreign radio stations combined) would undoubtedly be higher in the Soviet Union than in the rest of Eastern Europe at that time, at least in regard to the proportion of the total audience of foreign radio, because in the Soviet Union RL was being jammed, while the non-Soviet East European audiences had a wider choice of unjammed Western stations, including in some countries RFE. VOA also devoted a much greater effort to broadcasting to the Soviet Union than to Eastern Europe—the reverse of the relationship of RL to RFE. In 1968 VOA estimated its Soviet audience as 13 million people per week, evidently referring again to numbers of people listening at least once per week.[20] If both the 1966 percentage and the 1968 number were based on the number of radio receivers at one listener per receiver, a moderate increase of listeners from 1966 to 1968 would be indicated; if otherwise, a substantial decrease would be indicated.

The one precise Soviet figure on foreign-radio listening that is available is the outcome of a special poll that was conducted at the University of Vilnius in Lithuania. The poll was a consequence of a discussion of ideological problems among students in December 1967 in the Bureau of the Central Committee of the Communist Party of Lithuania. It found that 35.4 percent of the students at the university stated that they listened to the broadcasts of "capitalist radio stations."[21] Two major offsetting considerations affect this figure. The group is certainly not representative of the population as a whole; university students in an area of an uneasy minority nationality are likely to be more interested in foreign broadcasts than the general public, and the broadcasts are also more easily accessible in that geographical area. Some indications of a higher-than-average level of political interest appeared in that same poll, where 98.3 percent reported that they followed political information in the press, and 89.3 percent listened to Soviet and other socialist countries' broadcasts. Those figures compare to an average response in the area of 70 to 80 percent for similar questions in other Soviet polls.

On the other hand, the figure of 35.4 percent probably understates the actual amount of listening in the particular case. The polling method could not assure anonymity to the respondents. The poll was conducted by Komsomol activists who fanned out through the university, interviewing students, knocking on dormitory doors, and so on. Even if no identifications were requested or recorded, it is likely that many students would presume that they were recognizable and would be cautious about answering the question about foreign radio. That more than one-third declared an interest in foreign radio broadcasts shows a high degree of self-confidence.

Those three separate indications of foreign-radio listening are all consistent with one another, although with very broad margins of uncertainty. An independent correlation of the figures can be attempted by extension of the USIA estimates and the Lithuanian poll, using as a modifier the proportional weight that the Soviet authorities apparently assigned to VOA within the spectrum of all foreign radio stations. The proportion for VOA, about 30 percent, is what _RT_ appeared to assume in 1966-67, when it was carrying out its assigned task of counteracting foreign radio programs.

An assumption is required that *RT* was guided by unpublished results of polls on foreign-radio listening. The results of Krasilov's polling on the subject were available early in *RT*'s life.

Thus, if the USIA estimate for 1968 of 13 million Soviet listeners for VOA is multiplied by 3.3, one obtains a figure of 43 million for the combined audience of all foreign radio stations. If the Lithuanian poll figure of 35.4 percent is applied to the entire adult Soviet population, the result is 50 to 60 million listeners, depending on how one selects the lower age limit to define the adult population. The two figures are not far apart, although they are developed from maximally opposite starting points (a USIA estimate, a Soviet poll, and Soviet activities against foreign broadcasts). Given the many uncertainties in the various figures, the difference of 10 to 15 million—about 6 to 9 percentage points—is relatively insignificant.

There are many other variables that can affect the figures—for example, the definition of a listener, the definition of the adult population, the representativeness of samples, straightforwardness of responses, and so on. Some of them would affect one figure but not the other. The possibility of the USIA estimate being based on one listener per receiver would artificially reduce the lower figure but not the higher, while the overlapping of audiences of different foreign stations, which was not taken into account, would increase it. Also, the Soviet counterefforts, on which the modifier figure was based, may have been based more on a Soviet estimate of the influence of individual stations rather than on the size of the audience. In such a case VOA was more likely to have been given a proportionally greater emphasis than that based on the size of its audience, particularly in view of the continued jamming of RL, and, therefore, the derived audience figure is lower than it would have been if Soviet authorities were taking into account only the numerical size of audiences and not their type.

The number of the variations is great enough to raise the probability that they tend to cancel each other out. However, because of the size of the margin of uncertainty the variations would not be important unless they could affect the figure by a magnitude approaching 10 million. The most important part of the difference may arise from the assumption that the unrepresentativeness of the university sample, which would have a higher-than-average listenership, was balanced by deliberate understatements of interest in foreign radio given to the interviewers. It may well be that the proportion of listeners at the university was so high that even after a reduction in the poll result caused by false responses, the remaining figure was still substantially higher than the average for the population at large. Taking that into account, the lower of the two derived figures is probably closer to the true situation.

A further test of the audience estimates is their relationship to the information in the polls. According to the polls, in 1966-68 about one-fourth to one-third of the adult population had a direct interest in foreign broadcasts. In absolute numbers even the lower of those figures would mean that the audience for foreign radio was larger than the number of short-wave receivers available at that time, suggesting that the potential audience interest in foreign broadcasts was still short of saturation.

THE POLLS

A good reference point from which to begin the survey of the media and information polls is an early-1965 study that preceded the effective beginning of these polls. It was a study of 250 trainee propagandists who filled out anonymous questionnaires about their attitudes and opinions after completing their course. Disbelief in the propaganda they were about to disseminate was expressed by 13.2 percent. Another 24.8 percent did not answer the question.[22] That was a remarkably high negative response rate from such a group, and the conductors of the study made an awkward effort to try to explain it away.

The 24.8 percent "no answer" responses is suspiciously high, and it becomes even more suspicious when the breakdown by age, education, and Party membership reveals that it increases with education. The more highly educated had 17 percent negative responses and 28 percent "no answer" responses, compared to 8 and 21 percent for the less educated. It is not likely that the more highly educated were genuinely less able to evaluate the course, so the cause of at least the additional 7 percent of "no answer" responses can be attributed to a fear of revealing a negative opinion, probably from suspicions of the efficacy (or integrity) of the anonymous procedure. The combination of 17 percent plus 7 percent suggests a minimum of 24 percent skeptical of the credibility of their propagandist-instructors. And it is probably an injustice to the shrewdness of the less-educated group to presume that none of the 21 percent of their "no answer" responses was motivated by similar thoughts. Probably considerably more than one-fourth of the "no answer" responses represented concealed negative opinions.

The 24 percent disbelief was in a group of volunteer propagandists. Even allowing for pressures to volunteer and careerist-opportunistic motives, such a group would certainly be more attached to official values and credibility than more typical samples of the public. The figure, in any case, makes a comparison with the media poll results. Another way of making this comparison for the group as a whole would be to take the 13.2 percent overall negative average and add to it half of the 24.8 percent "no answer" responses. That procedure suggests, as a rough rule of thumb for the media polls of more heterogeneous population groups, that one-half of the "no answer" or "no opinion" responses to sensitive questions might be assumed to be concealed negative opinions.

The newspaper polls are interesting, in respect to radio listening and credibility, mainly for two pieces of information. They give the only known indication of what elite, presumably political, groups thought of the opinions of the general public, as distinct from themselves, and evidence of the near-topmost place that international affairs occupied in the interests of the public, evidence that is amply confirmed elsewhere. Detailed polls in the 1960s are known to have been taken of the readers of four of the central newspapers: Pravda, Izvestia, Trud, and Komsomolskaya Pravda.

The Izvestia poll, conducted in October 1966, was the first of its kind. Playing it safe, the researchers selected more than 25,000 readers from the subscription list in order to be sure of a representative group. The selection was made for occupational, class, age, and geographical balance, among others. As confidence was gained, later polls used smaller samples until the number was less than 4,000. In this first poll, about one-fourth were personally interviewed and the remainder given questionnaires to return. The procedure was not anonymous. On the critical question, whether the newspaper gave full and objective coverage to various categories of news, the following number answered negatively: for economic problems, 3 percent; for Soviet democracy (presumably domestic affairs), 3 percent; for international affairs, 1 percent.[23] The low rate of unfavorable response was considered surprising, and, as already related, a doublechecking of the procedures concluded that the lack of anonymity and the method of interviewing had inhibited the respondents.

The reason for the original skepticism was an unusual "prediction poll" that had been conducted at the start of the Izvestia poll. In that poll various experts—sociologists, journalists, and scientists—had been asked to predict the results of the main poll. The prediction of negative answers to the questions about the completeness and objectivity of the news ranged from 13 to 25 percent, with more than two-thirds falling between 15 and 20 percent. The predictions of partially negative answers ranged from 25 to 42 percent. Despite the lack of agreement with the actual results of the poll, the prediction of 15 to 20 percent negative opinions is instructive. It is not far from the quantities of negative opinions that turned up in some later, presumably more carefully conducted, polls.

Another aspect of the predictions is the fact that the experts who made them may well have been tuned in to the Party establishment. The experts were listed as "sociologists and economists," "journalists" ("well known" and "less known"), and scientists. Thus, there is a possibility that through their personal and professional contacts the 15 to 20 percent level of dissatisfaction they suggested reflected the beliefs of the Party leadership as to the situation at that time. Even if it is only an expression of the gut feelings of the experts, it is still interesting as a summary of insiders' viewpoints. In either case, it is certain that there were then no nonsecret, scientific polls from which an expert could derive his guess. No other reports of experts' opinions or predictions of results have been published.

Two years later, a similar poll of Pravda's readers was conducted. The group used was carefully selected to be representative of the subscribers and the poll consisted of 4,000 interviews and 5,000 mailed questionnaires. No significant amount of dissatisfaction with objectivity was reported. The closest that the reported results came to sensitive matters was in reference to a question about the amount of coverage of various categories of news. Satisfaction with the quantities of coverage was expressed by a high of 63 percent for news of other Communist parties, 58 percent for international affairs, and amounts down to 50 percent for various categories of domestic news.[24] Since those percentages were specified as "of those who answered" and the amount of "no answer" and other types of responses was not given, the meaning of the figures is not clear. However, unlike the Izvestia poll, the reportage of the Pravda poll did not give any impression of unhappiness or surprise at the results.

The reason for that relative complacency may have been that Pravda's readers were a special group, who used the paper for a particular purpose and had their own expectations about it, not centered on news in the conventional sense. Seventy-five percent of Pravda's readers were members of the Party (comprising about half of all members of the CPSU), compared to little more than 10 percent of the eligible adult population as a whole. Thus, they were obviously not representative of the general public, and they read Pravda not primarily as a source of general news but as an adjunct of their responsibilities as Party members and as an aid in carrying out their Party duties. The lesser expectations of the public about Pravda as a newspaper in the conventional sense, compared to Izvestia, have often been reported.

In one respect, however (and one that is significant in connection with the relationship of the Soviet press to foreign radio broadcasts), the readers of the two newspapers are similar. In response to the questions about the parts of the newspapers that were most popular or most read, both sets of readers designated international topics in second or third place on lists of nearly 20 subjects. Among Izvestia readers international commentary was in third place, attracting the interest of 69 percent of the subscribers. In the Pravda poll, bulletins on international events was the second most popular category, at 74 percent, and in third place was the category "Articles on International Affairs," at 63 percent.

The difference between the two sets of readers showed up in the first-place preferences of the pollees. Reflecting its official "chancelleristic" character, the most-read section of Pravda was "official bulletins," named by 81 percent of its subscribers. The top places in Izvestia were won by "morals," with 75 percent, and "surprising history," with 71 percent. Those sections are the closest to human interest stories that the daily press carries and also probably the most apolitical material in the newspapers. The analogous category in the Pravda poll, "morals and upbringing," was in fourth place, just behind the international themes, marked by 57 percent of the pollees. In both newspapers the various categories of domestic news and political themes were well down on the list, usually being marked as of interest by 40 percent or fewer of the readers. Perhaps showing a knowledgeable discernment of the real significance of legislative bodies in the Soviet system, Izvestia's readers put in last place, of interest to only 17 percent, "work of soviets," although Izvestia, as the formal organ of the soviets and the Council of Ministers, was directly charged with publicizing their activities.

The high level of interest in international news was confirmed by later surveys, some in much more extreme form. International news, of course, is the area in which foreign radio can offer the greatest competition and greatest contrast to the Soviet press. The fact that the Soviet public put that topic at the top of its interests means that foreign radio had become more influential in the public consciousness and of greater general interest than it would have been if popular interests had been distributed more evenly over the range of public affairs. It also means that the public's judgment of Soviet information policies and, therefore, of the credibility of the government had become dependent in larger proportion on that part of its performance where it was visibly weakest, and the relative importance of foreign radio as a political influence was enhanced beyond the proportionate size of its audience. It becomes a chicken-and-egg type of question, whether the public interest in international subjects increased the audience for foreign radio or whether the availability of foreign radio news on that area of affairs increased interest in the subject, because it was the only important field in which sufficient information could be obtained to form independent judgments.

The public's attitudes toward Soviet radio presumably were even more closely oriented on its comparison with foreign radio than were its opinions about the newspapers. While statistically controlled polling did not begin until 1966, there was at least one survey earlier that gave the researchers an indication of what was to come.

At some time prior to mid-1965 a voluntary mail poll about international-news coverage was tried. Of the 5,000 questionnaires distributed, 800 were returned. Twelve percent declared dissatisfaction with the radio news, and 16 percent with television news. The results were called "surprising," although one would expect that a poll that depended on a voluntary response would attract a heavier-than-proportional return from those who were dissatisfied. The questionnaire stimulated a number of letters of complaint about the quality of broadcast news. It also revealed preference by a narrow margin (37 to 35 percent) for radio over television for commentary on international affairs.[25] Additional soundings may have been taken in the succeeding 18 months, because, when the Izvestia poll began, despite the "surprising" label given to the probably overstated 12 to 16 percent negative opinion, the experts were expecting 15 to 20 percent dissatisfaction with news reporting.

The earliest more or less controlled poll of the broadcasting audience for which results were reported was done in Estonia in 1966 or early 1967. The Estonians sent out eight people on planned routes to distribute 1,300 questionnaires. While they could not guarantee that the sample obtained that way was strictly representative, they felt that they had an approximation of such a group. The interviewers were selected to exclude anyone who appeared to hold a position of authority, and the confidence they instilled brought a return of 1,160 questionnaires—almost 90 percent.

The poll concentrated on television, and the introductory comment was that it showed less dissatisfaction with the programs than did the letters received by the broadcasting organization. Evidently, that first poll had been undertaken with some trepidation, and there was relief that the mail could now be shown by this poll to be unrepresentative of the general opinion. (It was only two months after this report that a Soviet critic pointed out that television mail, along with statistics and analyses of it, was kept secret from the press and from researchers.)

Television polls in Estonia were analogous to radio polls in other parts of the Soviet Union because the Estonian viewers had a choice of foreign broadcasts, a choice available in other areas only in the medium of radio. One of the basic tasks of that first poll was the establishment of the parameters of that choice by checking on the visibility of the three possible channels. That determination showed that the relay of Central television (Russian) could be received by 71 percent, the Estonian television channel by 71 percent, and Finnish television by 66 percent. The significance of those percentages was immediately noted by the comment that those who had access to more than one channel were more critical.[26] Comparative figures on that point were not reported.

The poll apparently concentrated on determining the general preferences and desires of viewers. At least, if there was any detailed inquiry into opinions about the quality and characteristics of news, it was not reported. But, indirectly, it was suggested that news and the related problem of competition from foreign broadcasts, presented a major concern. For example, again without figures, it was reported that the Finnish channel was watched most by men and the intelligentsia, a possible hint that news was its main attraction. No mention was made of news on the Central Television channel (for which the Estonian broadcasting committee conducting the poll had no responsibility anyway), but it was found that the 30 most popular programs on the Estonian channel included only two that were pure entertainment, while three were solely informational, and the remainder mixed in character. On the other hand, when asked what they expected from television, 88.7 percent said they wanted something to relax them after work. The quantity who said that they were interested in programs about "work processes" was scrupulously reported to be .08 percent—which works out to slightly less than one out of the 1,160 responding. Because of the ostensibly contradictory responses to two sets of questions, the Estonian analysts concluded that the replies had been shaped more by the form of the programs than by the content.

However, when asked what they most valued about television, presumably without reference to particular programs, the largest number, a rather overwhelming 85 percent, said that it was news about world events and information about the life of other countries and peoples. The second most valued quality of television was the convenience of being able to watch it without going outside. The analysts added that they had other indications, the nature of which they did not specify, that showed that what was most appreciated on television was information, knowledge and emotion, presented in entertaining form. The largest complaint about television, from 78 percent of those polled, was that there were not enough original programs in Estonian.

Whether as a consequence of the interest in news revealed by the television poll or as a part of a previously worked out research plan, the Estonians followed up the television poll with a radio poll that went into evaluations of news programs. All the accounts of that poll have related it to the heavy competition to which Estonian radio was subjected from foreign news broadcasts, and the head of the news department of Estonian radio, who presented the most detailed account of it, described his own news operation as being primarily oriented around providing a rapid counter to foreign radio. Estonians had a choice of three local radio channels: the central radio relayed from Moscow, Vikker-Radio (an Estonian version of Mayak), and a channel specializing in intellectual material and classical music.

The poll showed that the most popular radio program in Estonia was the locally produced evening news, "Echo of the Day," which was broadcast every evening at 9:00 p.m. That was the program that the Estonians claimed to have driven VOA's Estonian program out of its time slot. It was listened to every day by 69.3 percent of the audience. The proportion was lower in the cities—64.5 percent—and higher in the countryside—78.1 percent. That was explained by shift work in the cities and greater opportunities there for outside entertainment, as well as more sources of news, exemplified by greater readership of newspapers. The second most popular program was the regular news (presumably the central radio relay), with 60.8 percent of the audience. After that, in declining order of popularity, were weekend musical programs, radio games, radio plays, and sports, with percentages ranging from 59 down to 37. Slightly more women than men listened to the news, and listenership increased with age: at 17 to 18 years it was 63 percent. Listenership also decreased with education: among university graduates only 57 percent listened regularly to "Echo of the Day." The trends for viewers of Finland's television were just the opposite in terms of sex, age, and education.

The poll apparently obtained numbers on the audience of foreign radio, but the figures were not reported. It was only stated that it was not a serious competitor to Estonian radio and that among foreign stations Finnish radio was first and VOA's Estonian broadcasts were second. But one set of figures was reported with some sense of dismay. That was concerning the views of the listeners on the promptness of Radio Estonia's news. Only 27.5 percent were generally satisfied with the speed of news reporting, while 36.4 percent said that there was significant delay on some questions, 7 percent said flatly that the news was slow, and a large 27 percent did not express an opinion. (It may be noted that those percentages add up to 97.9. Such discrepancies are not uncommon in the reporting of Soviet polls, and are rarely explained. It could be that they are a consequence of a manipulation of the figures, but in the case at hand it is difficult to see why the stated results should have been desired.)

The comment of the Estonian news director on the figures was that, unfortunately, the poll had made no attempt to distinguish between domestic and foreign news, but that they were inclined to think that the opinions about delay referred mainly to news from abroad.[27] It may be asked why that question was not asked. It was certainly an obvious question, and its omission was hardly likely to be a simple oversight. Perhaps the Radio Committee was afraid to probe for too precise an answer, because if foreign radio was to be declared not a serious competitor, it would be difficult to explain how so many people knew that the news on the local radio was frequently delayed.

If this summary of the Estonian news poll has made it sound as if the results were received calmly, almost complacently, it is probably because the accounts from which it was taken had been filtered through the directors of the Estonian radio system. However, the first presentation of this poll to an outside group produced a different reaction. It was in February 1968, at what was planned as

"The First All-Union Scientific-Theoretical Conference of Radio-journalists." The fact that only 27 percent considered the Estonian radio prompt was reported to the conference, and, according to the first account of its proceedings, the participants were affected so sharply that the nature of the meeting was changed. Everyone turned his discussion to this question, and instead of the planned meeting on theoretical topics, it became mainly a practical working session, centered on a relatively frank consideration of the future of Soviet radio. The majority of the participants apparently concluded that Soviet radio had no future unless it developed a better understanding of the importance of news.*

Next in chronological sequence was the Leningrad television poll. In April 1967, 1,916 residents of the city, selected to represent a cross-section of the population according to socio-economic categories, were surveyed. Of those, 69.5 percent were found to own radio receivers, and 87.4 percent had wired speakers. The number considering themselves regular listeners of radio was 64.5 percent. The number of owners of television sets was 1,646, so as they represented 86 percent of the total survey access to television was essentially equal to that of radio.

The television owners were questioned further to obtain their evaluation of programs. An overall judgment of television was sought by asking the set owners whether they were satisfied that they had bought a set. Satisfaction was expressed by 38.7 percent, while an almost equal number—39.2 percent—were dissatisfied. The remainder—22.1 percent—were listed under the category "difficult to say." That was hardly a vote of confidence in television, and succeeding questions were designed to pinpoint more precisely the sources of the dissatisfaction. Of those, two series that were reported seem relevant to the matter of confidence in the integrity of the information system. In one, set owners were asked what most of all dissatisfied them about television news. In the second, they were given a list of 12 different categories of television programs and asked to rate their satisfaction or dissatisfaction with each category.

To the question of what most of all dissatisfies them about television news, the responses were as follows: promptness, 11.6 percent; ability to understand, 5.7 percent; openness, 17.4 percent; variety of facts, 15.4 percent; on-the-scene reporting, 19 percent; no special complaints, 32 percent; rarely or never watch, 25.3 percent. The key categories are promptness and openness. "Openness" would seem to be a euphemism for truthfulness and sincerity. Since the adverb "most" ostensibly precludes multiple

---

*See pp. 93-95.

answers, the sum of these two answers—29 percent—is an indicator of the numbers holding a basic mistrust of the motives behind the presentation of the news. The other complaints are basically about style and technique, except for "ability to understand." The total of all responses is 126.4 percent. Even if all those who said they rarely or never watched news programs also signified a complaint or the lack of any, there probably were some multiple answers. Some light, although less than total clarification, is brought to this ambiguity by comparison with a similar discrepancy in the response to a differently-phrased question in the same poll.

In the second set of questions the viewers were asked to rate separately each of 12 categories of programs, one of which was news and current events. The results for the news and current events category were quite close to the response to the question about specific complaints but far different from the reaction to all other types of programs. For news and current events the results of the question were given as: satisfied, 38 percent; neither praise nor criticism, 20 percent; dissatisfied, 27 percent; rarely watch, 18 percent. The figure for dissatisfied is almost the same as that for those who chose the two characteristics bearing on the honesty of news presentations as their biggest complaint. And those who expressed themselves as unqualifiedly satisfied with the news programs were close to the same proportion as those who had no special complaint about them.

The biggest difference was in the number of people who said that they rarely or never watched the news. In answering the first question, 25.3 percent said they did not watch the television news, while only 18 percent said they did not watch the news when asked to give a general rating. There is no unambiguous way to account for that difference, particularly since no breakdown was given of how that group might have answered the other questions. The total of the responses to the second question was 103 percent, compared to 126 percent for the first question, so it may have been that there was less opportunity to give an opinion on the second question while simultaneously claiming not to watch, and a minimum of 7 percent therefore dropped the claim rather than forego the chance to give their opinion of the news. In either case, those who did not watch but still had an opinion about the news were more likely to have a negative opinion than a positive one. The claimed 18 to 25 percent lack of interest in news is smaller than that for the country as a whole, which runs closer to 30 percent, but for the sample at hand there is an indication that the true figure for genuine lack of interest is even smaller. The viewers were also asked about their reading habits, and it turned out that 86 percent read two or more newspapers a day. If one assumes that a person who reads that many newspapers is likely to be actively interested in public affairs, then a minimum of 4 to 11 percent of the total group who claimed not to watch the television news did so because they did not like it rather than out of simple lack of interest. The probability that news interest was that high in this particular sample is increased by the fact that it was solely urban, where the rural population, which had been shown to be less interested, comprised nearly 40 percent of a national sample, that the city was Leningrad, which is more sophisticated and more internationally oriented than other Russian cities, and that the group excluded those who did not own television sets, and was therefore likely to be of a higher-than-average level in its socioeconomic composition.

Additional information on the importance of news and the possible origin of the discrepancies in the reported amount of viewing comes from comparison with the ratings given to other types of programs. The special place of news stands out strongly. No other type of program, except for serious music and opera (which drew a 25 percent rate of rejection), evoked much dissatisfaction. The next highest negative rating was drawn by the category of general political programs, with 8.6 percent, and the remaining nine categories were lower. Also, those categories were reported to have yielded sets of responses that neatly totalled 100 percent for each of them. The one exception was serious music and opera, the type of program that evoked the second largest quantity of dissatisfaction, which had a response rate adding up to 101 percent.[28]

The distinctive treatment accorded to the results of the questions about news programs suggests that, if the figures were not deliberately manipulated, the pollers or the pollees, or perhaps both, had difficulty in deciding how to answer and to report questions on this subject—a sign of nervousness about the high percentage of negative opinions and of an understanding that the subject had a greater significance than the others. A second interesting comparison that could be made of the figures in the poll at hand is that between the rate for overall satisfaction with television and the rates for different types of programs. The number who said that they were so unhappy with the programs that they regretted having bought a television set was 39.2 percent. The bulk of that figure could be accounted for only by unhappiness about the presentation of news and current events. Complaints about other types of programs were too few to approach that figure. Thus, one could interpret the poll as indicating that the public considered news to be the most important function of television and, simultaneously, its most unsatisfactory aspect.

That interpretation of the Leningrad television poll can be compared to the figures of another television poll, which reported its results in quite a different form. In Sverdlovsk Oblast 4,500 television viewers were polled in 1968. No questions were asked, or at least none was reported, that bore directly on the quality or honesty of news. But the responses to two of the questions can be combined in a way that yields an interesting result.

For one of the questions, asking what the respondent expected from television, the responses were broken out in socioeconomic groups. The answers for workers and engineering-technical personnel, respectively, were: international news, 48.3 and 53.9 percent; extension of knowledge, 31.7 and 35.7 percent; national news, 37.7 and 39.6 percent; art, 30.4 and 43.3 percent; a way to kill time, 45.2 and 25.5 percent; entertainment, 42 and 37.9 percent. The profiles of the two groups were almost identical, the only differences being in the relative interests in using television for art and for killing time. Workers considered killing time as the second most important use of television and were least interested in art, while engineering-technical personnel exactly reversed the relative importance of the two uses. The listing again confirmed the high interest in international news, which was put in first place by both groups.

The pollees were also asked to construct their ideal television program schedule. There, an interesting disparity appeared. Among workers all but 26.3 percent and among engineering-technical personnel all but 25.1 percent included news in their weekday schedule. (The numbers excluding news on weekends was somewhat higher, especially among workers.)[29] The figures showed a general interest in news about equal to or slightly higher than the national average.

The difference between the figures on ideal scheduling and those on expectations (of which the report of the poll took no notice) may be an indication of the amount of basic dissatisfaction with the news broadcasts. There seemed to be a difference between the number who thought that television ought to show the news and those who thought that television news was worth watching. Among workers that number was 25.4 percent (73.7 minus 48.3), and among engineering-technical personnel it was 21 percent (74.9 minus 53.9). It is not entirely clear that that was what the difference meant, because nowhere was it explained what was intended by "expectations," or, more to the point, what the pollees may have thought it meant. It may not have been a precise figure of how many actually watched the news, but it is possible to interpret it as an indication of how many thought that the news was worth watching or hoped that it would become worth watching in the future. It is not possible to be certain that everyone who answered positively to the question about expectations also included news in his ideal schedule, but any deviations of that sort would only mean that the gap between those who were interested in news and those who retained hopes that they could get it from Soviet media was still greater than the 25 and 21 percent figures implied in that particular poll.

As uncertain as the raw data are, they do produce figures for quantities of basic dissatisfaction that are very close, at least within the same range, as those produced by very different types of polls, involving other types of groups, in different parts of the country.

The final poll in the series under discussion, although not the last chronologically, is the one poll that by itself probably had a great influence on the decision to resume jamming. In the only report of its results it was described as the first research on the effectiveness of foreign-policy propaganda. The State Committee, when it officially accepted the poll, described it as "on the effectiveness of radio and television broadcasts on international themes," and the first such research ever done; in greater detail its purposes were given as: "To estimate the interest of the population in broadcasts on international themes, to evaluate the weight of different sources of international information, to clarify to what degree listeners and viewers are satisfied with the coverage of international life, and their expectations."[30]

The poll was conducted jointly by the Scientific-Methodological Department of the State Committee and the Moscow Economic-Statistical Institute. They used 303 public correspondents (part-time, nonpaid staff) of the broadcasting organizations and some students from the institute. It covered 32 industrial centers and 11 rural districts. The State Committee concluded its brief note on the poll, the only public acknowledgment it ever gave to the poll's existence, with the comment that the results would be considered by the editorial boards of the various branches of broadcasting in order to make concrete suggestions for the improvement of radio propaganda.[31]

In sending the poll off to its editorial boards without substantive comment, the State Committee's intention probably was to bury it quietly. By the time the State Committee took that action the results had already been in for a year, and during the interim, jamming had been resumed. The State Committee was unwilling, insofar as can be determined, to discuss the poll in any form or give the slightest hint as to what it revealed. However, the Union of Journalists had already published some data collected by the poll.[32] Since the poll had been conducted by and for the State Committee for Radio Broadcasting and Television, it undoubtedly included questions about foreign-radio listening, although they were not revealed as such in the material released by the Union of Journalists. The union's article promised that a fuller version would be published in the latter part of 1968 in a volume to be entitled _Sociology and Ideological Activity_, but the book seems never to have appeared. A book with a similar title, _Sociology and Ideology_, did go to press at that time, but it contained only papers that had been presented at the World Sociological Congress two years earlier.[33] From what was published, however, it is possible to draw some fairly strong conclusions about the state of disarray existing in that ideological sector. The State Committee may well have been dismayed, it certainly had good reason to want to suppress and forget the poll.

The poll was conducted in 1967. It consisted of 5,232 questionnaires, administered according to a "statistically grouped model." The sample was large enough to enable it to be broken down into five different social groups. That portion of the reported results that is most relevant to foreign radio and the credibility of the Soviet media can be summarized in three tables. Table 2 is simply a survey of the relative uses of the different media and is interesting mainly because it confirms that the group surveyed was basically the same in its interests and uses of the media as those surveyed in other polls, although the table does give additional detail. The report of the poll commented additionally that women were less interested in news than men, except among students, and that collective farmers were more interested during the summer than at other times, because agitation campaigns were carried out at that time to take advantage of the convenience of finding them concentrated in the fields and at work assignments. The exact dates of the poll were not reported, but it was said that during the poll the issues at the center of attention were Southeast Asia and U. S.-Soviet relations, suggesting that the poll was conducted during the summer, around the time of the Johnson-Kosygin meeting at Glassboro. That would also seem to be the most logical time to reach collective farmers. If so, the figures for collective farmers, who were probably contacted in connection with the agitation campaigns, are artificially inflated and have anomalies that make them

TABLE 2

Sources of International Political Information
Used Daily, by Social Group
(percent)

Group	Press	Radio	Television	Lecture (monthly)
Workers	64.9	56.2	44.1	14.8
Eng.-tech. workers	78.7	50.0	35.7	14.7
Collective farmers	63.7	52.0	38.0	30.6
Students	70.4	34.7	30.2	14.0
Party and government officials	82.5	50.0	45.0	31.3

Source: Pavel Gurevich, "Concrete Sociology: The Thirst for Information," Zhurnalist (August 1968), Table 1.

not comparable with the figures for the other groups. Table 2 shows that among students there was not the usual marked preference for radio over television for news and that students used radio and television less than other groups. That is usually explained by pressures and competition for use of students' time and by a lower rate of set ownership for financial reasons. In all those respects the poll generally duplicates results found by other polls.

Tables 3 and 4 require extensive comment. Although the report of the poll took no notice of it, the "expectations" columns of Table 4 are identical to Table 3, except for the transposition of the rows for engineering-technical workers and collective farmers. However, the column headings, especially the third column, are not the same. That might be thought no more than an idle eccentricity (why was Table 3 published separately at all?), if it were not for the third column heading of Table 3, which was labeled precisely, "Answers to Sharp Questions on International Life." No less an authority than a sector head in the Department of Propaganda had already confirmed that the term "sharp questions" was, however regretfully, understood by the public to refer exclusively to subjects heard on foreign radio broadcasts.[34] Thus, whatever the composers of the poll may have intended, respondents affirmatively answering that question almost certainly had foreign radio in mind.

In the heading of the third pair of columns of Table 4 quotation marks have been added around the word "topicality" because the word does not seem to denote fully the meaning of the heading. What is usually meant in such polls is timeliness or promptness. The subject has often been discussed in the Soviet literature and has been included in a number of polls, but the word the Soviets have always used for this is operativnost' or one of its variants. The word used in Table 4 was zlobodnevnost', the technical definition of which is "actualness" or "actuality," a term whose awkwardness led to the use of "topicality" as a compromise. However, the Soviets have a special definition for the term zlobodnevnyye voprosy: "the burning topics of the day." While that can certainly include the concept of promptness and timeliness, it is actually broader and refers also to substantive content, its importance and reliability. The particular reason for using zlobodnevnost' instead of operativnost' must be connected with the fact that the former is actually a reform relation of the column labeled "sharp questions" in Table 3, and it was unlikely that Table 3 would have been labeled "sharp questions" if that specific phraseology had not been used by the polltakers. The use of zlobodnevnost' keeps the heading technically truer to its original meaning while disguising the import of the satisfaction rate on that point, which is concerned with much more than simply the question of the mechanical speed of reporting. The possibility of intentional disguise is enhanced by the transposition

TABLE 3

Interests According to Type of Program, by Social Group (percent)

Group	Concrete Facts	Commen- tary	Answers to Sharp Questions
Workers	49.0	28.9	56.6
Collective farmers	40.0	27.5	49.3
Eng.-tech. workers	62.9	40.2	72.4
Students	53.8	38.7	74.9
Party and government officials	61.3	55.0	81.2

Source: Pavel Gurevich, "Concrete Sociology: The Thirst for Information," Zhurnalist (August 1968), Table 2.

TABLE 4

Expectations and Degrees of Satisfaction with Broadcasts on International Themes, by Social Group (percent)

	Volume of Information		Persuasiveness of Interpretation		"Topicality" of Material	
	Exp.	Full Satis.	Exp.	Full Satis.	Exp.	Full Satis.
Workers	49.0	29.1	28.9	28.1	56.6	25.2
Eng.-tech. workers	62.9	18.0	40.2	18.0	72.4	23.4
Collective farmers	40.0	60.2	27.5	46.6	49.3	52.7
Students	53.8	21.6	38.7	22.1	74.9	27.8
Party and government officials	61.3	28.7	55.0	36.2	81.2	40.0

Source: Pavel Gurevich, "Concrete Sociology: The Thirst for Information," Zhurnalist (August 1968), Table 4.

of collective farmers and engineering-technical workers in Table 3. If the transposition of lines in Table 3 was not done deliberately to make the identicality of Tables 3 and 4 less obvious at a glance, it may have been the result of an accident during some hasty last-minute editing after the article was already set in type. The change in headings over identical data, the apparent nonappearance of the promised fuller report, the paucity of text and analysis in the Gurevich article (the text occupied only about twice as much space as the four tables), and the State Committee's silence all suggest that there was considerable difficulty about how to handle the results of the poll.

That background bears on the assessment of the significance of the figures. First of all, in terms of the reasons for interest in broadcasts about international affairs, the absolute level of interest between the different socioeconomic groups differed considerably. But within each group the relative importance of the three interests was identical. In all cases the most important reason for listening or watching was to get answers to "sharp questions"—i. e., to compare the Soviet reports with those of foreign radio. The least interest was in analysis and commentary. In general, the interest in "sharp questions" was almost double that of commentary, with the acquisition of specific facts falling in between. The one exception was the group of Party and government officials, who had a relatively higher interest in commentary relative to their interest in the other subjects, compared to the rest of the groups, but the order of precedence was the same. The higher relative (and absolute) interest of officials in the performance of broadcasting in the area of analysis and commentary may have been due not so much to a personal interest, but to professional concern over Soviet broadcasting's performance, a subject that would directly affect the officials themselves, since, regardless of their primary work, most probably also had some contact with the public in conducting propaganda activities.

The level of interest in "sharp questions" must have been disappointing, running as it did from 50 to 80 percent. If that were to be taken as the number listening to foreign radio broadcasts on a regular basis, it would far exceed the estimates of the foreign radio audience derived earlier in this chapter. Considering the number of radio receivers existing in the country, 50 to 80 percent listenership on a daily or near-daily basis seems a physical impossibility, especially after taking into account receivers in public places, out of order, not having short-wave capability, and so on. The highest figure—81 percent for officials—probably reflects access by many of those people to unofficial foreign information from sources other than foreign radio, such as the restricted TASS bulletins, surveys of foreign broadcasts, the Bulletin of Information, and other restricted publications and distributions. But the other four groups, whose interest in sharp questions ranged from 50 to 75 percent, could have received the bulk of their information only from foreign radio broadcasts as the original source. Undoubtedly, many of those people were receiving it second-hand or more indirectly (primarily, one would assume, by word of mouth), but the overall figures show that foreign radio had become a full-scale competitor of the Soviet information services.

Table 4 contains the figures on relative satisfaction with the broadcast news services. The most important information is conveyed by the differences between the figures in the third pair of columns. The implications of the changes in headings and the other matters of wording mean that these figures represent, in effect, answers to the questions, "Are foreign radio broadcasts important to you?" and "Do Soviet broadcasts effectively answer for you the questions they raise?" The numbers, at a minimum, who responded both affirmatively to the first question and negatively to the second are as follows: workers, 31.4 percent; engineering-technical workers, 49 percent; collective farmers, indeterminate; students, 47.1 percent; Party and government officials, 41.2 percent. Those figures are called minimum because they do not take into account those who might have answered both questions negatively. There is no way to determine those numbers, but the table shows that among collective farmers that response was certainly substantial, so there were probably significant numbers in the other groups as well. This effect masks some of the dissatisfaction among those who considered "sharp questions" important. The excess of satisfaction over interest among collective farmers may be no more than an artifact of the artificial conditions in which agitation campaigns—and probably the polling also—were conducted among them. On the other hand, the collective farmers could have been saying indirectly that, in effect, they were being bombarded with more information and propaganda than they cared to receive; perhaps even the polling was considered an unwanted intrusion.

The expressed rates of dissatisfaction—from 31 to 49 percent—are higher than those evolving from other polls—usually not greatly exceeding 30 percent. The probable cause was the exclusive concentration of the poll at hand on matters related to international affairs, the one area where foreign radio started on an equal footing with the Soviet media, in terms of access to the basic information. Other polls were usually broader and more diffuse, involving the gamut of public affairs, where foreign radio could not perform as efficiently because it did not have full knowledge of all matters of interest to the Soviet audience.

The results of the international-information poll probably contributed as a factor in the decision to resume jamming. The chronology of 1968 indicates that the basic decision on the resumption of jamming was probably taken around the time of the April plenum on ideology. The data from that poll were available by then. There is a note to that effect in Vestnik Moskovskovo Universita, Seriya XI, Zhurnalistika, No. 3, which was sent to the printer on March 23, 1968. The proponents of the resumption of jamming, who were then very active, could easily have exploited it to show that the Soviet media had totally failed to compete with foreign radio, even though they had had more than two years to do so, since that had been assigned as one of their top-priority tasks. Either Soviet information policy had to be radically liberalized, or the Soviet leaders faced the prospect of a large minority, perhaps even a majority, of important population groups becoming alienated from the political system out of frustration with its honesty on matters important to themselves.

That was the underside of the far more visible manifestations of protest, samizdat, and so on. It was more of a long-term problem than an immediate danger, but the resumption of jamming at least offered a short-range palliative while more basic policies could be considered. Repressive measures against the protesting elements were also increased at the time, but that would not be feasible for coping with the kind of passive dissatisfaction revealed by the polls. The connection between the two groups was that the former could act as a spark on the latter, igniting some kind of massive but unpredictable disruption during times when the system was undergoing unusual, perhaps economic, stress. A number of unhappy examples in Eastern Europe were at hand.

An overall estimate of the general state of public opinion—"feelings" might be a better term—about the Soviet system as measured, in effect, by attitudes about what is equivalent to its honesty, can be attempted by averaging out results from widely different types of polls. Table 5 summarizes them: 20 percent can be seen as a minimum figure of dissatisfaction. Combining the results of the polls with other factors previously discussed, the following seems to be a plausible estimate of the general state of discontent in Soviet society for the period 1966-68: generally satisfied, 40 to 50 percent; dissatisfied, 20 to 30 percent; unsure, indifferent, or opinions indeterminable, 30 percent. Discontent, of course, is an imprecise term, and this approach cannot define varying levels of intensity. It is clear, though, that the type of unhappiness expressed in the polls is likely to be felt more deeply in the upper socioeconomic levels of the population, especially by those designated by the Russian term intelligentsia.

That is a conservative interpretation of the meaning of the polls. One could just as easily conclude that the proportion of dissatisfied exceeded 30 percent. If so, the increase would be deducted mainly from the group of 30 percent classed as indeterminate. That 30 percent corresponds generally to the proportion of those who seem to show no interest in public affairs, as well as to some of the

TABLE 5

Summary of Key Indicators
from Opinion and Media Polls

Poll	Date	Nature of Key Indicator	Dissatisfaction (percent)
Propagandist trainee	1965	Instructors' credibility	24
Izvestia	1966	Experts' estimates	15-20
Estonia radio	1967	Promptness	38*
Leningrad television	1967	Promptness and openness	29
Sverdlovsk television	1968	Expectations and ideals	21-25
International information	1967	Preference for foreign radio	31-49

*Includes half the refusals to answer and half partially negative opinions; would be 20 percent without inclusion of latter category.

Source: Author's compilation.

"no answer" response rates in polls. Many of them are genuinely indifferent, but some part of the figure certainly represents people deliberately withholding their opinion, and most such opinions can be assumed to be negative. At least two other components of the "no answer" response and dissatisfied groups can be identified, but both are probably small, and they tend to cancel each other out.

One consists of the apparatchiki and government officials, who were identified in the international-information poll as having a high rate of dissatisfaction with media performance. Their interest is as much professional as personal, so it would be misleading to include them in the overall figures, insofar as the figures are being interpreted as indicative of personal dissent or disillusionment. However, the total of apparatchiki in the Soviet Union is not generally believed to be much more than a half million, and even if there are assumed to be several million government officials, taking them into account could not reduce the dissatisfaction figure by much more than one percentage point. On the other side, there is the phenomenon known as "internal emigration"; that is the term applied to those who are so disgusted with Soviet life that they withdraw entirely from all contact with public matters and live intensely personal private lives. They are unlikely to appear in the polls except in the "no opinion" group, but if they could be classified, they would have to be added to the total of the dissatisfied. Their numbers are unknown, but they are probably no more significant statistically, in comparison with uncertainties of ten-percentage-point magnitude, than are officials.

The 40 to 50 percent proportion classified here as generally satisfied are placed in that category as much as a remainder after the numbers of the other groups are deducted as from any positive evidence that identifies them in the polls. In considering whether the opinions about the media expressed in the polls can be extended to Soviet life in a broader sense, it should be recalled that the media are not only engaged in the dissemination of news and interpretation but are also the prime means of inculcating the hopes and promises of a better material and ethical life in the future, using the well-understood device of portraying "what ought to be" and "what will be" as "what is." If a significant number doubts the credibility of the media in their performance of handling the more conventional aspects of news, it is reasonable to suspect that it is also skeptical about the media's portrayal of basic Soviet accomplishments and perspectives.

Circumstantial evidence that the Soviet leadership so perceived the situation may be seen in the relation of the results of the _Izvestia_ poll to the evolution of the situation. It was suggested that the experts' estimates included there for comparison, although presented as the personal opinions of the individuals, perhaps reflected the prevailing view among leading circles, since those individuals circulated in the elite sectors of society, and had ample opportunity to absorb the views prevailing there. They estimated in 1966 that 15 to 20 percent of the population had little faith in the credibility of the media. However, at that time there was little inclination to resume jamming or to crack down on dissenting elements as harshly as was to be done after 1968. Thus, it would seem that a level of dissatisfaction around 20 percent was not considered cause for alarm. If the Soviet leaders became alarmed as suddenly as they seemed to after the beginning of 1968, and if they were paying attention to the more objective attempts to measure public opinion that apparently had begun only shortly before, then they must have become aware of a level of dissatisfaction that was considered to be substantially higher than 20 percent. To fit that situation the level of discontent could hardly have been much under 30 percent and could easily have been above that figure. However, the uncertainties in the poll figures that were publicly reported are too great to determine whether the amount of discontent increased substantially between 1966 and 1968 or whether the Soviet estimates of 1966 were too low. Probably a combination of both factors was involved.

CIRCULATION TRENDS

There are other indications that a fairly broad-based ideological malaise was developing in 1967. The most obvious was the fact that a decline in the circulation of the leading political periodicals set in at that time; the regime's ideological guardians considered that decline significant, treated it with evident embarrassment, and attempted to distort and eventually suppress discussion of the trend. Again, as in the case of the decline of radio mail, no attempt was made to explain it as a consequence of a natural development, such as the increased use of television. Table 6 depicts the changes in circulation of all newspapers and magazines with circulation higher than one million (excluding some specialized items such as the children's publication, Veseliye Kartinki).

The trend among the major newspapers of general content is particularly striking. After the removal of quota restrictions on circulation in the early 1960s, virtually all publications steadily increased their circulation for several years. But between 1967 and 1968 nearly all the largest "political" newspapers lost readership. The exceptions were Pravda, which continued to expand, and the Ministry of Defense's Krasnaya Zvezda, which held constant. However, Pravda was not regarded so much as a newspaper as an official bulletin for the professional needs of Party members, and it could be counted on to gain one subscriber for each increase of two in Party membership.

Perhaps the declines were a natural sequel to the recent surge of readership, but they seem to be more significant in a political sense in view of the reaction of the official establishment. The unsigned comment of the Union of Journalists became unhinged. In its annual review of circulation for 1968 the textual comment accompanying the table of figures said that there had been notable gains in circulation. A comparison with its own table of figures published a year earlier would show just the opposite. Additionally, the text said that Trud had gained 400,000 subscribers, while its own tables showed a loss of 100,000.[35] That those discrepancies were not simply a matter of carelessness became clear the following year when the Union of Journalists did not publish its summary of circulation trends, which had been an annual feature.

The situation of the major magazines was not so clear as that of the newspapers. The magazines had a less clear demarcation between those that emphasized political content and those that did not; they were generally less political as a whole, and their popularity was apparently influenced by idiosyncratic factors that cannot be simply categorized. However, an examination of Table 6 suggests that, on the average, magazines of less political emphasis fared better than those that were more political. Their overall

TABLE 6

Circulation of Major Newspapers and Magazines, 1967-70 (millions)

Name	1967	1968	1969	1970
Pravda	7.0	7.5	8.5	-
Pionerskaya Pravda	9.3	9.2	-	-
Izvestia	8.4	7.7	-	-
Komsomolskaya Pravda	6.9	6.7	-	-
Selskaya Zhizn	6.7	6.4	-	-
Sovetskaya Rossiya	3.1	2.9	-	-
Sovetskii Sport	2.5	2.6	-	-
Trud	2.4	2.3	-	-
Krasnaya Zvezda	2.4	2.4	-	-
Zirka	2.2	2.3	-	-
Nedelya	2.0	1.8	-	
Uchitelskaya Gazeta	2.0	1.2	-	-
Futbol	1.3			
Yunii Leninetz	1.1	1.4	-	-
Meditsinskaya Gazeta	1.0	-	-	-
Rabotnitsa	10.0	10.0	10.9	10.5
Zdorovye	8.0	8.0	9.5	-
Murzilka	5.6	5.6	5.6	-
Krestyanka	5.2	5.4	5.7	-
Krokodil	4.6	4.6	5.4	5.7
Nauka i Zhizn	3.6	3.6	3.0	-
Roman-Gazeta	3.0	2.2	2.6	-
Sovetskii Ekran	2.8	2.0	2.2	2.2
Vokrug Sveta	2.6	2.6	2.7	2.7
Sluzhba Byta	2.5	1.5	1.0	1.1
Ogonyek	2.0	2.0	2.1	2.0
Yunost	2.0	2.0	2.0	1.5
Za Rulem	2.0	2.0	2.5	2.6
Tekhnika-Molodezhi	1.5	1.5	1.5	-
Semya i Shkola	1.5	1.5	1.5	-
Politicheskoye Samoobrazovaniye	1.5	1.4	1.4	1.5
Smena	1.1	1.0	1.1	-
Radio	1.0	1.0	1.0	-
Za Rubezhom	0.7	1.1	1.3	1.4
Agitator	-	0.9	1.0	1.1
Kommunist	-	0.7	0.7	0.8

Sources: 1967: Zhurnalist (January 1967):18; 1968: Zhurnalist (February 1968):21; 1969-70: Mastheads of respective publications.

record was not impressive. Of the 21 largest, only five or six managed to show consistent increases in circulation after 1967.

Two magazines require special comment. Yunost, the country's most widely circulated serious literary magazine, showed some very interesting fluctuations. Its circulation had been two million in the mid-1960s, and then in 1966 it dropped back to one million. RFE's research department attributed the drop to the fact that after the Twenty-third Congress Yunost was the only "revisionist" monthly to publish an editorial of self-criticism and then adopt a less adventurous editorial policy. It also pointed out that the more conservative literary monthlies, Oktyabr, Zvezda, Neva, and Moskva, were then losing readers, while Novy Mir, Inostrannaya Literatura, Molodaya Gvardiya, and Znamya continued to gain.[36] In 1969 Yunost repeated the experience. In the middle of the year its editorial board was purged, most notably of Yevtushenko, and its editorial policy was curbed. After the changes, by the end of 1969, 500,000 readers dropped their subscriptions. The loss in 1966 was 20 percent; the loss in 1969 was 25 percent. Yunost's readers are unlikely to be representative of the population as a whole; nevertheless, the percentage of its readers sensitive to restrictions on its content was remarkably similar to the percentages doubting the credibility of Soviet news media turned up by the polls.

The second magazine whose statistics are particularly relevant is Za Rubezhom, which reprints translations of articles from the foreign press and carries original Soviet comment on international affairs. After its founding in the early 1960s, it was probably the fastest-growing Soviet magazine, and from 1967 to 1970, when a magazine could consider itself doing well if it did not lose readers, it doubled its circulation. That growth accords precisely with the polls' findings that international affairs was the subject of greatest interest to the Soviet public. The intensity of that interest was shown by a poll conducted in 1969 at the Kishinev Polytechnical Institute. About 1,000 students—day, night, and correspondence—were polled by questionnaire, basically in order to determine their attitudes toward the study of economics. One of the questions asked the names of the outside magazines that they read. The poll revealed that, in effect, they read nothing outside their personal field of study, except for materials about international affairs. Among all "social and political" magazines and newspapers, first place was held by Za Rubezhom, read by 49.1 percent of the students in the economics faculty and 73.9 percent of the engineering students. Second place went to another magazine on international affairs, Mezhdunarodnaya Zhizn (more theoretical and less informative), read by 22.6 percent of the economics students and 23 percent of the engineering students. No other magazine was read by as many as 20 percent of the students (excluding Ekonomicheskaya Gazeta, read by 62.1 percent of the economics students, presumably for academic reasons). In third place was Nauka i Religiya, and the fourth most popular magazine was yet another international publication, Novoye Vremya (the closest Soviet equivalent to a news weekly).[37]

The sociopolitical implications of that scale of interests are magnified when it is compared with what is known about trends in Soviet coverage of international news. There are no known measurements of the entire Soviet press on that matter—understandable when one considers the magnitude of the task—but one limited effort is highly suggestive. The COMCOM project at MIT selected at random 12 issues of Pravda for the years 1956, 1959, 1962, and 1965, and measured the amount of space given to each category of content in those years. There was a steady decline in the coverage of international news, with the released space being given over to domestic topics. The figures, in column inches, for each of the four years, for international subjects, were 4,476.5, 4,116.9, 3,496 and 2,947. Correspondingly, domestic materials in the same four years increased in the progression 4,940.1, 5,734, 5,921 and 6,980.5. The largest proportion of the decline in international news came from the systematic elimination of materials about China and its allies during the period of worsening of Sino-Soviet relations. That accounted for about one-third of the decline in international news in Pravda, but the decline was truly general. All categories of international news either declined in space or fluctuated up and down in relatively insignificant quantities.[38]

Had that study been extended beyond 1965 into the period of the Cultural Revolution, there probably would have been some reversal of the decline in international news in Pravda, if only because of the flood of vituperation and ridicule that was then directed at China by the Soviet press. But a large volume of information in one such narrow sector would hardly assuage the interest in the broad spectrum of international news. This measurement applies only to Pravda, but in view of Pravda's known function as a model and leader for the Soviet press as a whole, there is a probability that it characterizes a large sector of the press. The reasons for the reduction of international-news reporting remain conjectural. As was shown in previous chapters, it is possible to discern within the Soviet propaganda establishment a school of thought that holds international news per se as harmful and an interest in it by the Soviet public as "unhealthy." Conceivably, one might be seeing in those figures an influence of the proponents of that position.

It is more likely, however, that the decline in international-news reporting was not planned as such. It may have been an unintentional byproduct of natural developments connected with the growing complexity of Soviet society. Those would include the increasingly organized use of the press to promote special "campaigns"—particularly incessant in Khrushchev's time—and increased use of space for discussion of domestic issues, where on more and more occasions the presentation of different points of view was allowed. The space needed for those purposes may have simply squeezed out international subjects, which could not in any case have benefited from an opening of the press to broader discussion of issues, since foreign policy remained completely out of bounds as a subject on which any hint of public controversy could be allowed.

Whatever the causes of the restrictions on international news, the combination of the restrictions and the rising interest on the part of the public must have been a source of substantial frustration, if not irritation and antagonism, toward the authorities who might be held responsible for the situation. Even if the absolute quantity of international news increased after 1965, the gap between supply and demand almost certainly remained and perhaps increased. For a substantial segment of society that situation must be considered one of the major causes of the "credibility gap" between the government and the public.

CONCLUSIONS

In tracing developments along two levels of the Soviet political system, one level has followed the policies, attitudes, and official perceptions adopted by the Soviet leadership toward foreign radio broadcasting in the Soviet Union. The second has attempted to define the state of public opinion and feelings, about foreign radio in part but more often in respect to the information media in general and to related government policies that might underlie or condition governmental attitudes.

On the official level by the late 1950s and early 1960s Soviet authorities had relaxed their former wholly negative and defensive attitude toward foreign radio and had turned instead to a dual policy of making use of it for their own purposes and attempting to modify the content of foreign radio through informal and tacit bargaining with the West. The main feature of that policy was selective jamming according to content, frequently extending to item-by-item treatment of news programs.

Selective jamming enabled the Soviets to disseminate information to the public in support of governmental objectives that would have been inconsistent with overall Soviet information policy if published in Soviet media—e. g., news of individual Soviet nuclear tests, to demonstrate that they were detectable by the West without internal inspection—and information too sensitive or diplomatically too embarrassing to be officially propagated by the Soviet Union—e. g., unfavorable information about conditions in East Germany. Of broader significance, selective jamming was closely coordinated with major changes in Soviet policies and could be used in some cases as an indicator of future change, appearing earlier than any other overt indications: It gave, for example, the first sign of the reversal of the Soviet stance against concluding a partial nuclear test ban treaty.

Decisions on jamming, and on broadcasting policy in general, almost always coincide with major changes in Soviet policies or significant internal developments. There is also strong circumstantial evidence that they have been used as instruments in Kremlin power struggles. Thus, in examining the history and rationale of developments in that field, one can be reasonably sure that one is looking at aspects of decision making close to the center of the highest levels of the Soviet political process. The insights gained may sometimes be applicable to far broader areas of Soviet policy.

The decision to end most jamming in mid-1963, in addition to its role in furthering foreign policy, appears to have been based on a belief that the Soviet sociopolitical system had stabilized to the point that it could safely absorb additional uncontrolled information and that improvements in Soviet media would enable the Soviet information services to compete openly with foreign radio broadcasts and handle any questions raised by them. However, despite noticeable improvement, controls on Soviet information were never sufficiently reduced for the policy of open competition to succeed. The amount of listening to foreign radio increased, and by 1966 the experiment was visibly failing. One of the consequences was the use of foreign radio as a form of internal communications for the small groups of overt dissenters that appeared in 1966.

But those responsible for the management of propaganda and internal ideological cohesion made it clear that the aspect of foreign radio broadcasts that bothered them most was simply the constant supply of hard news, in itself not necessarily anti-Soviet or politically oriented, but constantly holding the Soviet press up to an unfavorable comparison and thereby undermining public confidence in the credibility of all aspects of the regime's dealings with the people.

By the beginning of 1968 the proponents of a hard line against foreign radio were engaged in a strong public campaign in support of their views. They appear to have been restrained between 1966 and 1968 by Brezhnev's personal intervention. The resumption of jamming in August 1968 was coincident with the invasion of Czechoslovakia, but the events there only influenced the timing of the resumption and were not the basic cause of it. The Soviets notably did not allege that the United States had reneged on any undertakings to impose restraints on the nature of program material.

The Soviets began serious investigation of basic public attitudes and audience reactions around 1965 and in connection with that explicitly cited problems presented by the existence of foreign broadcasting. The salient facts of those investigations, insofar as the limited raw data that were disclosed can be interpreted, are as follows. About 40 to 60 million people, with varying degrees of regularity, listen to foreign radio broadcasts. Major questions of public interest that are known mainly through foreign radio coverage reach and are of interest to 50 to 75 percent of various population groups. From 30 to 50 percent of the population consider the response of Soviet broadcasting to be inadequate. In addition, from 20 to 30 percent of the population, and perhaps more, seem generally to doubt the credibility of all Soviet information sources, and by inference, much of the basic ideological legitimacy of the system.

Those figures may explain the harshness of the repressive measures taken against the small groups of overt dissidents since 1966. The preference of the authorities for incarceration in mental institutions over public trials, despite the obloquy and harm to Soviet interests abroad, becomes more understandable. Those figures were also probably a major factor in the victory in 1968 of the proponents of the decision to resume jamming.

What cannot be definitively established is the connection between foreign radio and the creation of the situation crudely reflected in those numbers. There are direct and indirect Soviet statements to the effect that foreign radio broadcasts were mainly responsible for the ideological disarray. But such statements per se cannot be accepted at face value, because their originators have a clear self-interest in exaggerating, if necessary, the effects of foreign radio. Placing the blame on foreign radio excuses their own failures and glosses over any inherent defects in Marxist-Leninist concepts of social organization. There are certainly other influences that are intertwined with all the evolutionary trends connected with the modernization of a society. Among the most obvious of those are the rising levels of education, the more modern forms of lifestyles created by industrialization and urbanization, and the greatly increased mobility and means of internal, unofficial communication of the general population.

With the lack of hard data on the direct effect of foreign radio, the best comment on the importance of the broadcasts might be an indirect one of the Soviets themselves, from which an order of priorities can be inferred. On January 4, 1972, Congressman James H. Scheuer of New York had an interview in Moscow with Aleksandr Chakovsky, chief editor of Literaturnaya Gazeta. Scheuer was mainly interested in Soviet treatment of dissident writers and Jews and in restrictions on emigration to Israel, and he had come prepared with questions on specific cases. At the end of a somewhat labored conversation on those and related subjects, Chakovsky suddenly brought up the matter of VOA and RL and said that if the United States would change those broadcasts, the Soviet Union would change its treatment of dissidents and those who want to emigrate.[39]

Of course, the proposal was unofficial. Chakovsky may have introduced it only because he was under instruction to do so, in view of the fact that Scheuer had a vote on the forthcoming decision in Congress to continue appropriations for RL and RFE. The gist of the idea, however, was that the Soviets considered the broadcasts to have higher priority than the issues of the treatment of dissidents and Jews and were willing to sacrifice their position on the latter in return for concessions on broadcasts. Such would indeed be a very high priority. Subsequently, the Soviets held fast on those issues, even at the cost of angering Congressional opinion and jeopardizing the network of commercial and financial agreements with the United States (agreements aimed at overcoming the barriers to importation of U. S. technology, on which the Soviets were depending to overcome increasingly pressing economic lags). If Chakovsky raised the subject on his own initiative, he must have done so in knowledge of the place of foreign radio on the scale of Soviet priorities. He would have been one to know those priorities: In 1968 he had been selected, to all appearances, to spearhead the campaign for the resumption of jamming.

The level of concern about foreign radio demonstrated by the Soviet leaders at least raises the likelihood that foreign radio broadcasts have been an important cause of the existence in the Soviet Union of a moderately informed public opinion, to which the Soviet leaders have had to show deference. In practical terms, the most significant consequence of public opinion has been pressure on the regime to proceed more cautiously than would otherwise have seemed necessary, in order to reduce the possibility of meaningful movements of dissent emerging and coalescing.

The process by which foreign broadcasts influence events is indirect and gradual. Where specific links exist, they are concealed as well as Soviet and East European censorship and security measures can conceal them. One of the more visible recent links was in East Europe, where RFE is more predominant on the broadcasting scene than any single broadcaster is in the Soviet Union. The December 1970 protests triggered by restrictive new economic measures in Poland probably would have remained localized in the coastal cities and have been dealt with quietly by the Gomulka government before news of them became widespread had RFE not become aware of them through its monitoring antennas' ability to pick up at a great distance the signals of the small local stations. RFE's reporting of the situation to all of Poland caused the fall of the Gomulka government and its replacement by Gierek. The economic concessions by Gierek that subsequently placated the country were made possible only by the unprecedented Soviet act of granting Poland a hard-currency loan to obtain the necessary imports of consumer goods. In the year following that, helped no doubt by the change in U. S.-PRC relations, the Soviet Union itself decided to seek an easing of relations with the United States so that it could obtain the benefits of Western technology and resources to boost its faltering economic programs.

Foreign radio broadcasts may have been a factor in prompting the Soviets to seek more stable structures of security in Europe, based on lower levels of tension and using the situation to improve living conditions with the aid of expanded economic relations abroad. By the 1970s that was seen as the safest method of averting inside the Soviet Union the kind of popular outbreaks that have characterized four of the six Eastern European members of the Soviet bloc. Foreign radio's cumulative influence is less in addressing the specific issues directly or in promoting any ideological positions than in creating a general aura of skepticism and making the public less amenable to accepting at face value any explanations or sacrifices that the authorities may want to demand of it. The skepticism extends even to matters on which foreign radio is too insufficiently informed to speak meaningfully, because there have been so many other matters on which the authorities have been shown to be evasive or misleading.

The experience of the Soviet Union bears on the relationship between management of information and political stability in other political systems. If the Soviet Union, with its monolithic and massive control of information, is unable to prevent popular skepticism from reaching the levels suggested by its polls in the face of the comparatively small quantity of information that enters from abroad, it may be that many types of authoritarian systems, particularly those containing relatively educated and sophisticated populations, are inherently more subject to stresses and instabilities solely from the injection of uncontrolled information than has been apparent. If so, the world may see increasingly unstable political structures as its level of economic development grows and a greater proportion of the usually authoritarian-ruled less-developed areas become more educated and sophisticated. In addition, the struggle for control and access to the channels of international information flow will probably sharpen and become more central to the processes of international politics.

NOTES

1. Ithiel de Sola Pool, "The Changing Soviet Union," Current (January 1966):16-17.

2. Paul Hollander, "The Dilemmas of Soviet Sociology," Problems of Communism 14, 6 (1965):34-46; Zev Katz, "Sociology in the Soviet Union," Problems of Communism 20, 3 (1971):22-40.

3. Artem Flegontovich Panfilov, Radio SShA v psikhologicheskoi voine (Radio of the USA in Psychological Warfare) (Moscow, 1967), pp. 89-90.

4. David Wedgwood Benn, "New Thinking in Soviet Propaganda," Soviet Studies 21, 1 (1969):52-63.

5. V. N. Yaroshenko, "Studying the Radio Audience," Vestnik Moskovskovo Universiteta, Seriya XI, Zhurnalistika No. 1 (1966):27-39.

6. OIRT Information (June 1962):15-20.

7. Yaroshenko, "Studying the Radio Audience," pp. 27-39.

8. Boretskiy, "On Methods of Studying the Television Audience," Vestnik Moskovskovo Universiteta, Seriya XI, Zhurnalistika 3, (1967): 18-29.

9. B. A. Grushin, Mneniya o mire i mir mnenii (Opinions About the World and the World of Opinion) (Moscow, 1967).

10. Yaroshenko, "Studying the Radio Audience," pp. 27-39.

11. A. Tamre, "The Alphabet of Research," Sovetskoye Radio i Televideniye (June 1968):34-35.

12. B. Grushin, "Problems of the Audience," RT (June 1966):4-5.

13. Andrzej Sitinski, "Public Polls in Radio and Television Broadcasting," Radio and Television (Prague) No. 4 (July 1965):3-7.

14. Vasiliy Davidchenko and Vladimir Shlyapentokh, "'Izvestiya' Studies the Reader," Zhurnalist (February 1968):23-25; N. Kartseva, "Who, What, How?" RT No. 33 (August 1967):11.

15. Tamre, "The Alphabet of Research," pp. 34-35.

16. Rosemarie S. Rodgers, "The Soviet Audience: How It Uses the Mass Media," Ph. D. dissertation (MIT, 1967):22.

17. Ibid., p. 162; Alex Inkeles and Raymond A. Bauer, The Soviet Citizen: Daily Life in a Totalitarian Society (Cambridge, Mass.: Harvard University Press, 1959), pp. 181, 434.

18. Sergei Ivanovich Tsybov and Nikolai Federovich Chistyakov, Front tainoi voiny (Front of the Secret War) (Moscow, 1965), p. 112.

19. "Voice of America Says 43 Million a Week Tune in," New York Times, September 5, 1967.

20. Nan Robertson, "Soviet Resumes Jamming of the Voice of America," New York Times, August 22, 1968.

21. V. Nekrashas, "The Student and Life," Sovetskaya Litva, June 16, 1968.

22. A. G. Yefimov and P. V. Pozdnyakov, Nauchiniye osnovy partiinoi propagandy (Scientific Foundations of Party Propaganda) (Moscow, 1966), pp. 97-120.

23. Davidchenko and Shlyapentokh, "'Izvestiya' Studies the Reader," pp. 23-25; Kartseva, "Who, What, How?" p. 11.

24. Boris Yevladov, Anatoliy Pokrovskiy, and Vladimir Shlyapentokh, "4001 Interviews," Zhurnalist (October 1969):34-37.

25. N. Prokofieva and I. Gavrilova, "How the Turning Fork Sounds," Sovetskaya Pechat' (July 1965):23-25.

26. Rut Karemyae, ". . . Like Heavy Cannon in Battle," Sovetskoye Radio i Televideniye (July 1967):30-33.

27. I. Trikkel, "Radio in the Labyrinth of Communication," Sovetskoye Radio i Televideniye (July 1968):34-36; Kaazik, "'Ekho

Dnya.' Prestige, Rights, Duties," Sovetskoye Radio i Televideniye (September 1968):33-36.

28. Boris Firsov, "There Is No 'Average Viewer,'" Zhurnalist (December 1967):42-45.

29. L. Kogan, "We and Modern TV," Sovetskoye Radio i Televideniye (January 1969):22-25.

30. "From the Session of the Committee," Sovetskoye Radio i Televideniye (January 1969):15.

31. Ibid.

32. Pavel Gurevich, "Concrete Sociology: The Thirst for Information," Zhurnalist (August 1968):61-62.

33. L. A. Volovik, ed., Sotsiologiya i ideologiya (Sociology and Ideology) (Moscow, 1969).

34. Vasiliy Sitnikov, "Leninism in the Battle of Ideas," Zhurnalist (April 1967):8-10.

35. "240 Millions," Zhurnalist (January 1967):18; "Circulation Affairs," Zhurnalist (February 1968):21.

36. r. r. g. [Richard Rockingham-Gill], "Is TV Hitting Soviet Press?" Radio Free Europe Research Memorandum, January 3, 1967.

37. A. Kozhukhar' and I. Sarazhinskiy, "The Student and the Social Sciences," Kommunist Moldavii (February 1970):46-49, trans. in JPRS 50379, April 22, 1970, pp. 32-37.

38. Gayle Durham Hollander, Soviet Newspapers and Magazines (Cambridge, Mass.: Center for International Studies, MIT, 1967), pp. 41-43.

39. Memorandum by Department of State escort officer of conversation, James H. Scheuer and Aleksandr Chakovsky, January 4, 1972, supplied by office of Congressman Scheuer.

CHAPTER

6

EPILOGUE

On September 11, 1973, the Soviet Union again suspended jamming of VOA, BBC, and DW, leaving RL as the only major broadcaster still jammed. The broadcasting situation was thus restored to virtually the same as it had been from 1963 to 1968. Diplomatically, the issue of the flow of information and contacts had become linked with two major developments in relations between the Soviet Union and the West. Since the Nixon visit to the Soviet Union in June 1972 and the conclusion of U. S.-Soviet agreements on economic cooperation and other matters, criticism of the United States had almost disappeared from the Soviet press, but implementation of much of the agreements had become enmeshed with domestic U. S. criticism of Soviet repression of dissent and restrictions on emigration.

The other major set of diplomatic issues that had a direct relation to jamming revolved around the Conference on European Security and Cooperation (CSCE). That conference, encompassing almost all the nations of Europe in addition to the United States and Canada, had long been desired by the Soviet Union as a means of setting an official seal on the post-World War II rearrangement of boundaries and relations in Europe. After the Soviet agreement to stabilize relations with and between the two Germanies and on the status of West Berlin, the Western nations, which generally saw CSCE as primarily useful to the Soviet Union, could no longer postpone the conference. By mid-1973 the agenda and procedures had been settled, and the working sessions were scheduled to begin September 18, 1973. The three "baskets" into which CSCE was divided comprised measures a) to guarantee the postwar boundaries and security of Europe, b) to increase East-West economic and technical cooperation, and c) to improve the flow of information and contact between Eastern and Western Europe.

The nations of Western Europe considered that most of the benefits of the first two baskets would go to the Soviet Union and Eastern

Europe. Therefore, before the opening of the working sessions the Western nations, somewhat unexpectedly, united in determination that the negotiations on the third basket should result in meaningful relaxation of the iron curtain that had barred most informational, cultural, and personal contacts.

The suspension of jamming on September 11 thus strengthened the Soviet negotiating position on the eve of the opening of CSCE, and it simultaneously defused one of the arguing points of the opponents of the legislation needed to implement the U. S.-Soviet economic agreements. The White House only belatedly, and without the usual show of displeasure characteristic of its relations with the press at that period, denied the New York *Times* report of September 13 that Kissinger and Dobrynin had discussed the suspension of jamming on September 1.

The Soviets could calculate by that time that they had broken the back of the dissident movement. A series of trials and quiet consignments to psychiatric institutions had removed the boldest spokesmen from the scene. The *Chronicle of Current Events* had been suppressed after 28 bimonthly issues. Over 100,000 Jews, including most of the prominent advocates of emigration had been allowed to leave. The manuscript of Solzhenitsyn's *Gulag Archipelago*, the instrument of his upcoming deportation, or worse, had been unearthed by the KGB.

In mid-August Brezhnev, in a speech at Alma-Ata, had foreshadowed the decision on suspending jamming by reverting to his terminology of the mid-1960s in discussing the importance of a policy of an open provision of information to the public and adding that it was Soviet propagandists who should counteract the information from abroad. A few days later, on Soviet television Yuri Zhukov attacked VOA, a subject that had not been mentioned for months, urging Soviet citizens not to listen even to its music and "objective" information. A rear-guard action against the suspension of jamming was fought for several weeks, with a few articles in *Sovetskaya Rossiya* and *Krasnaya Zvezda*, the same publications that had always been against any relaxation of jamming. One article even appeared after September 11, but as in 1966, Brezhnev prevailed. By giving the KGB and the hard-line ideologists their head inside the Soviet Union he had won, if not a free, at least a leading hand for pursuing a policy of improving relations with the United States.

Unlike the situation in 1963, there was no attempt to link the suspension of jamming with RL and RFE. The summer of 1973 was the time of the U. S. Congressional debate over the continuation of funding for RL and RFE. A suspension of jamming of VOA at that time could have been used to influence the debate, but by September 11 the critical point in that decision process had already passed. Poland had its diplomats and agents all over Washington and Capitol Hill, promising to welcome VOA broadcasts and correspondents, to allow U. S. newspapers and magazines into the country, and so on, if RFE was terminated, but the Soviets seemed relaxed and content to issue routine propaganda attacks on the stations. By the end of 1973, when budgetary restrictions caused the discharge of some of the staff of RL and RFE, Soviet and East European sources were quietly passing the word that that was the beginning of the end of the stations. Emigrants and journalists have reported that in their respective contacts with the Soviet and East European security and diplomatic establishments they have been confidently assured that RL and RFE would be shut down but that it would be done gradually to save face for the United States.

Characteristically, the Soviet public tended to assume that if jamming had been suspended there must have been a deal of some kind. During the months following the suspension of jamming, the press reported that Soviet citizens and emigrants were complaining that VOA had "mellowed" or cut back its reporting on subjects likely to irritate the Soviet government. Allegations of new restrictions on VOA editorial policy were also made in the United States.

The United States did restore the arrangement on VOA's use of the 173 khz long-wave frequency. The long-wave transmitter near Munich was again deactivated, leaving 173 khz to the exclusive use of the Soviet Union. The Soviet Union then attacked VOA's sole medium-wave frequency in Eruope. That frequency, 1196 khz, on which VOA broadcast in several East European languages and English from a 300-kilowatt transmitter near Munich, had been used by VOA without challenge for more than 20 years. In January 1974 the Soviet Union began broadcasting on 1196 khz from a large new transmitter at Minsk, virtually obliterating the VOA signal. By choosing Minsk as the location of the frequency, the Soviets found almost the closest point on their territory to the VOA transmitter, thus creating the maximum possible interference.

After 1970 it became possible to conduct independent research on Soviet radio audiences. RFE had been performing such research since 1967 by polling the large number of East European visitors in Western Europe. With more than a million travelers a year visiting Western Europe, it was not difficult to contract with independent survey organizations, whose interviewers in theory did not know that their client was RFE, to poll 500 to 1,500 residents of each country each year, and to obtain a sample that could be weighted to approximate a demographic cross section of each country, except for Bulgaria. The results for the 1973-74 season, as published by RFE's Audience and Public Opinion Research Department, are shown in Table 7, expressed as the percentage of the total adult population that listens to each Western broadcaster.

Until 1970 not enough Soviet citizens were allowed to travel abroad to make surveys of Soviet radio audiences possible. After 1970 the numbers increased to the point where it was possible to

TABLE 7

Listeners to Western Radio
in Eastern Europe, 1973-74
(percent of adult population)

	Bulgaria N = 632	Czecho-slovakia N = 617	Hungary N = 1,134	Poland N = 1,338	Rumania N = 1,086
RFE	43	39	55	57	60
VOA	25	22	23	18	18
BBC	28	24	26	25	17
DW and Deutschlandfunk	1	22	9	2	6
Radio Luxembourg	18	28	15	14	9
Radio Vienna	3	*	13	1	5
Others	10	18	8	6	14
Do not listen to Western stations	47	24	33	30	28

*Undetermined.

make sample surveys, but it took several years to accumulate enough interviews to establish a statistical data base, and the sample was so far from being representative of the Soviet population that RL did not attempt to project the results to the population as a whole. The author requested RL to provide some of the raw data and thanks Radio Liberty for doing so. The tables that follow, while based in part on those data, were compiled by the author, and RL is not responsible for them. The author also thanks Murray Feshbach of the U. S. Department of Commerce for assistance in the use of Soviet census data.

Between 1970 and 1972 detailed information on listening interests and related socioeconomic status was provided by 1,680 Soviet citizens, none of them an emigrant or defector. RL, with some contribution from other European broadcasters, funded the contracts, but the European survey organizations or at least their interviewers were not told the identity of their clients. It appears that many of the interviews took place in a social context, without awareness of their purpose.

As could be expected, the group was much more educated, urban, and European than the Soviet population as a whole. Many, perhaps most, were associated with official delegations or governmental business in one form or another. The characteristic most closely linked to radio listening was education. For each broadcaster and for listening in general there was a distinctive educational profile. The question was whether the education-listening correlation for the survey group could be projected to the general population.

Of those approached 20 percent refused to provide any information. That was about the same refusal rate as the average for the population inside the Soviet Union. On any sensitive subject Soviet polling organizations, regardless of provisions for anonymity will rarely get less than 10 percent refusals to answer or "no opinion" responses, and that rate is usually in the 15- to 20-percent range.

It is not possible to make direct educational comparisons, because Soviet organizations rarely publish results correlated to level of education. There are probably two reasons for that. Characteristics that are considered ideologically "negative" often increase with the level of education. Publication of educational data would also call attention to the disproportionate distribution of formal education in the Soviet Union. Forty-four percent of the adult population has an elementary school education or less. The Central Statistical Administration omits most of those people in its census reports, although their number can be calculated from residuals. Soviet research organizations perhaps take that omission as a cue in publishing their own work.

Although educational comparisons are avoided, Soviet reports often use Marxist class categories of workers, peasants, intellectuals, and so on. It was possible to regroup some of RL's occupational categories into social-class categories and compare them with the State Committee for Broadcasting's 1967 poll of more than 5,000 representative Soviet radio listeners (see Tables 3 and 4). The results are shown in Table 8.

TABLE 8

Comparisons of RL and Soviet Polls
(percent)

	Listeners to Western Radio			News as Reason for Listening		
	Soviet	RL	Diff.	Soviet	RL	Diff.
Workers	56.6	61	4.4	49.0	54	5.0
Coll. Farmers	49.3	44	5.3	40.0	58	18.0
Eng.-Tech. Workers	72.4	69	3.4	62.9	71	8.1
Students	74.9	77	2.1	53.8	69	15.2

RL's tests of the statistical consistency of its data showed an accuracy of plus or minus five percentage points. In the eight categories in which comparison was possible with the State Committee, five fell within or just outside that margin. The three categories in which the differences were significant all concerned the question of whether news or information was a prime reason for listening. The RL poll asked that question specifically about foreign radio, while the State Committee's poll concerned reasons for listening to both Soviet and foreign radio for news on international subjects. That the distinction may account for the difference is also suggested by the fact that on that question the responses to the RL poll were consistently higher than to the Soviet poll, while on the more precisely defined question of listening to foreign radio the RL responses were in equal proportion higher or lower than the responses to the Soviet poll four years earlier.

Another basis for comparison is the relative weight of the individual broadcasters within the total audience. An estimate of the Soviet evaluation of the relative importance of the different foreign broadcasters was made in Chapter 4, based on the attention given to them by RT. The Soviet evaluation reflected in RT, if it was based on any hard data, probably derived from the survey work of the sociologist Aleksandr Krasilov, sponsored by the sections of the Central Committee Secretariat that were responsible for the press, radio, and related activities. Table 9 compares this Soviet evaluation with results of the RL poll.

TABLE 9

Relative Importance of Western Broadcasters, RL and Soviet Polls

	VOA	RL	DW	BBC	Others
Soviet evaluation	33	33	17	17	—
RL poll	38	27	18	17	—
Soviet evaluation	30	30	15	15	10
RL poll	27	19	13	13	28

The two upper rows compare the audiences on a scale of 100 for the four main Western broadcasters alone. The two lower rows make the same comparison for all Western broadcasters. The major difference is that the Soviet evaluation gives relatively more weight to RL and much less weight to "others" then does the RL poll. The reason for this could be that the presumed Soviet evaluation is that of the overall influence of the broadcasters, taking into account the type of programs and the type of audience, which vary substantially from broadcaster to broadcaster, while the figures derived from the RL poll are based solely on the relative sizes of the audiences.

Tables 8 and 9 show enough similarity between Soviet travelers and Soviet citizens at home to suggest that a projection of the characteristics of the first group will give an approximation of the listening interests of the entire adult population. Table 10 does that, based on the educational distribution shown by the Soviet census of December 1970. The rows labelled "Total" and the percentages in parentheses are for the population 16 years of age and older. Table 10 could overstate the actual number of listeners in that it assumes that radio receivers are evenly distributed and that the signals of the major Western broadcasters are audible throughout the populated areas of Soviet territory. The distribution of radio receivers is unknown, but there are probably proportionately more in urban areas than in rural areas. The effect of that distribution on listening is probably smaller than any differences in proportions, because in areas where there are fewer radio receivers there are likely to be more listeners using each receiver.

The unevenness in quality of signal in different areas of the Soviet Union probably causes a greater difference between the figures in Table 10 and the actual numbers of listeners than do variations in the availability of receivers. The effect would be particularly severe for RL, which has poorer equipment and worse reception conditions than the other major broadcasters. It is known that RL cannot be heard at all in large areas of the Soviet Union. As for other broadcasters, those areas tend to be those of thinnest population density, but for RL the effects of its small and obsolete technical plant probably reduce its actual audience to 10 to 20 percent less than the potential audience shown in Table 10. A 20-percent reduction in the audience shown for RL would bring it down to the high end of the 35- to 40-million range of listeners claimed by RL.*

Table 10 shows some internal inconsistencies that for the most part have a significant effect only on the audience shown for VOA. The number of occasional listeners (those listening less than once per week) shown for the individual stations—but not all stations combined—is too high. One category, "Rural Occasional Listeners of VOA," is higher than the total for occasional listeners of all Western broadcasters. That is not a mathematical impossibility

---

*First Annual Report of the Board for International Broadcasting, October 30, 1974, p. 10.

TABLE 10

Listeners to Foreign Radio in Soviet Union, by Educational Level, 1970-72 (millions)

Educational Level	VOA Urban	VOA Rural	VOA Total	RL Urban	RL Rural	RL Total	BBC Urban	BBC Rural	BBC Total	DW Urban	DW Rural	DW Total	All Western Stations Urban	All Western Stations Rural	All Western Stations Total
University															
Frequent	4.4	0.8	5.2	2.6	0.4	3.0	2.1	0.4	2.5	1.4	0.2	1.6	5.6	1.0	6.6 (60)
Occasional	—	—	—	—	—	—	—	—	—	—	—	—	1.6	0.3	1.9 (17)
Nonlistener	—	—	—	—	—	—	—	—	—	—	—	—	2.1	0.4	2.5 (23)
Total	9.3	1.6	10.9	9.3	1.6	10.9	9.3	1.6	10.9	9.3	1.6	10.9	9.3	1.6	10.9
Specialized Institution															
Frequent	3.4	1.0	4.4	1.4	0.4	1.8	1.0	0.3	1.3	0.8	0.2	1.0	4.1	1.2	5.2 (39)
Occasional	—	—	—	—	—	—	—	—	—	—	—	—	2.7	0.8	3.5 (26)
Nonlistener	—	—	—	—	—	—	—	—	—	—	—	—	3.5	1.0	4.6 (34)
Total	10.4	3.0	13.4	10.4	3.0	13.4	10.4	3.0	13.4	10.4	3.0	13.4	10.4	3.0	13.4
Secondary															
Frequent	13.4	6.2	19.6	5.6	2.6	8.2	1.7	0.8	2.5	2.0	0.9	2.9	15.3	7.2	22.5 (33)
Occasional	—	—	—	—	—	—	—	—	—	—	—	—	12.6	5.9	18.4 (27)
Nonlistener	—	—	—	—	—	—	—	—	—	—	—	—	19.1	8.9	28.0 (41)
Total	46.5	21.7	68.2	46.5	21.7	68.2	46.5	21.7	68.2	46.5	21.7	68.2	46.5	21.7	68.2
Elementary															
Frequent	10.5	12.9	23.4	3.5	4.2	7.7	0.3	0.4	0.7	0.3	0.4	0.7	13.1	16.0	29.0 (39)
Occasional	—	—	—	—	—	—	—	—	—	—	—	—	2.7	3.3	6.0 (8)
Nonlistener	—	—	—	—	—	—	—	—	—	—	—	—	17.8	21.7	39.4 (53)
Total	33.5	40.9	74.4	33.5	40.9	74.4	33.5	40.9	74.4	33.5	40.9	74.4	33.5	40.9	74.4
Total															
Frequent	31.7 (32)	20.9 (31)	52.6 (32)	13.1 (13)	7.6 (11)	20.7 (12)	5.1 (5)	1.9 (3)	7.0 (4)	4.5 (5)	1.7 (3)	6.2 (4)	38.0 (38)	25.2 (38)	63.3 (38)
Occasional	17.8 (18)	11.8 (18)	29.6 (18)	16.7 (17)	9.7 (14)	26.4 (16)	7.3 (7)	2.7 (4)	10.0 (6)	10.5 (11)	4.0 (6)	14.5 (9)	19.5 (19)	10.2 (15)	29.7 (18)
Nonlistener	50.2	34.5	84.7	69.9	49.9	119.8	87.3	62.6	149.9	84.7	61.5	146.2	42.5 (43)	32.0 (48)	74.5 (45)
Total	99.7	67.2	66.9	99.7	67.2	116.9	99.7	67.2	166.9	99.7	67.2	166.9	99.7	67.2	166.9

Note: Population in survey is 16 years of age and older. Frequent listeners are those who listen once per week or more. Totals do not add exactly because of rounding. Numbers in parentheses are percentages.

(an occasional listener of VOA could be a frequent listener to another station), but, nevertheless, it appears to be a consequence of the method that had to be used to separate the categories in the poll. The proportion of the population that listens to Western stations without listening to VOA is almost certainly higher than the six percent shown in Table 10.

The major reason for the apparent inflation in the number of occasional listeners was the insufficiency of information on the distribution of occasional listeners of the separate broadcasters according to level of education. The separate totals for each station's occasional listeners had to be calculated from a single ratio for that broadcaster, as if they were distributed in equal proportion in each educational group. The combined figures for all Western stations show proportionately more occasional listeners in the more highly educated groups, however. Because of the heavy concentration of population in the less-educated groups, the effect of using a single ratio for each broadcaster increases the number of occasional listeners from the less-educated groups much more than it reduces the numbers that would be shown for the more highly educated groups. Thus, the listeners shown for RL, BBC, and DW are understated, but probably by an insignificant amount, compared to the natural five percent margin of uncertainty. VOA's audience is significantly overstated because of its heavy concentration of listeners in the less-educated groups, where even a few percentage points can make a difference of several million listeners.

Another source of inaccuracy arises from the complexity of handling overlapping languages and program types between the separate broadcasters. The figures in the righthand column of Table 10 are for all Western stations in all languages. The figures for frequent listening of VOA, RL, BBC, and DW were intended to be for Russian-language programs only, but there were some data handling problems with those who listened to some stations in Russian as well as to other stations only in languages other than Russian. In addition, there may have been some confusion in the minds of those interviewed about the language definition of VOA's extensive musical programs. The major effect of those variations would be to increase the size of the audience shown for VOA, as compared to other broadcasters. But the artificial part of that bulge may be testimony to the popularity of Willis Conover's English-language musical program and also evidence of the sensitivity of the poll in detecting relatively small, but real, influences.

On balance, Table 10 may be within five percent accuracy for its totals shown for BBC, DW, and all Western stations combined. It probably overstates RL's totals by 10 to 20 percent, because of the inadequacies of RL's technical plant, and possibly overstates VOA's totals by 20 percent, mainly because of methodological problems in handling overlapping categories. In considering whether

Tables 8 and 9 might overstate the similarities between the RL poll's traveling sample and that of the Soviet population at home, there is one known difference that might introduce a systematic bias of political significance. All the Soviet citizens on whose behavior Table 10 is based had to be cleared by loyalty and security investigations before they were allowed to travel in the West.

The major broadcasters have very dissimilar audience profiles. Taking into account only frequent listeners, BBC and DW have similar profiles, with very few listeners in the lower strata but a steady increase to about 15 to 20 percent of the most highly educated part of the population. BBC's rate of increase is slightly higher than that of DW. RL has by far the flattest profile, with about 10 percent of listeners among the bulk of the population but a sharp upward hook to about 30 percent of the university educated. VOA has a "J"-shaped profile, with about 30 percent of the public among its listeners at the lower end, a slight dip in the middle, and then a rise to almost 50 percent at the upper end.

The differences in the shape of the profiles can be explained by the differences in overall program patterns of the broadcasters. RL is the only broadcaster with programs concentrating on in-depth treatment of Soviet political affairs, and it has the least differentiated audience. Basic factors, such as age and sex, have less effect on the frequency of foreign-radio listening in the Soviet Union than they do for radio listening, both domestic and foreign, elsewhere, although DW is preferred more by men than by women. Age and sex do affect preferences for types of programs. RL, however, may have the least differentiated audience in terms of age and sex distribution.

VOA's unique "J"-shaped educational profile arises from the fact that in the Soviet Union VOA has two separate audiences. One audience is primarily interested in the entertainment values of VOA's programs. That audience is younger and declines as education increases. The other audience is primarily interested in information, and it increases as education increases. The superimposition of those rising and declining curves gives the "J" composite. The trend is even more obvious if instead of showing percentages of total population, the curves are plotted as percentages of those who listen frequently to any Western broadcasters. The VOA profile, because of its overwhelming preference among the less educated, then becomes "U" shaped. A large proportion of the audience claims to be equally interested in the entertainment and informational aspects of VOA's programming, and that overlapping accounts for the relative shallowness of the dip.

Preference for types of programs is the primary factor in the Soviet listener's determining choice of a foreign station. An important secondary factor is the audibility of the signal. As could be expected, the rate of frequent listening declines for all broadcasters as the quality of reception worsens. The rate of decline seems to be slightly steeper for VOA than for the other three major broadcasters, and is definitely less steep for RL than for any of the others. Thus, it might be possible to discern the effects on listening of the suspension of jamming of VOA, BBC, and DW on September 11, 1973. The suspension of jamming of VOA, BBC, DW, but not of RL, by moving the average quality of signal upward along the slopes of the audibility curves of the first three, but not of RL, should increase the relative amount of listening of those three compared to RL. Table 11 shows the trend in listening over a period preceding and following the suspension of jamming. The percentages are not adjusted for demographic weights so they have little relation to the actual amount of listening inside the Soviet Union. However, each of the groups is essentially the same in its makeup, so the horizontal rows show proportional changes over time, and the columns show the proportional relationships between broadcasters at a given time. The figures for the 1970-72 period differ slightly from those used to make Table 10, because Table 11 shows only listening during the immediately preceding four weeks.

TABLE 11

Trends in Listening to Foreign Radio
in the Soviet Union, Russian-Language Only
(percent)

	1970-72 (N = 1,680)	Oct. 1972 to March 1973 (N = 321)	Oct. to Dec. 1973 (N = 190)
VOA	45	40	38
RL	29	30	29
BBC	19	14	24
DW	18	10	19

According to Table 11, there was no change in listening to RL before and after the September 1973 changes in jamming. VOA seems to show a long-term gradual decrease, and BBC an increase in listening. The changes are just barely larger than the margin of uncertainty in the poll, and are in any case very small compared to the overall amount of listening. The beginning of the reduction in listening to VOA occurred well before the suspension of jamming and seems unrelated to it.

A continuation of the trends in Table 11 would eventually lead to an equalization of listening between VOA, RL, and BBC, particularly among the more educated strata. The later samples were a little broader-based demographically: on average less educated and older. That could slightly reduce the apparent amount of listening shown in the last column of Table 11. The six-percentage-point decline in the number of university educated, for example, (all other things being equal), would reduce the reported rate of listening about one percentage point. The most important fact shown, however, by the preliminary data on which Table 11 is based is that the suspension of jamming on September 11, 1973, seemed to have no appreciable effect on listening to Western radio.

Part of the reason for the lack of change may be seen in Table 12, which shows the listeners' subjective evaluations of the quality of reception of each broadcaster. The quality of RL's reception, which continued to be jammed, showed absolutely no change. For all the others the end of jamming caused a significant decline in the numbers who felt that reception was poor. For VOA alone, however, was there a significant increase in the number of those who felt that reception was good.

TABLE 12

Listeners' Evaluation of Audibility of Foreign Radio Stations, Before and After Suspension of Jamming on September 11, 1973 (percent)

	Better Than Fair		Worse Than Fair	
	Before	After	Before	After
VOA	27	43	17	6
RL	14	13	31	28
BBC	23	23	39	7
DW	32	35	10	0

In general, listeners showed poor ability to distinguish between jamming, other kinds of interference, and natural changes in reception conditions. That is testimony to the overcrowded state of the airwaves as well as to ingrained suspicion of Soviet policy. (About one-third of listeners thought that jamming had continued even where there clearly was none.)

The combined impact of Tables 11 and 12 is to show that Soviet jamming has not been very effective as a deterrent to listening. Perhaps a realization of that has been a cause of the lessening of Soviet reliance on jamming since the beginning of the 1960s.

BIBLIOGRAPHY

Books and Monographs in English

Barnouw, Erik. The Image Empire: A History of Broadcasting in the United States, 3, From 1953. New York: Oxford University Press, 1970.

Bramstead, Ernest. Goebbels and National Socialist Propaganda 1925-1945. East Lansing: Michigan State University Press, 1965.

Buzek, Antony. How the Communist Press Works. London: Praeger, 1964.

Byrnes, Robert F., ed. The United States and Eastern Europe. New York: Prentice-Hall, 1967.

Codding, George, Jr. Broadcasting Without Barriers. The Hague: UNESCO, 1959.

Davison, W. Phillips. International Political Communication. New York: Praeger, for the Council on Foreign Relations, 1965.

Dizard, Wilson P. The Strategy of Truth. Washington: Public Affairs Press, 1961.

Durham, F. Gayle. News Broadcasting on Soviet Radio and Television. Cambridge, Mass.: Center for International Studies, Massachusetts Institute of Technology, 1965.

_____. Radio and Television in the Soviet Union. Cambridge, Mass.: Center for International Studies, Massachusetts Institute of Technology, 1965.

Elder, Robert E. The Information Machine. Syracuse, N. Y.: Syracuse University Press, 1968.

Havighurst, Clark C., ed. International Control of Propaganda. Dobbs Ferry, N. Y.: Oceana, 1967.

Henderson, John W. The United States Information Agency. New York: Praeger, 1969.

Hinton, Harold C. The Bear at the Gate: Chinese Policymaking Under Soviet Pressure. Washington: American Institute for Public Policy Research; Stanford, Calif.: Hoover Institution on War, Revolution, and Peace, 1971.

Hollander, Gayle Durham. Soviet Magazines and Newspapers. Cambridge, Mass.: Center for International Studies, Massachusetts Institute of Technology, 1967.

Horelick, Arnold, and Myron Rush. Strategic Power and Soviet Foreign Policy. Chicago: University of Chicago Press, 1966.

Inkeles, Alex, and Raymond A. Bauer. The Soviet Citizen: Daily Life in a Totalitarian Society. Cambridge, Mass.: Harvard University Press, 1959.

International Commission of Jurists. The Berlin Wall: A Defiance of Human Rights. Geneva, 1962.

Jacobson, Harold, and Eric Stein. Diplomats, Scientists, and Politicians: The United States and the Nuclear-Test Ban Negotiations. Ann Arbor, Mich.: University of Michigan Press, 1966.

Kruglak, Theodore E. The Two Faces of TASS. Minneapolis, Minn.: University of Minnesota Press, 1962.

Leive, David M. International Telecommunications and International Law: The Regulation of the Radio Spectrum. Leyden: Sijthoff, 1970; Dobbs Ferry, N. Y.: Oceana, 1970.

Markham, James W. Voices of the Red Giants. Ames, Iowa: Iowa State University Press, 1967.

Murty, B. S. Propaganda and World Public Order: The Legal Regulation of the Ideological Instrument of Coercion. New Haven, Conn.: Yale University Press, 1968.

Paulu, Burton. Radio and Television Broadcasting on the European Continent. Minneapolis, Minn.: University of Minnesota Press, 1967.

Salinger, Pierre. With Kennedy. New York: Doubleday, 1966.

Schlesinger, Arthur M., Jr. A Thousand Days. Boston: Houghton Mifflin, 1965.

Sorensen, Theodore C. Kennedy. New York: Harper & Row, 1965.

Sorensen, Thomas C. The Word War. New York: Harper & Row, 1968.

Tatu, Michel. Power in the Kremlin. New York: Viking Press, 1969.

Taubman, William. The View from Lenin Hills. London: Hamish Hamilton, 1968.

Vladimirov, Leonid [pseud.]. The Russians. New York: Praeger, 1968.

Whitton, John B., and Arthur Larson. Propaganda: Towards Disarmament in the War of Words. Dobbs Ferry, N. Y.: Oceana, for the World Rule of Law Center, Duke University, 1964.

Articles in English

American Academy of Political and Social Science, Propaganda in International Affairs: The Annals, vol. 398, (November 1971).

Benn, David Wedgwood. "New Thinking in Soviet Propaganda." Soviet Studies 21, (1969):52-63.

Berger, Marilyn. "Radio Moscow Hit by VOA 'Jamming.'" Washington Post, November 16, 1970.

Borra, Ranjan. "The Problem of Jamming in International Broadcasting." Journal of Broadcasting 11, (1967):355-68.

"Broadcasts Breed Dissent in Soviet." New York Times, July 14, 1968.

"The Case of Yuri Levin." Khronika Tekushchikh Sobytii, August 31, 1969. Reprinted in Problems of Communism 19, 2 (1970):50.

Document 63. Problems of Communism 17, 5 (1968):40-47.

Frankel, Max. "East-West Standstill." New York Times, May 17, 1963.

____. "Rusk Says Soviet Avoids Test Ban." New York Times, May 30, 1963.

____. "Test Ban Hopes Linger." New York Times, May 19, 1963.

Gaer, Felice D. "The Soviet Film Audience: A Confidential View." Problems of Communism 23, 1 (1974):56-70.

Grose, Peter. "Leaders in Soviet Fear West's Radio Is Ensnaring Youth." New York Times, March 25, 1966.

_____. "U. S. and Soviet Exchange Charges over Propaganda." New York Times, September 25, 1968.

Gwertzman, Bernard. "Soviet Scientist and Party Aide Clash on the Freedom of Ideas." New York Times, October 8, 1970.

Handler, M. S. "West Preparing Appeal to Soviet on Atom Testing." New York Times, May 26, 1963.

Harvey, A. McGehee. "A 1969 Conversation with Khrushchev: The Beginning of His Fall from Power." Life (December 18, 1970):48B.

Hollander, Gayle Durham. "Recent Developments in Soviet Radio and Television Reporting." Public Opinion Quarterly 31, 3 (1967):359-65.

Hollander, Paul. "The Dilemmas of Soviet Sociology." Problems of Communism 14, 6 (1965):34-46.

"Jamming Air Waves: How Soviets Operate." U. S. News and World Report (August 7, 1961):8.

Kamm, Henry. "Bulgarians Find U. S. Bias on Trade." New York Times, November 24, 1966.

Katz, Zev. "Sociology in the Soviet Union." Problems of Communism 20, 3 (1971):22-40.

Kubik, Leonid. "An Eight-Day Analysis of New Programmes on the Soviet Radio." Radio Liberty Research Note, October 25, 1962.

Levitin, A. E. "Listening to the Radio," Document 51. Problems of Communism 17, 4 (1968):107-9

Linden, Carl. "Khrushchev and the Party Battle." Problems of Communism 12, 5 (1963):27-35.

Lisann, Maury. "Moscow and the Chinese Power Struggle." Problems of Communism 18, 6 (1969):32-41.

Osborne, John. "Speaking to the Russians in a New Voice." The New Republic (November 6, 1965):9-10.

Phelps, Robert H. "U. S. Says Russians Step Up Jamming." New York Times, July 9, 1969.

Pool, Ithiel de Sola. "The Changing Soviet Union." Current (January 1966):12-17.

Robertson, Nan. "Soviet Resumes Jamming of the Voice of America." New York Times, August 22, 1968.

Rosenfeld, Stephen S. "'Left'-Handed Compliment: Effectiveness of 'Voice' Acknowledged by Pravda." Washington Post, March 18, 1965.

____. "Party's Journal Attacks Soviet News Censorship." Washington Post, July 11, 1965.

r.r.g. [Richard Rockingham-Gill]. "Is TV Hitting Soviet Press?" Radio Free Europe Research Memorandum, January 3, 1967.

"Russians Amiable at Radio Parleys." New York Times, May 3, 1959.

"Seeds of Poison." Washington Post, September 20, 1965.

Shabad, Theodore. "Soviet Press Told to Report Fully." New York Times, July 12, 1965.

Shub, Anatole. "Western Radio Forces Soviets' Hand." Washington Post, January 19, 1968.

"Soviet Aide Suggests Leaders Should Hold News Conferences." New York Times, April 5, 1971.

"Soviet Magazine Rebuts U. S. Radio." New York Times, May 1, 1966.

Sulzberger, C. L. "Foreign Affairs: The Coexistence Bazaar." New York Times, October 17, 1965.

____. "Foreign Affairs: The Two Ks and Germany." New York Times, November 6, 1966.

____. "How Khrushchev Changed His Mind." New York Times, September 11, 1961.

Unger, Aryeh L. "Politinformator or Agitator: A Decision Blocked." Problems of Communism 19, 5 (1970):30-43.

"Voice of America Says 43 Million a Week Tune in." New York Times, September 5, 1967.

Welles, Benjamin. "Voice of America Sends New Sound." New York Times, November 8, 1966.

Wicker, Tom. "U. S. and Russians Put Off TV Show." New York Times, March 8, 1962.

Other Sources

Foreign Broadcast Information Service, daily transcripts of radio broadcasts.

Foreign Relations of the United States, 1945. Vol. V: Europe. Washington: Government Printing Office, 1967.

Foreign Relations of the United States, 1946. Vol. VI: Eastern Europe; The Soviet Union. Washington: Government Printing Office, 1969.

Gayer, John H. Interview, Valley Forge, Pa., July, 1966.

Lisann, Maury. "The Politics of Broadcasting to the USSR." Ph. D. dissertation, Johns Hopkins University, 1973.

Memorandum of conversation, James H. Scheuer and Aleksandr Chakovsky, January 4, 1972.

Rodgers, Rosemarie S. "The Soviet Audience: How It Uses the Mass Media." Ph. D. dissertation, Massachusetts Institute of Technology, 1967.

Rusk, Dean. Interview, April 21, 1971. ____. Letter to Maury Lisann, June 1, 1971.

Thompson, Llewellyn. Interview, April 30, 1971.

U. S., Congress, House, Committee on Appropriations. Departments of State, Justice, and Commerce, the Judiciary, and Related Agencies Appropriations for 1965: Hearings. 88th Cong., 2nd sess., 1964.

_____. Committee on Foreign Affairs, Subcommittee on International Organizations and Movements. Modern Communications and Foreign Policy, Part X, Winning the Cold War: The U. S. Ideological Offensive: Hearings. 90th Cong., 1st sess., 1967.

_____. Committee on Foreign Affairs, Subcommittee on National Security Policy and Scientific Developments. Satellite Broadcasting: Implications for Foreign Policy: Hearings. 91st Cong., 1st sess., 1969.

U. S. Congress. Senate. Committee on Appropriations. Departments of State, Justice, Commerce, the Judiciary, and Related Agencies Appropriations for 1968: Hearings. 90th Cong., 1st sess., 1967.

United States Information Agency. Background on Radio Jamming, press release, November 1959.

Voice of America. Monitoring Records, 1961-63.

_____. Scripts of News Broadcasts (Russian), 1961-63.

Soviet Books

Bunyakov, P., and V. Komolov. Tri tsveta a odna mast' (Three Colors but One Suit). Moscow, 1957.

Golyakov, Sergei. Voina bes vystrelov (War Without Shots). Moscow, 1968.

Grushin, B. A. Mneniya o mire i mir mnenii (Opinions About the World and the World of Opinion). Moscow, 1967.

Kaftanov, S. V., ed. Radio i televideniye v SSSR (Radio and Television in the USSR). Translated by Joint Publications Research Service, No. 4838, August 3, 1961.

Lapitskiy, Isaak M. Koroli lzhi i sensatsii (Kings of Lies and Sensations). Moscow, 1967.

Mikhailov, M. P., and V. V. Nazarov. Ideologicheskaya diversiya—vooruzheniye imperializma (Ideological Diversion Is the Armament of Imperialism). Moscow, 1969.

Narodnoye khozyaystvo v 1962, SSSR (The National Economy in 1962, USSR). Moscow, 1963.

Panfilov, Artem Flegontovich. Radio SShA v psikhologicheskoi voine (Radio of the USA in Psychological Warfare). Moscow, 1967.

Spravochnik partiinovo rabotnika (Handbook of the Party Worker). 3d ed., Moscow, 1961; 4th ed., Moscow, 1963; 6th ed., Moscow, 1966; 7th ed., Moscow, 1967.

Tsvigun, S. K. Nevidimiy front (Invisible Front). Baku, 1966.

Tsybov, Sergei Ivanovich, and Nikolai Fedorovich Chistyakov. Front tainoi voiny (Front of the Secret War). Moscow, 1965.

Tunkin, Grigory Ivanovich. Ideologicheskaya borba i mezhdunarodnoye pravo (Ideological Struggle and International Law). Moscow, 1967.

Uledov, Aleksandr Konstantinovich. Obshchestvennoye mneniye sovetskovo obshchestva (Public Opinion in Soviet Society). Moscow, 1963.

Vlasov, A., I. Ivanov, A. Panfilov, and O. Stroganov. Strategiya lzhi (Strategy of Lies). Moscow, 1967.

Yefimov, A. G., and P. V. Pozdnyakov. Nauchnyye osnovy partiinoi propagandy (Scientific Foundations of Party Propaganda). Moscow, 1966.

Yegorov, V. N. Pravda o imperialisticheskoi propagande (The Truth About Imperialist Propaganda). Moscow, 1963.

Zasurskiy, Ya. N., ed. Sovremennyye burzhuaznyye teorii zhurnalizma (Contemporary Bourgeois Theories of Journalism). Moscow, 1967.

Zhiveinov, N. I. Operatsiya PW (Operation PW). Moscow, 1966.

Soviet and Related Articles

"About the New in the New Style," editorial. Sovetskoye Radio i Televideniye (December 1962):1.

Afonin, M. "Reportage from America." Sovetskaya Pechat' (October 1959):7-15.

_____. "What Worries the Preachers of Imperialism." Sovetskaya Pechat' (October 1963):60-61.

Alekseyev, E. "Read, Misters, Krylov." Pravda, August 21, 1966.

Aleskovskiy, M. "Applause and Whistles." Sovetskaya Pechat' (February 1965):38-41.

_____. "What to Turn On: The Radio or the Television Set?" Sovetskaya Pechat' (January 1964):32-34.

Anokin, I., and D. Prudchenko. "Absolutely, Yes!" Sovetskoye Radio i Televideniye (March 1963):1-2.

"Anti-Sovietism: One of the Main Trends in the Ideology of Imperialism Today." World Marxist Review, Information Bulletin No. 57, (Toronto: Progress Books, October 25, 1965):5-20.

"Anti-Sovietism—One of the Main Trends in the Ideology of Modern Imperialism," editorial. Kommunist No. 10 (July 1965):64-77.

Bannov, Boris. "Violence and Propaganda." Zhurnalist (October 1968):64-65.

Barmankulov, M. "Battle on the Air." Prostor (Alma Ata) (August 1968):110-14.

"A Beginning in Kyaariku: The First All-Union Scientific-Theoretical Conference of Radio Journalists 'The Present, Man, and Radio.'" Zhurnalist (May 1968):28-29.

Belyayev, V. "World Agency." Sovetskaya Pechat' (February 1964): 20-27.

Bogomolov, Anatoliy. "News Comes to You." Zhurnalist (January 1967):45-47.

_____. "You're Watching the Television Set Less!" Zhurnalist (June 1967):39-41.

Boretskiy, R. A. "On Methods of Studying the Television Audience." Vestnik Moskovskovo Universiteta, Seriya XI, Zhurnalistika No. 3 (1967):18-29.

"Britain Through the Eyes of Soviet People?" Literaturnaya Gazeta (February 7, 1968):9.

Budantsev, Yuri, and Vladimir Derevitskiy. "On This Day and Hour: The Telescreen and the Event." Zhurnalist (March 1967):46-47.

Bugayev, Ye. I. "Tribune of Millions." Sovetskaya Pechat' (May 1965):6.

Chakovsky, A. "On Audacity Real and Feigned." Sovetskaya Rossiya, January 27, 1968.

Cherkasov, V. "The Brown Face of 'Deutsche Welle.'" Sovetskoye Radio i Televideniye (July 1969):40-42

Chernyavsky, V. "Filthy Loudspeaker." Druzhba Narodov, (February 1967):212-19.

"Circulation Affairs." Zhurnalist (February 1968):21.

"The 'Cultural Revolution' and the Hungweipings." RT No. 5 (January 1967):11.

Danilov, V. "Political Information. How to Conduct It?" Pravda, August 3, 1967.

Davidchenko, Vasiliy, and Vladimir Shlyapentokh. "'Izvestiya' Studies the Reader." Zhurnalist (February 1968):23-25.

Demchenko, V. "Political Information: Our Experience." Pravda, October 27, 1966.

Demichev, P. "The Construction of Communism and the Tasks of the Social Sciences." Kommunist No. 10 (July 1968):14-35.

"The Disgraced Baron." Izvestiya, September 15, 1966.

Domoratskiy, Ye. "The Search Ought to Continue." Sovetskoye Radio i Televideniye (July 1961):25-27.

Dyachenko, Valentin. "The Desire to Learn Is a Sign of Strength." Zhurnalist (September 1967):38-40.

Dzhus', I. "Around the Sharp Questions." Pravda, January 26, 1967.

Firsov, Boris. "Mass Communications." Zhurnalist (February 1967): 50-52.

_____. "There Is No 'Average Viewer.'" Zhurnalist (December 1967): 42-45.

"For the Further Improvement of Radio Broadcasting and Television," editorial. Sovetskoye Radio i Televideniye (July 1962):1-4.

"For the People's-Worker, the People's-Creator." Sovetskaya Pechat' (April 1963):33-36.

"From the Session of the Committee." Sovetskoye Radio i Televideniye (January 1969):15.

Giller, A. "As an Advocate for Bonn." RT No. 13 (July 1966):7.

Golovanov, V. "A Visit to 'Voice of America.'" Sovetskoye Radio i Televideniye (November 1968):38-40.

Golyakov, Sergei. "An Alliance of Dirty Hands." Komsomolskaya Pravda, March 17-18, 1966.

_____. "Here Among Us in America." Zhurnalist (July 1968):62-63.

Goryunov, D. "The Main Theme." Sovetskaya Pechat' (January 1966):1-6, 18.

_____. "On a Great Campaign." Sovetskaya Pechat' (June 1964):1-7.

"The Great March Towards Communism," editorial. Sovetskaya Pechat' (April 1966):1-3.

Gribachev, N. "What a Day to Come . . ." Komsomolskaya Pravda, July 25, 1968.

Gromov, A. "The Arithmetic of German Wave." RT No. 2 (April 1966):7.

_____. "The Special Mission of Mister Gardner." RT No. 1 (April 1966):11.

Grushin, B. "Problems of the Audience." RT No. 10 (June 1966):4-5.

Gurevich, Pavel. "Concrete Sociology: The Thirst for Information." Zhurnalist (August 1968):61-62.

Gusev, G. "Silhouettes and Call-Signs." Sovetskoye Radio i Televideniye (October 1968):5-8.

Ilichev, Leonid. "Widen the Front of Ideological Work." Sovetskaya Pechat' (December 1959):67-68.

Ilina, A. "Value the Honor of the Journalist." Sovetskaya Pechat' (January 1963):37-38.

_____. "Voice of the People." Sovetskoye Radio i Televideniye, No. 6 (1959):1-2.

Ilyin, T. "Radio Broadcasts and the House on Yubileinaya." Sovetskaya Pechat' (October 1962):40-41.

"An Interview with the Deputy Chief Editor of Latest News and Mayak Leonid Vernerovich Gyune." Sovetskoye Radio i Televideniye (December 1967):5-6.

"Intrigues, Forms and Contents." Sovetskaya Pechat' (September 1966):28-30.

Ivanovskaya, N. "About the Program 'Vremya.'" Sovetskoye Radio i Televideniye (May 1968):30-33.

"The Journalist at the Microphone," editorial. Sovetskaya Pechat' (September 1963):1-3.

Kaazik, F. "'Ekho Dnya': Prestige, Rights, Duties." Sovetskoye Radio i Televideniye (September 1968):33-36.

Kaftanov, S. "Use Better the Powerful Possibilities of Radio." Sovetskaya Pechat' (December 1959):59-60.

Kalashnik, M. "Ideological Work Is the Business of All Communists." Kommunist Vooruzhennykh Sil No. 21 (November 1966):10-18.

Karemyae, Rut. ". . . Like Heavy Cannon in Battle." Sovetskoye Radio i Televideniye (July 1967):30-33.

Kartseva, N. "Who, What, How?" RT No. 33 (August 1967):11.

Kazakov, G. "In a Hundred Languages of the World." Sovetskaya Pechat' (October 1962):33-36.

Kenzhebayev. T. "Timeliness Is the Sister of Success." Sovetskoye Radio i Televideniye (March 1963):8.

Kharlamov, Mikhail. "A Mighty Weapon of Our Ideology." Pravda, May 7, 1963.

_____. "A Powerful Means of Ideological Work." Pravda, May 7, 1964.

Khazanov, A. "Experiment? No! Practice." Sovetskaya Pechat' (October 1966):20-22.

Khrushchev, Nikita Sergeievich. Interview, CBS, June 2, 1957.

____. "Speech to the Congress of the Union of Journalists, November 14, 1959." Sovetskaya Pechat' (December 1959):2-8.

Kitayev, V. "Without Information There Are No Newspapers." Sovetskaya Pechat' (January, 1961):36.

Kogan, L. "We and Modern TV." Sovetskoye Radio i Televideniye (January 1969):22-25.

Kolesov, N. "Stop, Instantly." Sovetskoye Radio i Televideniye (August 1967):2-5.

Korobeinikov, V. "What Is Miss Hollander Looking After?" Sovetskoye Radio i Televideniye (June 1968):38-39.

Kosin, V. "Twenty-six Issues of 'RT.'" Pravda, November 20, 1966.

Kosygin, Alexei. "Election Speech at Minsk." Sovetskaya Belorussia, February 15, 1968. Translated in Current Digest of the Soviet Press 20, 7 (1968):15.

Kozhemyako, V. "A Word for Each." Pravda, May 31, 1967.

Kozhukhar', A., and I. Sarazhinskiy. "The Student and the Social Sciences." Kommunist Moldavii (February 1970):46-49. Translated in Joint Publications Research Service, No. 50379, April 22, 1970, pp. 32-37.

Kraminov, Daniel. "The Battle for Minds and Hearts." Zhurnalist (August 1969):34-37.

Krutov, Fed. "New Trends." Sovetskaya Pechat' (November 1962): 36-38.

____. "We Go to 'Mayak': 120 Days of Work of the New Radio Station." Sovetskaya Pechat' (December 1964):38-40.

____. "Yesterday, Today, and Tomorrow." Sovetskaya Pechat' (September 1965):35-36.

Kruzhilin, Yu. "Seven and a Half." Sovetskaya Pechat' (June 1966): 38-39.

Kudenko, Oleg. "The 108 Hour Day." Sovetskaya Pechat' (August 1963):28-31.

Kulikov, V. "Falsity in the Ether." Sovetskaya Pechat' (October 1963):56-58.

Kurtinin, M. "This Has Long Agitated Us." Sovetskaya Pechat' (May 1966):10-11.

Kuryanov, M. "Information Is the Base of Political Agitation." Pravda, May 28, 1969.

Laptev, I. "Soldiers of the Party: A Tale About the Communists of One Shop." Kommunist No. 12 (August 1968):46-55.

Latysh, E., and P. Chernyshev. "About the Agitator and the Politinformator." Pravda, December 25, 1967.

Luchai, V. "Special Broadcasts." Sovetskoye Radio i Televideniye No. 6 (1959):5.

Lyadov, V., and V. Rozin. "The Intelligence Service and the BBC." Izvestiya, December 17, 1968.

Matveyev, V. "The Ice is Breaking." Sovetskaya Pechat' (October 1959):16-17.

"Mayak." Sovetskaya Pechat' (September 1964):30.

"Meeting of Historians of the Present Day." Zhurnalist (April 1967):11, 14.

Melenkov, I. Partiinaya Zhizn No. 12 (June 1957):48-50.

Merkulov, A., and N. Nikolayev. "On the Banks of the Terek." Sovetskaya Pechat' (June 1960):32-33.

Mikhailov, V. "The Publicism of Fact on the Central Television Program 'Vremya.'" Sovetskoye Radio i Televideniye (January 1969):40-41.

"Mission of Peace." Sovetskaya Pechat' (September 1959):4.

Mochalov, B. "Party Work in the Institute." Kommunist No. 10 (July 1966):32-43.

Nakropin, O., and V. Samarin. "The BBC on Land and the BBC on the Air." Sovetskoye Radio i Televideniye (August 1969):40-43.

Nebenzya, A. "Political Upbringing of the Masses." Kommunist No. 10 (July 1966):15-24.

Nekrashas, V. "The Student and Life." Sovetskaya Litva, June 16, 1968.

Nepomnyashchy, K. "Black Sky Bosses and Lackeys." Izvestiya, August 22, 1968.

Nikolayev, A., and K. Ushakov. "High Vigilance Is the Armament Against the Probes of Imperialism" Kommunist No. 11 (July 1968):93-102.

Nikolayev, K. "Promptness and Depth." Pravda, December 14, 1967.

"Not on Instructions, but by Conviction—Readers' Dialogue." Pravda, July 31, 1968.

Nozhin, Ye. "The Law of Precedence." Sovetskoye Radio i Televideniye (May 1969):34-36.

Observer. "Slanderers on the Air Waves." Izvestiya, April 14, 1966.

Official Department. "In the Department of Propaganda of the CC, CPSU." Zhurnalist (July 1968):78.

_____. "In the Department of Propaganda of the CC, CPSU." Zhurnalist (August 1968):78.

"On the Matter of 'Vremya.'" Zhurnalist (June 1968):15-17.

Osipov, Vladimir. "The Keys of the BBC." Zhurnalist (May 1968): 56-59.

"Our Knowledge, Strength, and Weapons." Pravda, October 4, 1966.

Petrov, A. "Cosmos—The Televiewer Without Intermediaries." RT No. 28 (July 1967):11.

Pilotovich, S. "Party Life: Knowledge and Consciousness." Pravda, March 26, 1969.

Pinter, Ishtvan. "A Den of Poisoners of the Ether." Izvestiya, March 6, 1966.

Polyanov, N. "The Great Responsibility of the Press." Sovetskaya Pechat' (September 1959):1-3.

Popov, L., and Afanasyev, V. "Step Up the Struggle Against the Illegal Production and Use of Radio Transmitters." Sovetskaya

Yustitsiya No. 13 (July 1970):13-14. Translated in Joint Publications Research Service, No. 51100, August 5, 1970, pp. 96-100.

"The Present Day and Our Tasks." Sovetskaya Pechat' (November 1966):3.

Prokofieva, N., and I. Gavrilova "How the Tuning Fork Sounds." Sovetskaya Pechat' (July 1965):23-25.

"Publicists of High Ideals." Sovetskaya Pechat' (July 1964):1-17.

Rapokhin, A. "Radio, Man, and His World." Sovetskoye Radio i Televideniye (May 1968):5-7.

____. "The Tribune of the Millions." Selskaya Zhizn, May 7, 1970.

"Renewal," editorial. Sovetskoye Radio i Televideniye (December 1963):1-2.

"The Reporter," editorial. Zhurnalist (June 1968):5-7.

"Revolutionary Vigilance," editorial. Sovetskaya Rossiya, March 11, 1969.

Rodionov, B. "Meeting Battle." Izvestiya, June 28, 1966.

Rodionov, Nikolai N. "Speech to the 23rd Congress of the CPSU." Pravda, April 5, 1966.

Sagal, G. "Life and the Silver Screen." Sovetskaya Pechat' (October 1963):25-26.

____. "The Most Difficult Is to Guide the Pen Along the Paper." Sovetskaya Pechat' (October 1966):39-41.

Samarin, V. "Almost Fifty Days per Day." Sovetskoye Radio i Televideniye (October 1969):42-44.

"The Screen of Millions," editorial. Zhurnalist (September 1968):2-3.

Sergeichuk, K. "The Goal Is Maximum Speed and Reliability." Ekonomicheskaya Gazeta No. 28 (July 1969):6.

"The Sharpest Front of the Class Struggle," editorial. Sovetskaya Rossiya, April 13, 1968.

Sherkovin, Yu. A. "Persuasion, Suggestion, and Propaganda." Vestnik Moskovskovo Universiteta, Seriya XI, Zhurnalistika, no. 5 (1969):28-42.

Shevlyagin, D. "The Invincible Power of Marxist-Leninist Ideas." Pravda, June 14, 1967.

Shkondin, M. V. "The Tools and Credo of American Propagandists." Vestnik Moskovskovo Universiteta, Seriya XI, Zhurnalistika, no. 6 (1968):91-93.

Shmelev, A. B. "Some Views on the Means of Forming Public Opinion." Vestnik Moskovskovo Universiteta, Seriya XI, Zhurnalistika, no. 1 (1969):19-24.

Shpakov, Yu. "The Logic of the Fall." Sovetskaya Rossiya, May 28, 1968.

Shumakov, A. "Intellectual Vertical." Sovetskoye Radio i Televideniye (February 1968):18-20.

Sitinski, Andrzej. "Public Polls in Radio and Television Broadcasting." Radio and Television (Prague) (July 1965):3-7.

Sitnikov, Vasiliy. "Leninism in the Battle of Ideas." Zhurnalist (April 1967):8-10.

Skachko, N. "On New Frontiers." Sovetskoye Radio i Televideniye (August 1963):1-2.

____. "Times, Times." Sovetskaya Pechat' (January 1962):21.

Sluck, Aado. "Commentators' Work." Radio and Television (Prague) (April 1968):48-50.

Smirnov, G. "Democracy, Freedom, and the Responsibility of the Individual." Pravda, December 4, 1967.

Snastin, V. "The Main Direction," editorial. Sovetskaya Pechat' (May 1964):1-6.

"Soviet Radio," editorial. Pravda, September 22, 1965.

"The Soviet Way of Life," editorial. Sovetskaya Rossiya, May 15, 1970.

"Statement of the Ministry of Foreign Affairs of the USSR." Pravda, September 15, 1961.

"The Strength of the Press Is in Partymindedness," editorial. Zhurnalist (December 1968):2-3.

Stuk, A. "On the Wave of Slander." Literaturnaya Gazeta (July 31, 1968):2.

Sviridov, N. "Party Concern for the Upbringing of the Scientific-Technical Intelligentsia." Kommunist No. 18 (December 1968): 36-45.

Tamre, A. "The Alphabet of Research." Sovetskoye Radio i Televideniye (June 1968):34-35.

"To Be an Ideological Fighter," editorial. Sovetskaya Rossiya, June 5, 1968.

"To Perfect the Strike Forces of the Ideological Front." Sovetskaya Pechat' (July 1963):5-12.

Tolkunov, Lev. "The Word Is the Deed." Zhurnalist (July 1967):2-5.

Trikkel, I. "Radio in the Labyrinth of Communications." Sovetskoye Radio i Televideniye (July 1968):34-36.

Tsvetov, V. "How Many Pairs of Pants Does a Japanese Have?" RT No. 12 (March 1967):12.

Tsvigun, S. "To Struggle with the Ideological Diversions of the Enemies of Socialism." Kommunist No. 11 (July 1969):102-12.

"240 Millions." Zhurnalist (January 1967):18.

Uskova, G. "How to Improve the Broadcasts of 'Latest News.'" Sovetskoye Radio i Televideniye No. 3 (March 1957):6-8.

Vasilenko, N. "The Press and the Small Screen." Sovetskaya Pechat' (March 1966):36-39.

Vasilyev, B. "Provocateurs at the Microphone." Sovetskoye Radio i Televideniye, no. 5 (1958):28-29.

Veselovskiy, Viktor. "Twelve Points of Courage." RT No. 12 (July 1966):4.

Vishnyakov, K. "On Leningrad Radio and Television." Sovetskoye Radio i Televideniye No. 5 (1959):3.

Vlasov, V. "News Is First of All." Sovetskoye Radio i Televideniye no. 5 (August 1961):11-13.

"The Whole Heart with the Party," editorial. Zhurnalist (August 1968):2.

"Why Is the Magazine Becoming a Rarity?" RT No. 29 (July 1967):4.

Yakovlev, A. "Television: Problems, Perspectives." Kommunist No. 13 (September 1965):67-81.

_____, I. Chuprinin, and Yu. Orlov. "A Powerful Means of Propaganda." Sovetskaya Pechat' (June 1965):1-5.

Yakovlev, Boris. "Yet Again About 'Vremya.'" Zhurnalist (February 1969):27-28.

_____, and A. Leonov. "Disinformation—A Weapon of 'Psychological Warfare.'" Pravda, June 25, 1966.

Yanuitis, I. "We Work for the Radio Listeners." Sovetskoye Radio i Televideniye, no. 10 (October 1962):4-5.

Yaroshenko, V. N. "On Some Psychological Aspects of Radio Broadcasting." Vestnik Moskovskovo Universiteta, Seriya XI, Zhurnalistika, no. 6 (1969):55-65.

_____. "Studying the Radio Audience." Vestnik Moskovskovo Universiteta, Seriya XI, Zhurnalistika, no. 1 (1966):27-39.

Yegorov, A. G. "Strengthen and Develop Leninist Style in the Work of the Press." Sovetskaya Pechat' (March 1965):1-8.

Yevladov, Boris; Anatoliy Pokrovskiy and Vladimir Shlyapentokh. "4001 Interviews." Zhurnalist (October 1969):34-37.

Yevstafyev, Aleksandr. "To Converse with the Russians in a New Language." RT No. 21 (September 1966):10.

Zalutskiy, A. "It's Time to See the Birth-Certificate." Sovetskoye Radio i Televideniye (December 1963):23-25.

Zazerski, Ye. "The Force of Propaganda Is in Truthfulness." Pravda, August 18, 1965.

Zhidkov, Vladimir. "In Order to Persuade . . ." Zhurnalist (November 1969):30-32.

Zhukov, Yuri. "Arms of Truth." Sovetskaya Pechat' (December 1959):45-46.

Zimanas, G. "New Standards of Effectiveness." Sovetskaya Pechat' (January 1962):20-21.

Zimyanin, M. "An Affair of Our Honor." Sovetskaya Pechat' (May 1966):3.

Supplementary List*

Govorit Moskva (1958-). Biweekly newspaper of the Party Committee of the State Committee for Radio Broadcasting and Television.

Hollander, Gayle Durham. Soviet Political Indoctrination: Developments in Mass Media and Propaganda Since Stalin. New York: Praeger, 1972.

Hopkins, Mark W. Mass Media in the Soviet Union. New York: Pegasus, 1970.

Price, James R. Radio Free Europe—A Survey and Analysis. Washington, D. C.: Congressional Research Service, Library of Congress, March 22, 1972.

Stepakov, V. I. Partiinoi propagande—nauchnuyu osnovu (Party Propaganda on a Scientific Basis). Moscow, 1967.

Whelan, Joseph G. Radio Liberty—A Study of its Origins, Structure, Policy, Programming and Effectiveness. Washington, D. C.: Congressional Research Service, Library of Congress, March 22, 1972.

---

*Items on this list were not used in the preparation of this book.

INDEX

ABOUT THE AUTHOR

MAURY LISANN has been employed by the Hazeltine Electronics Corporation and the Economic and Political Studies Division of the Institute for Defense Analyses. He has been a consultant to the National Aeronautics and Space Agency, the Voice of America, and the Board for International Broadcasting.

His articles on Soviet and Chinese politics have been published in the United States, Britain, and Germany.

He received his Ph. D. from the School of Advanced International Studies of Johns Hopkins University.

RELATED TITLES
Published by
Praeger Special Studies

COMMUNICATIONS AND PUBLIC OPINION:
A Public Opinion Quarterly Reader*
edited by Robert O. Carlson

FOREIGN AFFAIRS NEWS AND THE BROADCAST
JOURNALIST
Robert M. Batscha

MASS COMMUNICATION AND CONFLICT
RESOLUTION: The Role of the Information Media
in the Advancement of International Understanding
W. Phillips Davison

MASS COMMUNICATION RESEARCH: Major
Issues and Future Directions*
edited by W. Phillips Davison and
Frederick T. C. Yu

THE ROLE OF COMMUNICATIONS IN THE
MIDDLE EAST CONFLICT: Ideological and
Religious Aspects
Yonah Alexander

THE USES OF COMMUNICATION IN DECISION-
MAKING: A Comparative Study of Yugoslavia
and the United States
Alex S. Edelstein

---

*Also available in paperback as a Praeger Special Studies
Student Edition.